HOPELESSLY DIVIDED

HOPELESSLY DIVIDED

THE NEW CRISIS IN AMERICAN POLITICS AND WHAT IT MEANS FOR 2012 AND BEYOND

Douglas E. Schoen

ROWMAN & LITTLEFIELD PUBLISHERS, INC.
Lanham • Boulder • New York • Toronto • Plymouth, UK

Published by Rowman & Littlefield Publishers, Inc.
A wholly owned subsidiary of
The Rowman & Littlefield Publishing Group, Inc.
4501 Forbes Boulevard, Suite 200, Lanham, Maryland 20706
www.rowman.com

10 Thornbury Road, Plymouth PL6 7PP, United Kingdom

Distributed by National Book Network

British Library Cataloguing in Publication Information Available

Library of Congress Cataloging-in-Publication Data

Schoen, Douglas E., 1953–
  Hopelessly divided : the new crisis in American politics and what it means
for 2012 and beyond / Douglas E. Schoen.
    p. cm.
  Includes index.
  ISBN 978-1-4422-1523-8 (cloth : alk. paper) — ISBN 978-1-4422-1525-2
(ebook)
  1. Political parties—United States—History—21st century. 2. Divided
government—United States—History—21st century. 3. Two-party systems—
United States. 4. Right and left (Political science)—United States—History—
21st century. 5. Populism—United States—History—21st century. 6. United
States—Politics and government—2009– 7. United States—Politics and
government—2001–2009. I. Title.
  JK2261.S357 2012
  320.973—dc23

                                                            2011047878

∞™ The paper used in this publication meets the minimum requirements of
American National Standard for Information Sciences—Permanence of Paper
for Printed Library Materials, ANSI/NISO Z39.48-1992.

Printed in the United States of America

CONTENTS

INTRODUCTION

I've been a practitioner in the political process—as a pollster, strate-gist, and consultant—for forty years. I've polled for mayors, members of Congress, and a president (Bill Clinton), and I've worked for candi-dates of both political parties in the United States as well as candidates overseas. Although I've never been a lobbyist or a fund-raiser, I've seen our political system close up, I know it intimately, and my experience working within it is long and varied.

Over the last decade, I've written books about political reform and finding bipartisan solutions (*The Political Fix*); about the need for third parties (*Declaring Independence*); and about the growing discontent in the country (*Mad as Hell*, with Scott Rasmussen). All of those books were about, in one way or another, *process*: how the political system works, what's wrong with how it works, how it might be made to work better.

This book is different.

This book is not about process, but crisis: a crisis of our democracy, of our economy, of the legitimacy of our political system, and ulti-mately, of our society. The indications are clear: political and economic institutions across the board, from Congress to the Federal Reserve, have lost the confidence of the American people. The approval rating of Congress matched an all-time low in September 2011. Both political parties have low ratings, too, and self-identified Independents are now the largest American voting bloc. Americans elected a historic figure, Barack Obama, as president in 2008, amid excitement and hope for the future—but have become disillusioned as he, too, has been sullied by the partisan warfare in Washington. His two predecessors, George W. Bush and Bill Clinton, also came into office amid high hopes and pledges to change a system and a whole manner of politics. Like Obama, however, their best intentions of changing the way Washington works were overwhelmed in a tide of partisan warfare.

The state of things in Washington might not trouble so many people if the nation were doing well otherwise. But on Main Street, things are bleak. We have a deep-seated economic crisis—one that, while not matching the Great Depression in unemployment figures in its overall devastation, has in its own way become a unique and almost equally crippling phenomenon. Unemployment and underemployment figures combined reach something in the neighborhood of 18 percent; millions of Americans, middle-aged with dependent children, haven't worked in a year or more and have lost jobs in industries that won't be coming back here. In September, the Census Bureau released new figures showing that nearly one in six Americans lives in poverty—a record 46.2 million people. The U.S. poverty rate is the highest of any major industrialized nation.

Meanwhile, the gap between rich and poor in America is already the largest in the industrialized world. And it continues to grow. Real income for all Americans, except the super-rich, has declined.

Clearly these problems have had a long foreground; they didn't just suddenly happen. But for the first time, there is a clear linkage between these crises and the failures of our political system. When the financial crisis hit in 2008 and the federal government responded with the plan to purchase the "toxic assets" of failing banks (what came to be known as TARP), no one was very happy about it—but there was also substantial agreement, at least in the broad political center of the country, that such a systemic rescue was probably necessary. Nobody liked it, but at a certain level, it was accepted. And of course, many still argue today that TARP did in fact save the U.S. financial system.

I'm not going to take a position on that one way or the other. To me, what is more important is where we are now three years later. The consensus that supported TARP is long gone. The prevailing view now is that our widespread political paralysis has *caused* the debt and deficit crises we face, along with the structural employment problem, the threat to entitlement-program solvency, and their concomitant effects. Standard & Poor's, in downgrading the U.S. credit rating for the first time in history in August 2011, made this point explicit: that the United States' inability to address these woes was a political failure of the system to step up and act.

That failing system, I submit, more than unemployment figures, debt, or deficits, is the principal reason why so many today believe the United States faces a prolonged period of decline.

The purpose of this book is to explain why and how this happened. We have become hopelessly divided, not only by the actions of politicians and political parties but also by structural forces, including:

- The concentration of political power in Washington, D.C.
- The role of fund-raising and campaign money in dominating the political process and thwarting the public will
- A strengthened party system that enforces ideological obedience at the expense of individual action and bipartisanship
- The enduring, and growing, power of lobbyists
- A political system that at nearly every point—from Super PAC money to the redrawing of congressional districts—has become undemocratic and unrepresentative.

These forces, and others, have not just corrupted our politics; they have rendered our politics ineffective, even impotent, in solving any of the important problems the American people face every day. These forces run deeper than either party or any one politician or even presidential candidate. No one person can correct this alone. The problems must be addressed structurally.

We need fundamental, systemic change. In my concluding chapter, I offer some ideas for solutions that might help us get there. But to be frank, I've done that in other books—and I think I have some good solutions, but that's not my goal here. My deeper interest in writing this book is to set out clearly and definitively the challenge we face as a democratic society.

The system we have today, as it presently operates, no longer serves the American people. It is neither sustainable nor worthy of a nation dedicated to representative democracy.

I make no claim to be free from association with this tarnished system—far from it. I've worked in the system my whole career, and I've benefited from it, even from some of the parts that I complain about.

I've climbed my share of ladders. Now I want to offer my perspective as an insider, one who knows the system intimately, to make the severity of our present situation clear—as well as how vital it is that we take steps to change it, now.

That's what this book is about.

1

AMERICA ON
THE BRINK

*Washington is home to a vertiginous tangle of industry
associations, activist groups, think tanks and communications shops. These forces have overwhelmed the government that was originally conceived by the founders.*

*Republican politicians don't design policies to meet
specific needs, or even to help their own working-class
voters. They use policies as signaling devices—as ways to
reassure the base that they are 100 percent orthodox and
rigidly loyal . . . As for the Democrats, they offer practically nothing. They acknowledge huge problems like wage
stagnation and then offer . . . light rail! Solar panels!*

—David Brooks, *New York Times*, June 14 and 16, 2011

There is an increasingly serious crisis in American politics—a crisis
that was rarely discussed until recently yet explains much of the
dysfunctionality and dissatisfaction that we see every day. Our system
has simply stopped working, and both the politicians and the people
know it. Moreover, the political class—political leaders, business elites,
and those in the information and technology vanguard—have explicitly
come to function on their own behalf. They've put ordinary, mainstream Americans in a subsidiary, indeed inferior, position.

As a result, the political class is very happy with how things are going
in America, while everyone else suffers, economically and politically.
Ordinary people, regardless of ideology or social position, have come

to believe that an unrepresentative, self-interested elite has rigged the system against them.

To be sure, the public has splintered ideologically. Those on the right want to dramatically reduce the size and scope of government, while those on the left want bigger government, more stimulus, and higher taxes on the wealthy.

Regardless of ideology, mainstream Americans believe the system no longer works on their behalf; that the American Dream no longer is a reality for them and their families; and that their institutions—those that they were brought up to cherish—have largely failed them and their fellow citizens.

And the political elite has either tuned out ordinary, mainstream Americans or come up with schemes to manipulate them in a variety of ways. The elite helps politicians of the right and left raise huge war chests for campaigns, support massive lobbying campaigns for special interests, and more frequently, deploy huge amounts of secret campaign funds independently to protect their interests. Moreover, they cater to an increasingly polarized electorate with blatant appeals to the political extremes. They create, facilitate, and maintain electoral rules that play to these extremes.

The result is an unsustainable system that perpetuates a self-selecting, self-satisfied elite and increasingly alienates a restive and frustrated electorate that substitutes ideology for thought, anger for judgment, and alienation for commitment.

Something has to give, and soon.

THE FAILURE OF THE POLITICAL CLASS

For the last several years, the American people have withstood one blow after another: a financial crisis, a housing and foreclosure crisis, an unemployment rate far higher than we've seen in generations, stagnating middle-class incomes, and a general sense of a declining quality of life and diminished prospects for the future. Substantial percentages of Americans tell pollsters they've lost faith in the American Dream. The nation faces a genuinely frightening debt profile, a federal deficit at record highs, states and municipalities near bankruptcy, and no real sense that job recovery is in sight in the near or even distant future.

In my life, now is the most difficult time I can remember in this country, and it's made worse by the prevailing sense that our political leaders in Washington, both Republican and Democrat, have no answers for it. One might even conclude, from watching their endless partisan squabbling and failure to come to compromises on monumental issues, that they feel it might not be in their interest to find answers—as if the system they've set up, painful as it has become for everyone else, is serving them rather nicely, thank you very much.

In fact, that's how most Americans *do* tend to see it.

What else should they conclude about a system in Washington which, in summer 2011, held a gun to the head of the American economic and financial system with an absurd, incredibly destructive battle over raising the federal debt ceiling?

Never before had the U.S. government seen anything like it: a battle to the finish between the two parties over what had been, for decades, a routine transaction: raising the nation's credit limit so that it could continue to make payments to the creditors of its national debt, not to mention fulfill a host of other obligations. At the eleventh hour an agreement was reached, but the damage was done: Standard & Poor's, citing dysfunction and rampant partisanship in Washington, downgraded the nation's credit rating for the first time in American history.

Even that wasn't the end of it: barely a month and a half later, the two parties were at it again. This time, the issue was provisions for disaster relief in a short-term government funding bill known as a Continuing Resolution—again, a fairly routine mechanism in Washington. Democrats wanted to insert the higher funding number from a Senate version of the bill, while Republicans insisted that any increased funding had to be offset by spending cuts. Inside baseball? Normally, yes—except that, just like in the debt-ceiling fight, both sides refused to budge. Without a deal, the federal government would have shut down. Once again, Americans watched as their elected representatives spent most of their energy on partisan warfare instead of bipartisan solutions.

And so Americans have lost almost all confidence in their political institutions, especially the two parties—Democrat and Republican—that have been at the heart of the political system for over 150 years. Americans see in the two parties little but partisanship, self-interest, ideological obsession, and a prevailing desire to hold on to power at all costs, including the cost of national interest. They view government as being insulated from the problems of ordinary Americans, almost solely responsive to organized special interests or to financial elites. An ABC News poll in June 2011 found 69 percent of those polled described themselves as dissatisfied or even angry with the way the federal government is working. Less than one in five has any confidence left in government. Some 70 percent of Americans believe the nation is on the wrong track.

Perhaps most striking of all, millions of Americans have lost their faith in the American Dream. They no longer believe that, under the current system, their children will enjoy the same opportunities. I've seen this in my own polling. In an April 2011 poll of unemployed and underemployed men I conducted for *Newsweek* and the Daily Beast, 42 percent of respondents said that they felt the American Dream was out of reach for them; 18 percent said they weren't sure. About 75 percent said that they didn't have the money to live the way they wished, while 65 percent said they had tapped their retirement savings to get by. Last fall, an ABC News/Yahoo poll's findings were similar. Just half the respondents believed that the American Dream still existed, while nearly the same portion said explicitly that it was a thing of the past. Not surprisingly, those who earned over $75,000 had the most confidence in today's American Dream.

The implications of such an outlook cannot be overstated. It goes to the fundamental nature of the crisis we face today, the observable fact that for millions of Americans, the system no longer works. If the only demographic group that retains belief in the American Dream is the wealthy—and even then, by not much of a majority—then the American meritocratic ideal has clearly fallen on hard times.

Those hard times have eaten away at a defining American trait—optimism—both in the short and long term. Consider the findings of a *Newsweek* poll conducted by my firm, Douglas E. Schoen, LLC, in May 2011:

> Three out of four people believe the economy is stagnant or getting worse. One in three is uneasy about getting married, starting a family, or being able to buy a home. Most say their relationships have been damaged by economic woes or, perhaps more accurately, the dread and nervousness that accompany them.

As our *Newsweek* survey demonstrated, the magnitude of the nation's problems, combined with the vacuum of leadership, has had a debilitating effect on American confidence in the future and on the core values and principles of our society.

Though I can't prove it, I'd be willing to bet that throughout American history, in good times and bad, there has *never* been a time when a majority of Americans didn't believe that the future held great promise or that their children wouldn't have the chance for a better life. Until now.

Unfortunately, this widespread despair is grounded in troubling realities. Consider the situation we face:

- A national debt of over $14 trillion
- A federal budget deficit projected to reach $1.5 trillion in 2011, the highest in American history
- Our major entitlement programs—Medicare, Medicaid, and Social Security—headed toward bankruptcy
- An exploding wealth gap between the rich (and super-rich) and the poor: 14.5 to 1, nearly double the 7.69 to 1 figure from 1968, according to the 2010 census
- Failing education and health-care systems and crumbling infrastructure
- Falling living standards for millions in the middle class, with no hope for improvement
- An unemployment rate still holding at 9 percent

The problems confronting the country today are quickly becoming immediate threats to our well-being, both in the short and long term. Look no further than our frankly terrifying debt picture: a spring 2011 report from the Peterson Institute for International Economics estimates that the nation's debt as a percentage of GDP, which currently stands at 65 percent, will surge to 155 percent in 2035 under a "best-case" outlook, while a darker projection would have it reaching 302 percent of GDP. The Peterson Institute report—which notes that "debt ratios of around 200 percent of gross domestic product are at the extreme limit of what advanced economies can experience without becoming destabilized"—reads like a description of a slow onset of Armageddon.

Meanwhile the Federal Reserve System (the Fed), writes esteemed financial market analyst Martin Weiss, is printing money around the clock, doubling the nation's monetary base in just the last two years. Fed chief Ben Bernanke, Weiss writes, "has made it crystal clear that he will continue burying the world in newly created dollars to finance our record federal deficits."[1] The result is that global investors are dumping dollars on a massive scale, and the IMF is considering going off the dollar as the world's reserve currency. Weiss warns of consumer prices exploding in the near future.

While alarmism is never helpful, it must be said that the United States faces issues truly disturbing in their magnitude and severity. And Washington's inability, or unwillingness, to put forth genuine solutions makes the situation even more dire. When the parties do focus on major problems, they either cannot articulate rational solutions or they become mired in partisan warfare, falling back on reckless ideological positions.

MAINSTREAM PAIN, ELITE PROSPERITY

This loss of faith in the American Dream underscores the other fundamental source of division between the mainstream and the political class. Besides seeing the world very differently, the two groups are also *faring* very differently in today's economy: one group is prosperous, while the other, for the most part, has been engulfed in economic distress matched only by the Great Depression. Within the mainstream, the economic suffering is acute, broadly dispersed, and chronic. The Great Recession, as it has been called, might be, given different historical eras and economic structures, equal to that calamity or even worse. To give a brief picture:

- The United States has lost a net $7.7 trillion in household wealth since the meltdown, and Americans' home equity has declined 35 percent.
- As of September 2011, six million Americans have been out of work for twenty-seven weeks or more; in summer 2010, some 4.7 million Americans had been out of work for over a year.[2]
- The unemployment rate jumped 102 percent from 2007 to 2009.
- One in five Americans is either unemployed or underemployed.
- One in eight mortgages is in default or foreclosure, and millions more homes are on the brink.
- One in seven Americans is on food stamps.
- The U.S. median household income declined $2,241 from 1999 to 2008—even before the start of the Great Recession.[3]

- The price of a college education, meanwhile, has grown 467 percent since 1985, putting higher education out of reach for many middle-class students and burdening others with crushing debt.[4]

No wonder a recent poll showed that nearly half of Americans surveyed believe the nation is in a depression. And 44 percent, according to an NBC/*Wall Street Journal* poll in June 2011, believe that the nation is headed back into recession.

Meanwhile, corporate earnings are at their highest in history—according to the *New York Times*, fourth-quarter 2010 profits at American businesses were up an astounding 29.2 percent, the fastest growth in more than sixty years. Collectively, American corporations logged profits at an annual rate of $1.68 trillion. Since 2007, Wall Street profits have risen 720 percent. The top one-hundredth of one percent of households now makes an average of $27 million per household (the bottom 90 percent of American households makes an average of $31,244). While families dissolve under the blows of unemployment, while fifty-something professionals look in vain for work and college graduates work odd jobs in lieu of entry-level professional positions that can help them pay down their loans, the political class keeps cashing in—whether in Washington or on Wall Street.

Those most directly responsible for the 2008 financial crisis have gone unpunished, often rewarded with more lavish payouts and positions of leadership. The insiders' club continues to thrive; its members have made full recoveries from the financial meltdown and the Great Recession—if they were even thrown off stride at all.

Just consider the fate of the leadership of Fannie Mae, the federal mortgage broker whose liquidity crisis—and bailout—has so far cost taxpayers $162 billion. Tom Donilon, who served as general counsel of Fannie Mae, is now President Obama's national security advisor. Bill Daley, who served as a director, is the president's chief of staff. Franklin Raines, the disgraced CEO, left Fannie Mae with a golden parachute valued at perhaps as much as $240 million. Neither he nor anyone else associated with the Fannie Mae scandal has had to give any money back, let alone face any civil or criminal charges.

But while Fannie Mae went bust, Americans were evicted from their homes, and personal bankruptcies and foreclosures reached record highs. With that trail of destruction left behind them, the political class is only further enriched, empowered, and in effective control of government.

What the electorate sees when it looks at Washington is a political class that, over the last decade especially, has consistently made decisions on the great issues of the day that benefit the wealthy, the powerful, or the politically connected. No event of recent years has provoked this response more vividly than the government's handling of the financial crisis.

To be sure, what the political leadership in Washington faced in the fall of 2008 was truly daunting: nothing less than the threat of a systemic meltdown of our financial system. Some, like Federal Reserve chairman Ben Bernanke, told Republican and Democratic lawmakers that failing to act risked a Great Depression scenario. And three years later, it's certainly possible—though probably not provable—that what the federal government did in enacting the Troubled Asset Relief Program (TARP) and bailing out firms such as AIG, Bear Stearns, and Goldman Sachs really did prevent just such a scenario.

As far as mainstream Americans were concerned, though, the government was coming to the assistance of the very actors who had helped create the crisis (as it would later come to the aid, under President Obama, of some other groups whose worthiness was hotly contested—auto workers and public-sector employees among them). Further, poll data show clearly that the steps the federal government took in fall 2008 were opposed by the broadest cross section of Americans—the American mainstream. Yet the political class went ahead anyway, with barely a pretense of consulting their constituents.

All of this helps explain why millions of Americans now question the system itself and no longer believe that the political parties, in their current form, are capable of solving our most pressing problems. Republicans and Democrats seem to expend far more energy on politics than on problem solving; partisanship trumps everything in a system increasingly resembling, as former Republican congressman Mickey Edwards wrote in *National Journal*, "a battle between warring tribes."

Another lobbyist put it this way:

The legislative calendar used to be set up in a way where elected officials were in town, got to know their colleagues, and built broad-based bipartisan coalitions. That doesn't happen anymore. Today it is all about partisanship, political battles, and most of all, fundraising, 24/7. It makes it much harder for me to even reach them unless I have money at my disposal to get them to come, sit and pay attention. Other than that it is politics, politics, politics with bashing the other side at the top of the list.

It's unlikely that there has ever been such a wide disconnect between elected officials and the people they are elected to represent. As a result, there is real doubt, for the first time since the Great Depression, in our democracy's ability to meet the needs of the American people—let alone to maintain our position as a preeminent world power.

Worst of all, there is an overarching sense of national decline—economic, financial, and social—and a sense that, if we don't analyze our problems systematically and begin to address them, we might be headed for something much worse than that. As *U.S. News & World Report* publisher Mortimer Zuckerman wrote in June 2011:

> A new generation is coming of age that looks over its shoulder and sees a government in disarray, unable to make the wise and tough decisions to get things done and instead passing them off to some other body or future generation. Too many of us see a political leadership that lacks the character or capacity to build a consensus for the kind of constructive bipartisan compromise we have known even in fractious political times.[5]

The forces driving the polarization today are rooted in the parties themselves. Compromise has become virtually taboo in Washington because the parties have been captured by ideology, special interests, and—most of all—political money.

HOW PARTISANSHIP TRANSFORMED AMERICAN POLITICS

America's two-party system was once the envy of the world. We evolved a system in which Democrats and Republicans shared power in Congress and fought contentious and spirited elections for legislative and executive seats but also worked across the aisle to craft bipartisan solutions to the most pressing challenges. Moreover, the parties were subject to the will of the people: most candidates could not hope to win office without campaign donations from a substantial, broad-based section of the electorate—from blue-collar workers to professionals, college students to the elderly, urbanites and suburbanites to rural residents.

As I'll detail at length in a later chapter, all of this has fundamentally changed. A system once responsive to changing issues and changing tides of public opinion has become a massive, supremely powerful organism that exists to serve itself.

At the center of the story is campaign money—money to an extent never before seen in American politics. The kinds of money that candidates now raise through outside donors has become the most important source of funding for their campaigns, much more important than the old-fashioned individual donations that once powered campaigns and tied candidates to their constituents.

For a few years, culminating with Barack Obama's campaign in 2008, it looked as if the Internet might change this dynamic in its ability to attract individual donors and inspire "viral" public campaigns to raise funds for inspiring candidates. The Internet retains significant democratizing potential, and it's particularly potent for candidates with strong ideological appeal, like Republican congressman Ron Paul. But the battle uphill is much steeper now in the wake of the Supreme Court's landmark 2010 decision in *Citizens United*, which legalized unlimited independent expenditures to support or oppose federal candidates, effectively removing restrictions on political donations by corporations or unions. Then in May 2011, a Virginia federal judge ruled that the ban on companies contributing directly to federal candidates is unconstitutional. These decisions swing the balance heavily back in the direction of big money in politics. Often, this money comes from undisclosed sources.

It's true, of course, that President Obama historically tapped popular donations for his successful 2008 presidential campaign. He brought in a record amount of funding from ordinary Americans, but that didn't change the fact that his campaign was bankrolled by the same kinds of special-interest money that every modern candidate requires—including boatloads of Wall Street cash. (And in a clear sign that his team is ramping up for the 2012 presidential race, representatives of the Obama campaign held a closed-door meeting in spring 2011 with Wall Street donors—some of whom, like JPMorgan Chase's Jamie Dimon, have expressed disillusionment with the president.) Given the way the game is played today—with analysts estimating that Obama might spend $1 billion on his reelection campaign—candidates have little choice but to seek out the richest, most powerful donors.

On the Democratic side, which includes public-employee unions, who have essentially made the Democratic Party into their own subsidiary, exercising unprecedented power over the election of politicians who will then determine their pay, benefits, and job security. On the Republican side, the relationship between party elites and financial and business-interest groups is every bit as lucrative, and every bit as corrupt. The party can't afford not to pay heed when major donors urge relaxation of financial regulations or when private health insurers push for the loosening of restrictions under the new health-care law.

The pervasive and accelerating influence of campaign money has fundamentally transformed our politics, changing the dynamic of how politicians spend their time, how they see themselves, and, certainly, how they cast votes. This is because the campaign money comes from donors who expect specific results for their cash. Instead of receiving large sums from an aggregate of the population, the candidate receives money from special interests, whether in the financial industry, ethanol industry, Big Pharma, oil, automotive, or others. Or the candidate gets money from unions, professional organizations like the AMA, or social or civil-rights organizations. It's pay to play: buy off your representative, and get results.

One implication of monied politics is that our representatives are beholden to their funders in a way that separates them from their constituents. Another implication, related to the first, is that this dependence on special interests exacerbates partisanship and ideological polarization among elites. Since big-money donors and special interests don't represent anything like a broad swath of the electorate, their expectations distort the process. And the special interests, whether public-sector unions or industry lobbyists, have perfected the art of political activism and pressure to ensure that favored candidates stay on the right side of their issues.

Every sign going forward is that the political system will grow even more polarized, the two parties will be even less willing to put forth constructive solutions, and candidates will defer only to those willing to spend the most money—paying less and less attention to ordinary voters. With the possible exception of the Gilded Age, I'm not sure the United States has ever faced a time when, to such an extreme degree, the nation's political system has been so captured by outside money— and the system's workings so obviously put to the use of those who either write the checks or cash them.

The capture of the two parties by political money and interest groups has fostered the ideological and partisan obsessions driving both parties to political extremes—and alienating the electorate. There are other factors, too, including the party primary process, which encourages and facilitates the selection of candidates well to the right or left of most Americans. Congressional redistricting has made it easier for the parties to redraw the map of the country into "safe" districts for one party or the other—thereby diminishing, if not eliminating, the need for candidates to find common ground with the broader electorate.

It creates what we see in Washington on issue after issue: paralysis. There is no agreement on a single major issue facing the nation, several of which are approaching emergency status. There is no common ground, no bipartisanship. In fact, the very notion of bipartisanship has been sullied by the behavior of the political class. Instead of cooperating, the parties just play to their bases.

THE BUSH/OBAMA DECADE

The factors I've just cited are, I believe, essential to understanding how the political parties have run so far aground. At the same time, however, politics can never be separated from individuals whose leadership, for good or ill, can shape the environment in which these forces operate. In the American political system, no figure has more of that kind of influence than the president of the United States.

One of my arguments in this book is that the last decade in American political life has created an unprecedented breakdown in the compact that once existed between Americans and their political leaders. In fact, the compact no longer exists. Two presidents helped destroy what was left of it: George W. Bush and Barack Obama.

Bush ran for president as a so-called compassionate conservative. He was a conservative who understood social sympathy, entitlement programs, and bipartisanship. He famously ran as "a uniter, not a divider." It's hard to think of another presidential slogan that became more discredited—unless you consider that Bush succeeded, by the end of his presidency, in uniting most of the country against him.

Bush championed enormous tax cuts for the wealthy, which most economists agree did little or nothing to stimulate economic growth. He created a massively expensive new entitlement, the Medicare prescription drug program. He launched a war of choice in Iraq which, nearly a decade later, has cost the nation three-quarters of a trillion dollars and has no clear resolution in sight. He attempted to privatize Social Security, successfully gutted a generation's worth of sensible regulations—from environmental protection to financial policy—and showed little if any interest in curbing the growth of federal spending, which rose steadily on his watch. Then, in the fall of 2008, Bush engineered the financial bailouts. By the end of his two terms in the White House, Bush had approval ratings comparable to Jimmy Carter's.

No wonder, then, that Barack Obama ran so successfully as a candidate who would bridge the partisan divide. We're not Red or Blue, he famously said, we're American. That was music to the ears of millions, who wanted the conciliation Obama promised just as they had embraced Bush's pledge to "change the tone in Washington." In an election year in which Bush's Republicans were bound to be punished for his policies, Obama won easily, becoming the nation's first African American president—a potentially transformative, unifying moment in the nation's history.

But Obama proved just as partisan as Bush. His demeanor differed from Bush's in that he was more cerebral and deliberative, but the results were a Democratic mirror image of Bush-era partisanship: Obama pushed the most divisive piece of social legislation in the last half-century, the Patient Protection and Affordable Care Act (also called, usually derisively, Obamacare). The bill earned not a single Republican vote and made it through Congress only through hardball parliamentary tactics. It has faced a range of legal challenges ever since and may yet be repealed. Majorities favor doing just that.

With health-care reform, Obama managed to drive extreme responses from both sides. By initiating such an ambitious government program, he provoked impassioned opposition from the right's anti-statist voices. But by failing to deliver health care as a single-payer, government-guaranteed program, he sparked a populist uprising on the left—especially as it contrasted, in the left's eyes, with record Wall Street bonuses and pay, massive rounds of housing foreclosures, and crippling rates of unemployment and underemployment.

The president's nearly trillion-dollar stimulus didn't really stimulate the private-sector economy. It did save the jobs of public-sector workers and fill the pockets of democratic interest groups—and it did help give birth to the Tea Party movement, which became a major force on the right, as the 2010 midterm elections showed. Finally, Obama continued the Bush-style bailouts, rescuing General Motors and propping up major banks through the policies of Treasury Secretary Tim Geithner. On the left, howls for redistributive policies only increased. Left-wingers accused Obama of abandoning their agenda, and they have dug in harder than ever, pushing an almost religious commitment to higher taxes on the wealthy along with other cherished causes. They have embraced the Occupy Wall Street movement and have sought to associate themselves with the core analysis of the protesters—standing up for the 99 percent against the 1 percent. While the protesters themselves may well represent a fringe movement, the sense of disproportionate treatment of the rich versus the poor and working class is something that is firmly etched in the American consciousness regardless of ideology or worldview.

I'll examine this more closely in my chapter on left-wing populism.

Nearly three years into his term, Obama occupies a position similar to Bush: he gets few, if any, votes from the opposing party on just about any initiative. He polarizes the electorate. Whether he intended to be or not, he is seen as deeply partisan, as Bush was before him—a figure not willing to compromise with the opposition.

Under these two presidents, the Republican and Democratic parties have become almost uniformly partisan, unable and unwilling to make deals in the time-honored fashion of the past. There are no deals, because there is no agreement. Within the political class, everyone is dug into the trenches. And so, over the last several years, the American people have started digging in, too.

DIVISION IN THE MAINSTREAM: THE POPULIST REVOLT

My Fox News colleague Pat Caddell summed up extremely well the discontent ordinary people feel about the way politics in America works right now:

> The language, the discourse of politics right now has nothing to do with the way people feel. If you listen to these two parties talk about issues, about Medicare and etcetera. They're in it, it seems, to preserve their jobs. Somebody is going to get up and start talking the way Donald Trump did. About China, about "we don't have work here." Someone's going to get into this whole Wall Street thing. The Fannie Freddie scandal, the looting of the country, the bailouts. And it's going to appeal to a

coalition of people that don't fit the normal context of politics. (pollster Patrick Caddell, Fox News, June 12, 2011)

Ordinary Americans have responded to the extreme polarization in Washington by either becoming cynical and disengaged—withdrawing from the process completely—or by embracing more extreme solutions in the form of left- and right-wing populism. Seeing no answers coming from Washington, ordinary Americans have reached out for solutions that seem to make sense in the vacuum of leadership. We often hear that the American people are polarized, and that's true—just look at the last decade's presidential maps—but our popular divisions have been driven and deepened by divisiveness in Washington.

In fact, the partisan and ideological polarization so embedded in our politics today works something like a feedback loop. It is a dynamic, not static, process. Start with the division between the political class and the mainstream that I've described, a substantial portion of which is driven by the polarization between elites, which in turn leads to political paralysis and alienation of the electorate. Americans' mounting frustrations with chronic problems that go unsolved, and their disgust at a self-serving political class, drives them to seek solutions of their own—and these solutions vary. In short, they can be broken down into left-wing and right-wing populism: one side that calls for wealth redistribution and increased government oversight of the private sector, while the other calls for a much smaller government across the board. Both sides want an end to Washington's symbiotic relationship with Big Business and financial elites.

As we've seen over the last several years, the clashing visions of left- and right-wing populism create further polarization—the sense that the American public itself is splitting apart. Seeing this increased political strength coming from the most adamant parts of the ideological spectrum, Republicans and Democrats redouble their efforts to stay ideologically pure, thereby capturing votes of the energized populists and other elements in their "bases." And on and on it goes, polarization feeding upon polarization.

On the right, for example, the Tea Party has in just a few short years attained veto power within the GOP. If you're not squared up with them, you're not going far in today's Republican Party. Right-wing populists also include the supporters of Ron Paul and the devoted following that antipoliticians such as Sarah Palin and Michele Bachmann enjoy. The brief presidential fling of Donald Trump, as well, owed to a populist message—blunt talk about Chinese trade policy, for example—that appealed to many on the right.

On the left, we see reinvigorated union activism especially in response to battles with state governments on employee benefits, as in Wisconsin and Ohio—exemplified by the better than 63–37 vote to overturn the new collective bargaining law in Ohio—as well as a renewed policy push for wealth redistribution in late 2011, stimulated and facilitated in substantial measure by the Occupy Wall Street movement.

Intellectually, Robert Reich typifies this impulse with his calls for restoring the 70 percent top-income tax rate. The left has also dug in its heels on almost any kind of entitlement reform, as if "saving Medicare" without changes to the system were somehow possible. Environmentalists and foreign-policy isolationists have also been increasingly emboldened on the left in recent years, pushing for, respectively, a hugely expanded role for the EPA and a retreat from American leadership in the world. Democratic Party special interests, like the groups that pushed hard for health-care reform, have shown a renewed power and strength that they did not possess in the centrist Clinton years.

The important thing to remember about the electorate's turn to populism is that it is a symptom, not a cause, of partisan polarization in Washington. It is the ideological obsessions of the political class—so crystallized over the last decade in the Bush and Obama presidencies—that have led to the fundamental loss of faith in the system. And it is this loss of faith in the system that has driven the partisan divide at the popular level.

These are, in the end, two distinct universes. The loss of popular confidence in our political system intensifies and exacerbates a popular political divide, because people with no faith in their leaders are bound to come to different conclusions about what should be done. It all starts at the top, with a political class that is no longer self-correcting, only self-perpetuating.

WHERE ARE WE HEADED?

We've become essentially Two Americas: the political class and the American mainstream. In the 1960s, we famously heard about the problems of the Other America. Back then, this term referred to the problems of those who lived in rural poverty, particularly in Appalachia. Nearly fifty years later, most of the American mainstream has become the Other America to our ruling elites—a world they have little genuine contact with and barely understand.

This rift between ordinary Americans and the political class is the key, I believe, to understanding why our democracy no longer works. Though it has been discussed from time to time, it has never been analyzed and understood fully. That's why I wrote this book. I believe the political mainstream/political divide is at the heart of our problems today and that we need to understand it better—to get a sense not just of the 2012 election, but of the longer-term implications for American politics and indeed, American life.

It has become an American political cliché to say that an approaching election is the most important of our lifetimes. We're bound to hear the same thing about the 2012 election. Whatever the validity of that claim, most Americans won't need much reminding about how high the stakes are.

The last decade in this country has been, by any accounting, enormously difficult for most Americans, and there is little sign at the moment that this is about to change. No matter which party and candidates prevail this November, they will have to face challenges of rare scale and magnitude. As bad as these problems are, however, they tend to obscure the underlying pathology that is eating away at the viability of our political system.

We're in a crisis for our national identity and future. No one knows what's coming next, or whether anything or anyone can break the polarization that has paralyzed political leadership in Washington and divided the American people. As divisive and hostile as our political dialogue often is, one can still hear within it, especially at the popular level, the desire for unity as Americans.

September 11, 2001, and the days and months afterward, as awful as they were, showed how deeply those desires ran. Three years ago, when Barack Obama was elected president, the nation had a moment again to savor and reflect. Even though millions hadn't voted for him, only the most hardened partisans could fail to acknowledge the historic implications of America electing a black man as its chief executive. It was difficult not to feel pride that night. And in spring 2011, nearly ten years after 9/11, the brief but joyous celebrations that took place across the country when Osama bin Laden was killed by U.S. forces showed, again, that the American people devoutly wish for this kind of national unity.

I am by nature an optimist, and I don't think things are hopeless by any means. But breaking through the polarization is going to be a very daunting challenge.

Three years ago, when Obama was elected, people felt a surge of hope not just because of his historic significance but because of the kind of campaign he'd run: hopeful, uplifting, optimistic, deeply American in every good sense—and capped off by an explicit pledge to bridge the political divide. It didn't happen. Not even close.

Before Obama, George W. Bush promised compassionate conservatism only to stand by and let Karl Rove and others push hard-right policies that alienated a full half of the electorate from the get-go.

As I described briefly above, and will show in more detail in this book, there are strong, almost gravitational, forces driving the parties to behave and govern in this way. Examining all of the forces at work and the groups involved is essential to formulating a coherent analysis of what has brought us to this point and what the future might look like.

In the next chapter, I'll delve much more deeply into the political class/mainstream divide. I'll describe the political class in detail—who's in it, what characterizes its members, how it thinks and operates, with examples from recent history. I'll show how the divide is widened by the political class's consolidation of power and influence, and I'll describe some of the issues and events of recent years that have widened the gap—including the Great Recession and financial crisis, growing income inequality, and the corrosive effect of partisan politics and campaign money.

In chapter 3, I'll take an up-close look at the gap between the American mainstream and the political class on a host of issues—using mostly my own proprietary polling data. In chapter 4, I'll briefly describe how this Great Divide has left the American mainstream grasping for political answers—and finding them, increasingly, in a reawakened populism, whether of the left-wing or right-wing variety.

Chapters 5 through 8 will examine this new populism from both sides of the ideological spectrum. In chapters 5 and 6, I'll look at the principles that motivate left-wing populism and look at some recent history that has prompted a populist upsurge on the left; then I'll show how the left-populist impulse works in Washington today and the pressure it puts on the Obama administration to meet lofty progressive expectations. In chapters 7 and 8, I'll examine the principles that under-pin right-wing populism and discuss how this conservative disposition reawakened in the waning years of the Bush administration and then exploded in reaction to the financial bailouts and Obama's stimulus and health-care initiatives. Then I'll analyze its power and dynamics on the current scene, in which the Tea Party has become perhaps the central player in GOP politics.

Of course, not all Americans are left-wing or right-wing populists. What about everyone else? In chapter 9, I'll briefly profile the Inde-pendents, a segment of the electorate generally recognized as the largest—and the one that might be the angriest, too. Neither party can win without them; and neither can count on them, either, as In-dependents have swung radically over recent years, consistent only, it seems, in their discontent.

Finally, in chapters 10, 11, and 12, I'll examine in depth some of the means by which the political class has gained, maintained, and increased its power over the years. With a chapter each on money in politics, lobbying, and redistricting, I'll describe a system that, contrary to popular image, works rather efficiently—the problem is, it only works for its insiders, not its constituents.

In my conclusion, I'll share some reflections on the urgency of our political predicaments from my own perspective of a long career in political consulting. Whichever policies we choose to support going forward are less important than an honest recognition of the crises that we face.

Understanding the issues this book examines is one step, I believe, in recognizing this reality. Only by doing so can we begin to restore the viability of our democratic system.

2

THE MAINSTREAM/ POLITICAL CLASS DIVIDE

And in fact Republican and Democratic office holders and their retinues show a similar presumption to dominate and fewer differences in tastes, habits, opinions, and sources of income among one another than between both and the rest of the country. They think, look, and act as a class.

—Angelo Codevilla

Of all the problems the United States faces today, the most ominous is one rarely named: the massive divide between citizens and their leaders.

In June 2011, with the American economy struggling under an unemployment rate of 9 percent, Rasmussen Reports asked people if they agreed with this statement: "The gap between Americans who want to govern themselves and politicians who want to rule over them is now as big as the gap between the American colonies and England during the 18th Century."

Forty-five percent of all likely voters, and 55 percent of what Rasmussen defines as mainstream voters, agreed with that statement. In a May 2011 Rasmussen survey, 60 percent of all voters said that the U.S. government did not have the consent of the governed.

Think about those numbers. They reflect a deep-seated, corrosive loss of trust in the political institutions that have defined American representative democracy. By one central criterion—does the system serve the people?—our own political system has stopped working, at least for most of us. For a select group of political and financial elites, the system works just fine.

The federal branch of our two-party democracy has become a system that by its very nature cannot find solutions to major issues, from record deficits to a debt crisis to massive unemployment. Neither party has a serious jobs agenda, even after three years of debilitating unemployment rates. These problems and others are simply not adjudicated; they are hidden beneath blizzards of partisan warfare or obscured by temporary fixes or half measures that fool no one. The struggles of millions of Americans with stagnant incomes, lost jobs, soaring education costs, and continuous rounds of housing foreclosures count for little beside the machinations of a political class that puts its interests ahead of ordinary people.

Before I go further, I should say that I'm quite aware of how strong, and perhaps even extreme, these words sound. I've never been an alarmist. In nearly forty years working in politics as a consultant and pollster to members of Congress, senators, governors, and presidents—and for Republicans as well as Democrats—I've always been a proud centrist, someone who believed in our system of free markets and free enterprise and in the United States taking an active and leading role in the world. I've never thought much of "us against them" arguments, whether they came from left-wing unionists or right-wing social conservatives.

But over the last several years, I've become alarmed by the failures of our system to address both the broad issues facing our federal government and the everyday hardships of average Americans. I've reluctantly concluded that the problem is not about individuals or parties. It's a problem of an entire system. The American ideal of a citizen government has been overrun by elite-driven government. This would be bad enough philosophically, but it also happens to have real-world effects: vital issues are allowed to fester until they become existential crises and a citizenry loses both its standard of living and its trust in our political and economic system.

It is a system awash in political cash, a system that continues to reward insiders and do their bidding to the exclusion of ordinary people. It is a system that rewards reckless corporate behavior with government bailouts while doing little if anything to assist middle-class Americans trying to stay in their homes. It is perpetuated by a revolving door between the private sector and Washington that links most of the same people to one another. They forge alliances that come in handy when the going gets rough—like, say, in the fall of 2008, when having a former Goldman Sachs CEO, Hank Paulson, serving as Treasury Secretary proved a lifesaver for not only current Goldman CEO Lloyd Blankfein but also for most of the Wall Street establishment. It didn't work out so well for Main Street. In 2010 alone, 3.8 million Americans foreclosed on their houses. But since 2007, with the exception of minor players like hedge-fund entrepreneur Raj Rajaratnam or Goldman Sachs trader Fabrice Tourre, no principal figure in the housing bubble or financial crisis has been prosecuted.[1]

That almost no one could be brought to account for what the nation has suffered in fraud and deception underscores the fundamentally self-dealing nature of the system. Angelo Mozilo, CEO of Countrywide Financial and one of the leading purveyors of the subprime disaster, is as good an example as any. Although charged by the SEC with insider trading and securities fraud, Mozilo faced no criminal charges, paying civil penalties in a private settlement with the Commission. Numerous politicians in Washington over the years, including Connecticut senator Chris Dodd, have received sweetheart mortgage financing from Countrywide. The company placed Dodd and others into a program called "Friends of Angelo."[2]

Dodd was chairman of the Senate Banking Committee at the time. You can find examples of insider dealing like this behind most of the crises and scandals of recent years: a collaborative nexus between regulators and regulated, government and business, colluding together for their own benefit while taxpayers pay the cost.

That so many in Washington and on Wall Street weathered the storms of recent years—the rich getting richer, income inequality in the United States reaching record levels—suggests a system run by and for the wealthy that has effectively bankrupted the rest of the country. The housing crisis, the financial crash, the Great Recession, the loss of millions of manufacturing jobs—we've seen one devastation after another, yet those in positions of privilege and power have flourished. The underlying causes remain unsolved, threatening greater crises to come.

The Republican and Democratic parties have done so little to address this dysfunctional, collusive culture because, for the most part, they're part of it. Their members spend their energies courting wealthy donors, political-action committees (PACs), and powerful special-interest groups. While these groups—from NARAL, Emily's List, and labor unions on the left to the NRA, the Club for Growth, and Goldman Sachs on the right—don't represent the broader electorate, they have increasingly large resources that have enabled them to skew the political process and drive the nation apart. Other organizations—called 527s or 501(c)(3)s after the section of the U.S. tax code that allows them to organize—operate outside the scrutiny of the normal electoral process and can raise unlimited funds to influence campaigns and outcomes. In fact, some campaigns are now funded by more outside, secret money than money from either the candidate or the party committees. The days of candidates raising their own money based on levels of overall popular support are long gone.

And behind the parties and their PACs operate a select network of "super elites"—wealthy and powerful individuals who exert inordinate influence on our politics.

Super elites like the Koch brothers, for example, have donated over $100 million to right-wing causes over the last several years, along with tens of millions through their various organizations, such as Americans for Prosperity, which have played an important role funding campaign ads against Democrats and advocating favorable deregulatory policies for fossil-fuel industries. On the left, George Soros, the billionaire chairman of the Open Society Institute, has spent millions to defeat Republican candidates and push left-wing positions on drug legalization, assisted suicide, and health-care reform.

No wonder, then, that most Americans view both parties as undemocratic. They have little opportunity to gain access to a closed system and get their voices heard. Millions have become disillusioned, cynical, or angry, and many have embraced populist answers on the far left or far right of the spectrum. A crucial dynamic underlies all of this: the profound division between mainstream Americans and a governing elite, what I along with many others call the political class.

America is a divided country, but not in the way you usually hear. The fundamental divide is not Red versus Blue, or Republican versus Democrat. The divide has to do with an unbridgeable gap between those in positions of power and influence—especially in politics and business—and everyone else on the outside looking in. There is the America of Washington D.C., which is satisfied with the two-party system, and there is the America of the rest of the country, where three-quarters of the people are unsatisfied with the state of their country and deeply worried about their future.

On one side, we have the vast American mainstream, the most varied electorate in human history. They believe in hard work, the rule of law, free enterprise, self-governance, and a general principle that Americans should be free to do as we wish so long as we're not hurting someone else. They are liberals and conservatives, libertarians and progressives, Tea Party members and unionists. They have struggled mightily over the last decade against stagnant incomes, diminished employment prospects, and perhaps most of all, a sense of powerlessness—a belief that those in positions of power and privilege hold all the cards and couldn't care less what they think or want. They see the political class with remarkable unanimity, as elites motivated by little but self-gain. They see big government and big business, despite their adversarial rhetoric, as allies, united against the will and interests of the American people. And on a host of the most important issues facing the country over the last few years—from TARP to the Wall Street bailouts, from the auto bailouts to health-care reform—they stood firmly opposed to the political class.

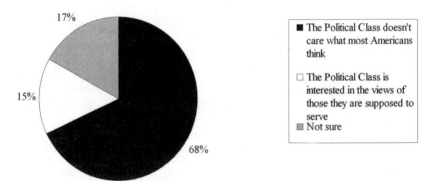

Figure 2.1. National survey of 1,000 likely voters in July 12–13, 2010.

On the other side is a governing class in Washington increasingly insulated from public accountability, while a financial elite, what some call a "super class," not only enjoys the fruits of prosperity but also increasingly puts their wealth to work in shaping political outcomes. Instead of serving the public, these elites have set up the system so that our laws and political processes serve *them*.

I don't believe that the United States can continue indefinitely under a system that divides us into such stark categories of rulers and ruled. The divide between the political class and the American mainstream explains, I believe, the dysfunctional, angry, polarized state of our politics today. On a multitude of issues, the two sides are irreconcilably opposed.

To begin with, on that Rasmussen question about the gap between Americans and their leaders being as great as during Revolutionary times, *0 percent* of the political class agreed—while 95 percent disagreed.

WHAT IS THE POLITICAL CLASS?

In my 2010 book with Scott Rasmussen, *Mad as Hell*, we briefly summarized the nature of the political class:

> This exclusive club comprises chieftains in business, government, and the media, who manage the public and private sectors, and for whom our system is fundamentally rigged. They control the nation's banks, think tanks, the flows of news and information, and virtually every lever of power and influence across society. They attend elite schools, are members of elite organizations, and operate within insular social circles.

Because of their extraordinary and concentrated power and the sophistication of the industries they manage, the odds are tilted obscenely in favor of the political elite. Their top-rate educations provide them with access to sophisticated careers. Their managerial positions in technologically complex sectors in government and business allow them to game the system they control to their own self-interest. And their wealth and social status insulates them from the forces of globalization and economic decline that have ravaged almost everyone else.

This all remains true. Think of the political class as the American meritocratic elite: a small group of influencers from business, government, academia, and media who occupy the most prestigious institutional positions in American society. While its membership is extremely small, the political class exerts enormous power and influence.

The political class includes Republicans, Democrats, and Independents. Genuine policy differences exist among them but are less important than their shared goals and outlooks, perhaps the most important of which is the conviction that they are the people best suited to run

America's government, to make political decisions, and to affect social change. They differ on specifics, but they all agree that "ordinary" Americans possess neither the talent nor the temperament to make these decisions. In short, the political class has essentially co-opted and subverted the American democratic system for its own gain.

Political class members are driven by something more powerful than political ideology: self-interest and a desire to benefit from government, whether economically, politically, or socially. But fundamentally, what distinguishes the political class from the mainstream has less to do with the social or professional position than with their outlook and their behavior—in short, the way they see the world and how they act as a result.

That's why we came up with the Political Class Index, a set of three questions that separate these elites from everyone else:

1. Generally speaking, when it comes to important national issues, whose judgment do you trust more, the American people or America's political leaders? *Those in the mainstream say the American people; those in the political elite say political leaders.*
2. Some people believe that the federal government has become a special-interest group that looks out primarily for its own interests. Has the federal government become a special interest group? *Mainstreamers say yes; the political elite says no.*
3. Do government and big business often work together in ways that hurt consumers and investors? *Mainstreamers say yes; the political elite says no.*

Based on exhaustive research, Scott Rasmussen determined that 55 percent of Americans could be classified on the mainstream side of the political divide, while only 7 percent make up the political class. When "leaners" were included, those figures increased to 75 percent and 14 percent, respectively.

So the political class is vanishingly small, but its power and influence are immense. Over the last several years, several other writers have taken note of the pervasive power of the political class and how its members operate. One of its core characteristics is insularity.

In a 2010 *American Spectator* article, right-wing thinker Angelo Codevilla points out that the members of what he calls the Ruling Class tend to be clustered in cities like New York, Boston, Washington, Los

Angeles, and San Francisco, but also university cities, especially those that harbor high-tech jobs, such as Austin and the Raleigh-Durham/ Chapel Hill triangle, and that with such geographical clustering goes cultural clustering: political and social elites tend to have the same reference points, and they also tend to be deeply cut off from the interests most ordinary Americans pursue. The political class in Washington, of both parties, has certain things in common:

> Regardless of what business or profession they are in, their road up included government channels and government money because, as government has grown, its boundary with the rest of American life has become indistinct. Many began their careers in government and leveraged their way into the private sector. Some, e.g., Secretary of the Treasury Timothy Geithner, never held a non-government job. Hence whether formally in government, out of it, or halfway, America's ruling class speaks the language and has the tastes, habits, and tools of bureaucrats. It rules uneasily over the majority of Americans not oriented to government.[3]

My notion of the political class, however, is broader than Codevilla's Ruling Class, which tends to exempt Republican/conservative–type thinkers and business elites—especially entrepreneurs, oil executives, and the like. I see the political class as including not just the Washington leadership class but those in multiple other professional sectors who either work closely with government or *have learned to use government to foster their own advancement and enrichment.* A good example is Texas billionaire T. Boone Pickens, an oil and gas magnate who began championing wind and solar power when government subsidies for alternative energy became the norm in Washington.

Some of these individuals (like Pickens, who chairs the hedge fund BP Capital Management) are also members of a separate, almost adjunct class to the political class, which many have come to call super elites or the super class—those of such overwhelming wealth that they have essentially become a separate culture unto themselves. As journalist Chrystia Freeland has written, this new class of "jet-setting meritocrats" believes itself, in somewhat Ayn Rand–like fashion, to be composed of "deserving winners of a tough, worldwide economic competition." They are often dismissive of the less successful—which is basically everyone else. They have become, Freeland writes, "a transglobal community of peers who have more in common with one another than with their countrymen back home."[4] Perhaps their emblematic member is Steven Schwartzman. Schwartzman is CEO of the Blackstone Group, a private-equity firm, who also sits on the boards of a range of foundations and councils, including the World Economic Forum. (Schwartzman's notorious comment comparing President Obama's desire to raise taxes on top-bracket earners to Nazism is a vivid example of this class's sense of entitlement and lack of perspective.)

It's not difficult to imagine how such a super class, along with political and other business elites, could come to very different conclusions than people on Main Street.

There is the unmistakable sense among the political class that they are something like a guardian class that knows what is best for the American people. As Glenn Greenwald has written: "It has long been the supreme fantasy of establishment guardians in general . . . that American politics would be dominated by an incestuous, culturally homogeneous, superior elite who live in (Washington) and who have often known each other since prep school." *New York Times* columnist David Brooks explicitly lauded such an ideal when he paid tribute to the British political system, which, he wrote, was "dominated by people who live in London and who have often known each other since prep school. This makes it gossipy and often incestuous. But the plusses outweigh the minuses." The implication was that insiders knew best and could function most effectively with minimal popular interference.

This American elite, while more democratic than it was a half century ago, has in some ways not changed that much. Certainly political-class proving grounds, like Ivy League colleges, have opened up their admissions processes substantially over the last few decades. Yet most kids attending elite colleges—four out of five, according to sociologist Joseph Soares—come from families in the top quarter of America in terms of income, education, and professional status. Only about one in twenty elite-college students come from the bottom half of the family-income tier.[5] So political class members-in-training not only come from self-selected family and income groups but also they spend their formative years around people much like themselves.

All of these reinforcing factors—family background, educational attainment, professional status—create key tendencies within members of the political class.

As a class it tends toward self-selection, which perpetuates its structures, assumptions, and practices. The kinds of individuals who tend to rise high in party politics, let alone run for president, usually have certain common features. They are often, if not always, independently wealthy. They come most often from a legal background. And they tend to be the kinds of personalities for whom ambition colors nearly every move. They're adept at "going along to get along," the better to attract and leverage the kinds of people who can help them—even if it means violating ethical codes, personal or professional, that they'd vowed to honor.[6]

That last trait is essential in today's political world, where attracting the right funders and doing the bidding of the right special interests is indispensable to winning, and holding onto, political office. And it also helps ensure that political class members become insulated from their constituents, because their constant inward focus on pleasing the right individuals and groups—almost all of them inside the Beltway—quickly cuts them off from the rest of the country.

The political class' belief in its own superiority and natural fitness for governance fosters another characteristic: closed-door decision making. Think of the major policy efforts of the last several years, from Wall Street bailouts to trillion-dollar stimulus packages to massive health-care reform legislation. All of them were opposed by the American mainstream. They were created and implemented by political elites who simply disregarded the popular will.

The political class, being deeply incestuous, is also extraordinarily self-protecting.

In Washington, of course, such "watching your back" practices are part of the culture in both parties. It could be Washington's "Senator from Wall Street," Chuck Schumer, helping to gut the financial reform bill's requirements on banks. Schumer, after all, was tight with Goldman Sachs CEO Lloyd Blankfein, having once shared a stage at a Democratic fund-raiser to sing "nostalgic furniture-store jingles" with the Goldman boss.[7] It could be Richard Fuld, Lehman Brothers' last CEO, who left the failed company in fall 2008—with $72 million in compensation for his final year and no demand from Washington that he give any of it back. Or it could be a congressman like the GOP's Joe Barton, who came to the defense of BP during its 2010 oil spill—the largest in the history of the petroleum industry—by calling President Obama's insistence that the company put cash into a relief fund "a tragedy." CEO Tony Hayward showed how political class habits cut across national boundaries when he complained, at the height of the crisis, that "I want my life back." He soon got his wish, stepping down from BP to begin enjoying a pension of at least £10 million.

Perhaps no example better illustrates how interconnected political class elites both look out for one another and enrich one another than the case of Fannie Mae. *New York Times* columnist Gretchen Morgenson's book on the financial crisis, *Reckless Endangerment,* documents how in the 1990s Fannie executives, led by then-CEO James Johnson, looted $2.1 billion of $7 billion in guaranteed congressional funds. With that public money, Johnson and his well-placed cronies paid themselves higher salaries and bonuses and also doled out money to selected interest groups in exchange for their political support. They lavished money on sympathetic members of Congress in exchange, again, for their political support—because Fannie's loose subprime-lending practices were arousing worries among some legislators and prompting calls for stricter regulation. Those complaints went nowhere, thanks to the Fannie loyalists in Congress, especially Democrats with close ties to the broader banking industry, like Representative Barney Frank and Senator Chris Dodd.

By the time the dust had cleared, subprime had wrought unimaginable havoc on the nation's housing market, middle-class living standards, and our debt picture. James Johnson had left Fannie Mae a decade earlier, eventually clearing around $100 million. His welcome within the portals of the political class showed no sign of diminishing: Barack Obama named him to a three-person committee to vet vice presidential candidates in June 2008, although Johnson was roundly criticized for his ties to Angelo Mozilo of Countrywide Financial and soon stepped down. Otherwise, despite becoming what Morgenson and her coauthor Joshua Rosner call "corporate America's founding father of regulation manipulation" and a key figure in the financial crisis, Johnson paid no price whatsoever.

Why not? So many Americans ask. Part of the answer—an unsatisfying one—is that all of this is typical. The insiders' culture in Washington is fundamentally self-serving. As David Brooks wrote about Fannie Mae, the worst thing about the scandal is that it involved nothing illegal on its face—this is just the way Washington works.[8]

On top of all of this, the political class has a built-in self-righteousness—both in terms of the credit it feels it deserves as well as its anger and irritation when it receives public rebuke. When political class members hear criticism, even outrage, coming from their constituents, they often fall back on rhetorical devices. One is to invoke common sense: they claim what they're doing is simply the only logical option and paint impassioned popular opposition as emotional and irrational. Political leaders' reactions to public outrage at TARP often took this tack, suggesting that the people just didn't understand such a complicated problem. In the summer of 2009, when town halls around the nation revealed intense opposition to the Obama administration's health-care plan, Democrats could barely contain their contempt for their own constituents. During the debt-ceiling standoff of summer 2011, those who opposed extending the nation's credit were portrayed as irrational while those supporting the extension insisted that it was the only conceivable solution.

Another tactic of self-defense is to invoke selflessness and political courage. A good example of this came in October 2010, when President Obama appeared on the *Daily Show* with Jon Stewart. Asked about the contentious health-care reform debate, the president said that many of his fellow Democrats had voted for the bill, even in the face of popular opposition, because they believed "it was the right thing to do." They nobly pursued the public good, in other words—even though their constituents' view of the public good was quite different from theirs.

Certainly political courage is much needed today, and standing up for "what's right" is exactly what we need. The problem is that political elites are standing up for what's right in their own minds, with often no attempt to reconcile those ideas with the wishes of the people who elect them. The political class has lost the sense that they are *representatives* of other people, not those people's *leaders.* They have internalized the dynamics and levers of power so deeply that they believe their role is not to represent others but to make decisions for them.

Or, in the case of the super elites, they believe the government's role is to serve their interests should they get into trouble—regardless of whether that remedy is ethical or even legal, let alone whether it will have destructive effects on ordinary people. The CEOs of the many disgraced financial giants of recent years, as well as super-rich hedge-fund managers and financial innovators, have all shared this assumption.

By now, the chasm between what people of this kind and what mainstream Americans think, do, and believe about the issues facing us is so wide as to threaten our national future. Let's take a look at how the divide developed and expanded over recent years.

WHAT DRIVES THE DIVIDE

One simple way of understanding the break between the political class and ordinary Americans is to track how well the actual views of the American people are reflected in the laws and policies the political class implements. The alienation of the American people from their governing elites is impossible to separate from this essential fact: that while we still have a democracy in terms of elections and laws, our leadership class has adopted deeply undemocratic habits in pursuing policies contrary to the will of the majority of Americans.

In a 2004 article, the late political scientist Samuel Huntington cited numerous scholarly studies that clearly documented the growing gap between policy elites and the public, even when public opinion changed in one direction or another. The hinge point seems to be the 1970s, when there was still 75 percent consistency between public opinion and actual government policy; but that number steadily dropped in ensuing decades. It was down to 67 percent by the mid-to-late 1980s, just 40 percent by the early 1990s, and just 37 percent by the mid-1990s. These declines track individual policy areas, from foreign policy to economic policy to social issues.[9]

More recently, over the last decade, the gulf between popular preference and the actions of our elites has taken on a much more disturbing cast—because it comes against the backdrop of enormous problems and metastasizing crises. In times like we live in today, we cannot afford to have such a disconnect in our democratic arrangements. Without popular support and some degree of trust, government faces a crisis of legitimacy, leaving it little basis on which to unify the electorate, ask for sacrifice (if necessary), or otherwise rally a democratic citizenry to action.

Unfortunately, that's the situation we find ourselves in—and developments of the last decade and a half, both in Washington and beyond it, have only made it worse.

The Great Recession

There aren't many parallels to what the nation has been living through on an economic level. Where it is having its deepest, starkest impact is on middle-class Americans, the heart and soul of the national mainstream. According to Chrystia Freeland, the job numbers—9.1 percent unemployment, with an average time of unemployment of nearly forty weeks—"depict an unemployment crisis that is deeper and more sustained than at any time since 1948, when records first started to be kept."[10] The middle class has taken it on the chin not just on jobs, but in the aftermath of the housing crash. While stock-market prices fell more than house prices during 2007 to 2009, houses made up a much larger share of the middle class's gross assets than did stocks for the rich. The middle class took a much bigger hit, then, on the decline in home prices than the top 20 percent took from stock-price decline.[11]

And things may get worse before they get better, since stagnant incomes make middle-class Americans less appealing constituencies for CEOs and shareholders of American companies, already eyeing overseas emerging economies.[12] And the energy in Washington seems focused on deficit cutting, not job creation.

All of this, of course, leads to an inequity in who bears the burden for the hard times and fosters distrust, anger, and disillusionment—best reflected in the figures I cited in chapter 1 on the decline of the American Dream. As it dawns on millions that unemployment, housing instability, and financial distress may be part of their lives for the long term, a sense of betrayal and even rage are palpable. The American Dream, as publisher Arianna Huffington put it, "has become an American nightmare." If you want one sentence that might best summarize Americans' disgust, it's this: Washington, D.C., is the one of the few cities in the country where housing values are going up.[13]

Exploding Income Inequality

Hand in hand with that feeling of disgust is the nation's exploding rate of income inequality over the last few decades. Current estimates put the rate of income inequality at somewhere near that of 1928, the year before the stock market crashed and helped create the Great Depression.

Other estimates are even worse. Between 1970 and 2005, the American Gini coefficient, a technical measure that gauges income inequality, has increased by more than 20 percent. On the Gini coefficient, a "0" score would indicate complete income equality, while a "1" would indicate complete inequality, where one person would be responsible for 100 percent of income. In those thirty-five years, the coefficient increased from 0.39 to 0.47, the largest gap between the very rich and the very poor since the early twentieth century, the earliest time for which there is available data.[14] The United States currently has the third-highest inequality and poverty rates in the OECD countries—after Turkey and Mexico—and the gap has accelerated over the last ten years.

Between 1993 and 2008, the top 1 percent of Americans captured 52 percent of all income growth in the United States.[15] Our richest 10 percent earn an average of $93,000, the highest in the OECD, while our poorest 10 percent earn an average of just $5,800.[16] Even with economic productivity gains of close to 20 percent, the middle class has seen virtually zero income growth. A June 2011 Pew poll found that over the past year, between a quarter and one-third of those earning less than $75,000 had trouble paying for medical care, paying a mortgage or rent, and feared either being laid off or suffering a pay cut in the next year.[17]

These trends have been enormously painful, obviously, for millions of Americans, and they have fostered no shortage of explanations—and reactions, including resurgent populism within the electorate. Certainly the globalization of the American economy, with its accompanying downsizing and outsourcing, has played an important role in driving working-class and middle-class salaries down, when it hasn't actually been eliminating jobs altogether. Globalization led to the loss of five million U.S. manufacturing jobs since the inception of NAFTA in 1997. While millions of American families contend with these extraordinary losses, the political elite in business and government have enjoyed increased corporate profits and decreased tax liabilities.

The technological revolution of the last thirty years, which automated so many jobs, seems mostly to have benefited those with advanced degrees—thereby broadening the income gap. Over the last thirty years, adjusting for inflation, weekly earnings for the 74 percent of consumers without a college degree fell about 10 percent—while those with bachelor's degrees or higher saw their incomes increase about 20 percent.[18] And high rates of unemployment, and long periods of time spent on unemployment, mean that millions will see their skills diminish and grow out of date—making it all the more difficult to recover their previous income levels.

Meanwhile, executive pay has risen substantially since the financial crisis. One year after the financial crisis, the top twenty-five hedge-fund managers were paid an annual salary, on average, of $1 billion.[19] Is it any wonder that so many Americans believe that government and business collude together against ordinary people?

The Financial Crisis and Its Aftermath

Probably the most emblematic period in the recent history of the elite/
popular divide was the fall of 2008, when the U.S. economy faced a
financial crisis rivaled by few, if any, in its history. The crisis was preceded by two decades of deregulation and irresponsibility on the part
of the political elite on Wall Street and in Washington. The Federal
Reserve, the SEC, and private Wall Street regulators all failed—really,
flat-out refused—to monitor the risks associated with the derivatives
market. The Fed kept lowering interest rates, prompting a marked
increase in unchecked subprime-mortgage lending, which led to a
housing bubble that proved nearly fatal for the U.S. economic system.
Yet the crisis mostly enriched the political class further. Some lost
money in the short term, but they were for the most part bailed out by
Washington and recovered their losses. Most are doing as well or better
today—unlike millions of Americans, who lost homes, jobs, and liveli-
hoods, and may never recover.

Panic on Wall Street and in the financial markets sparked a near
bank run on money-market mutual funds in September 2008 and
raised fears of a liquidity crisis. Overleveraged investment houses,
such as Lehman Brothers, collapsed. Washington stepped in to contain the damage. Urging lawmakers to adopt a $700 billion emergency
bailout to buy back the banks' "toxic assets," Federal Reserve chairman Ben Bernanke and then–Treasury Secretary Hank Paulson spoke
classic political-class language to the legislators: "If we don't do this,
we may not have an economy on Monday."[20] There was, yet again,
only one possible, commonsense answer. A problem of enormous
magnitude would be addressed behind closed doors, with no national
discussion or debate.

What became TARP, the Troubled Assets Relief Program, was supported nearly unanimously by Democrats and Republicans in Congress.
The media, from *The Nation* to the *Wall Street Journal*, urged its passage to stave off what everyone called "systemic collapse." This may
well have been an accurate assessment of the situation, as I suggested
earlier. Some argue otherwise. But what we do know for sure is that at
the time, the majority of the American people didn't buy it. Americans
of all political orientations strongly opposed TARP. They believed, as
they still do today, that the nation's economic meltdown was caused by
a combination of criminal behavior by financial executives and collu-

sion with Washington politicians, who benefited from close ties to Wall Street and looked the other way for years.

Mainstream Americans would later oppose the government's shifting strategy to buy up equity in the banks, as they would later oppose the bailout of the U.S. automotive industry—and as they would later oppose the institution of a massive new health-care entitlement. All of these things, too, were implemented by the political class in contravention of the public will.

Today, when Republicans and Democrats talk about the financial crisis, they speak in tones much closer to the populist revulsion of their constituents three years ago. Democratic congressman Philip Angelides released a report in June 2011 that placed primary blame for the financial meltdown on self-dealing Wall Street figures and called the entire episode an "avoidable crisis." Republicans have pointed the finger at Fannie Mae and Freddie Mac, the prime beneficiaries of the subprime shell game, and their backers in Congress. For the left, the crisis was driven by private-sector greed; for the right, the crisis was the result of misguided and corrupt government policies.

Whichever analysis you prefer, the American people had the broad conclusion right, and the political class had it wrong: the financial crisis was, indeed, a failure of the system and a stark example of government and business working against the interests of ordinary people. Washington insiders—liberal and conservative, Democrat and Republican—were convinced that the free flow of capital and a free hand for major financial institutions in creating financial products were good policies for our economy and would regulate themselves. Some argued that Washington regulators and politicians had been "captured" or overrun by Wall Street figures, but the truth is that the crisis was a collaborative effort. Other than a few principled figures, like Brooksley Born of the Commodities Futures and Exchange Commission, Washington happily went along with the deregulatory ride. The resulting catastrophe was wholly engineered by the political class.

Meanwhile, three-plus years later, just 13 percent of Americans, according to Rasmussen research, believe that the government has been aggressive enough in pursuing possible criminal behavior by major Wall Street bankers. Some 64 percent say the government has not been aggressive enough. Another 23 percent are not sure. No wonder, then, that 51 percent of Americans believe the federal government is more concerned with making Wall Street firms profitable than making sure the U.S. financial system works well for all Americans. Only 22 percent say the government is more concerned with making the system work for all.

The financial crisis, devastating as it was in real terms to American households, was just as devastating in another vital respect: it shattered, perhaps irreparably, any lingering faith in the integrity of the two parties in Washington.

Political Money and Partisan Politics

When you have two political parties whose members have to spend an increasing portion of their time raising money and dealing with lobbyists, you have a prescription for disconnection from the needs and concerns of ordinary constituents. According to Jacob Hacker and Paul Pierson, the last thirty years have been crucial in driving a larger and larger wedge between political leaders and their constituencies, mostly because of political money. "Of the billions of dollars now spent every year on politics . . . only a fairly small fraction," they write, "is directly connected to electoral contests. The bulk of it goes to lobbying."[21]

Advocacy organizations and corporations spend staggering sums to influence politicians and policy. Corporations now spend $3 billion annually on lobbying expenses, nearly twice what they spent a decade ago. Political candidates are awash in money, too: in 2009 to 2010, the top twenty Political Action Committees contributed $52,890,689 to candidates.[22] And the 2010 election cycle saw the rise of "Super PACs," which, thanks to the Supreme Court's ruling in *Citizens United v. Federal Election Commission*, are now legally permitted "to raise unlimited amounts of money from individuals, corporations and unions to fund independent expenditures."[23] The Super PACs will be a potent force on both sides in driving efforts to influence control of the House and the Senate.

President Obama has notoriously rewarded donors or major fundraisers with jobs, positions, and government contracts. A recent report from the Center for Public Integrity found that, while Obama took office two years ago vowing to banish "special interests" from the White House, nearly two hundred of his biggest donors—called "bundlers"—have landed coveted government jobs and advisory posts, won valuable federal contracts for their business interests, or attended White House events. A Public Citizen report in 2008 said that George W. Bush, over his eight years in office, had appointed about the same number of bundlers to administration posts. So Obama is way ahead of his predecessor's pace.

This is all in keeping with the underlying logic of the system: the problems just compound one another and grow worse. The need for political money fosters the need for still more political money. Tinkering at the edges of the system or giving lip service to reform won't make a bit of difference.

AMERICAN DIVISION

A political system that needs such cash to function can't possibly be closely connected to everyday concerns—and as poll after poll shows, it isn't. Radical reforms are needed if there is to be any hope of a return to meaningful constituent representation. The American people feel that the issues they most care about aren't even being addressed, let alone solved. Let's take a look at some of them.

3

THE DIVIDE
A Data Portrait

The estrangement that mainstream Americans feel from the political elite shows every sign of approaching a point of no return. As I'll show in this chapter, that divide is measurable and empirically demonstrable through extensive polling data. These data paint a stark picture of a democratic government that has lost touch with its constituents, fostering a sense of public betrayal and an estrangement between the vast majority of ordinary Americans and their political leaders. Within the electorate, the sense pervades that the political class has not only managed to benefit from the conditions that have caused so much damage to so many Americans—but in many respects, that the political class also **created and fostered** those conditions.

As my poll data reflects, the American people's outlook is fundamentally different from that of the political class on a whole range of issues. Mainstream American discontent comes through clearly and unambiguously. Where the political class acknowledges problems but believes that the country is on the right track toward recovery, the mainstream says it's on the wrong track. Where the political class finds American society generally fair, the mainstream now disagrees. And where the political class says America's best days are in the future, the mainstream says that they're in the past.

Despite the economic downturn, the political class believes the American Dream is alive and well, while mainstream Americans profoundly disagree.

As my data will show, this radical disjunction between the political class and the mainstream has created a fascinating, and surprising, secondary division: the gulf that now exists between the political class and a group that I'll call the ultrarich. These Americans—whom I define as those with total personal investible assets over $1 million, and whom I polled separately[1]—have moved, over the last few years, toward a viewpoint more or less aligned with that of the American mainstream. That is, they, too, broadly feel that our leaders in Washington have failed to address the problems the nation faces, that our system is corrupt and compromised by special interests, and that the American future may well be less bright than the past. On many issues, I found a bigger gap between the political elite and mainstream Americans than between the ultrarich and the mainstream.

I had chosen to talk to wealthy individuals as part of my research because I wanted to confirm where they would fall along the mainstream/political class divide—fully expecting that they would be much closer in their attitudes to the political class, given their success. A decade ago, perhaps that would have been the case. Not now.

On reflection, I think there is a relatively simple explanation for the ultrarich's move toward a mainstream viewpoint. The worsening dysfunction in Washington from 2008 to 2011 eventually alienated this group in a similar way (if not always with the same severity) that it has the mainstream. If 2008 was a crisis of the financial markets, 2011 was a crisis in governance—and for those with considerable personal wealth, the difference between the two was significant and troubling.

During the 2008 financial crisis, political and financial elites in Washington and on Wall Street cooperated closely. They sparked an uproar from mainstream Americans with their bailout packages, of course—but whatever one's view of those decisions, a systemic meltdown was averted and financial stability, at least for the next several years, was reestablished. The Dow Jones Index, after losing over 40 percent in 2008 and sinking to a low of 7,552.59 for that year, broke 12,000 again in early 2011.[2]

But the cooperation between government and finance broke down later in 2011, creating a financial crisis of political making that culminated with the debt-ceiling fiasco and the eventual downgrade of U.S. credit for the first time in history. As former Bush administration Treasury official Neel Kashkari told the *Wall Street Journal* in August 2011,

"Washington has told markets: 'You are on your own now.'"[3] And as a former executive board member of the World Bank and the IMF told the *Wall Street Journal* in August 2011:

> What we are seeing in the financial markets reflects to a large extent the inability of governments to put their fiscal house in order and even to cooperate among themselves.

The sense of being unable to rely on institutions that have been at the heart of American stability has made the ultrarich feel embattled and even fearful of the future—if not for themselves, then for their children. While they can still afford their lifestyle, their view of the future has changed: they're no longer so sure that the system will work for their kids. They think the system has come apart.

Admittedly, this feeling of discomfort is not nearly equal to that felt within the American mainstream, which has been impacted to a much greater degree by the Great Recession than either the ultrarich or the political class.

In fact, this represents one of the few areas on which the three groups broadly agree. The political class, mainstream, and the ultrarich all agree, for instance, that the economy is not delivering the jobs we need; that the economic elite is thriving in the current economy at the expense of ordinary Americans; and that higher taxes are needed on the rich to raise revenue and protect working people. They also agree that special interests have too much power in government and that Washington benefits the rich and powerful over ordinary people.

These points of agreement, however, cannot obscure the much deeper divide between the political class and the American mainstream. The groups diverge on everything from specific policy solutions to more perceptual questions and overall outlook. Despite the nation's difficult circumstances, the political class remains generally optimistic and forward-looking; but the American mainstream has become increasingly pessimistic, even cynical. I believe that the crisis of legitimacy that I described in chapter 2 underlies these differences: the political class, retaining its confidence in the system and belief that government still serves the people, remains hopeful about the future. The mainstream, having lost faith in our democratic institutions, increasingly regards the future with apprehension—a rare, if not unprecedented, state of affairs in middle-class America.

The data that follow, unless otherwise indicated, are drawn from my original survey research in two separate polls:

1. A national survey of one thousand randomly selected American voters. Specifically, we will be comparing the findings for those voters we classify as being part of the political class[4] with that of the mainstream.
2. A survey of two hundred ultrarich Americans.

As the data below show, on many of the most defining questions in our political life, Americans and their leaders simply inhabit different realities.

THE DATA

State of the Nation/Overall Well-Being

If there is a fundamental piece of data that summarizes the mainstream point of view—that summarizes, really, the entire divide—it is this: a plurality (47 percent) of **mainstream** Americans say that the American Dream is out of reach, and only 11 percent of **mainstream** Americans say that their children will achieve the American Dream. Just 8 percent of **mainstream** Americans think of the American Dream as "alive and well," while 83 percent say that it is at least somewhat broken.

Two-thirds (66 percent) of the **mainstream** say that they don't make enough money to make ends meet, and 61 percent say that their personal economic situation will either get worse or stay the same over the next few years. (In contrast, just 12 percent of the **ultrarich** and 32 percent of the **political class** say they do not make enough money.)

The **mainstream** is divided fairly evenly over whether they think their personal economic situation will get better, worse, or stay the same over the next few years—while the **political class** remains confident that its future prospects are bright.

Given these findings, it should not come as a surprise that a solid majority (58 percent) of **mainstream** voters are "very angry" that the economy is stagnating while big corporations post record profits.

When asked about the direction the country is heading, 60 percent of the **political class** said that the country was headed in the right

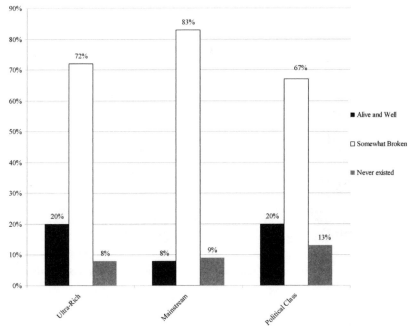

Figure 3.1.   American dream.

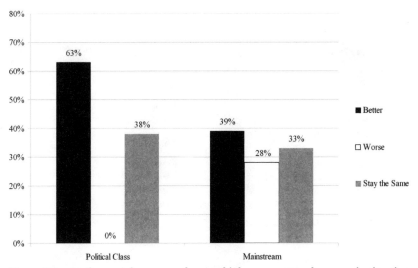

Figure 3.2.   In the next few years, do you think your personal economic situation will get better or get worse, or will it stay the same?

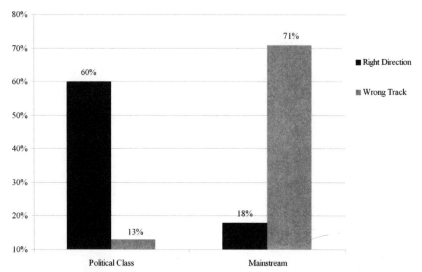

Figure 3.3. Are things in the country heading in the right direction or are they off on the wrong track?

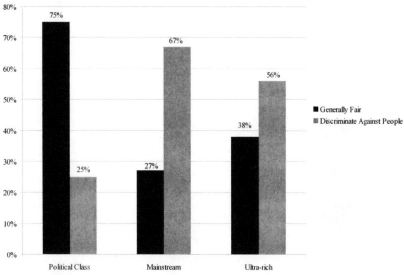

Figure 3.4. How fair is America?

direction, while 13 percent said it was on the wrong track. For the **mainstream**, the results were virtually opposite: just 18 percent said right direction and 71 percent said that the United States was on the wrong track.

By a 75 percent to 25 percent margin, the **political class** said that American society was generally fair. Both the **mainstream** and the **ultrarich** said the opposite.

The **political class** was far more optimistic as well about the future of the country than either the **mainstream** or the **ultrarich**. A solid majority (71 percent) of the **political class** thought that America's best days were in the future, while a narrow majority of the **ultrarich** and two-thirds (65 percent) of the **mainstream** thought that America's best days were in the past.

The **political class** overwhelmingly agrees that leaders are responsive to the serious issues facing the country (86 percent). The majority of both the **mainstream** (76 percent) and the **ultrarich** (66 percent) disagree.

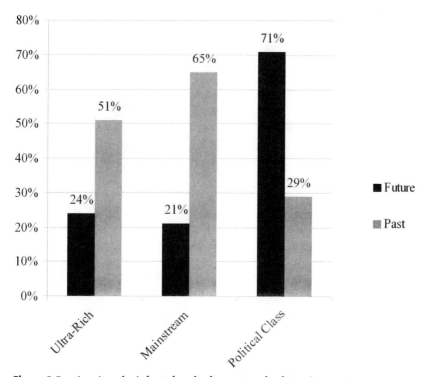

Figure 3.5. Are America's best days in the past or the future?

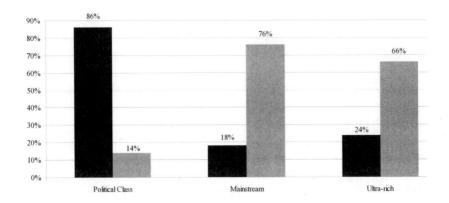

Figure 3.6.   How responsive are our leaders to the serious issues facing us today?

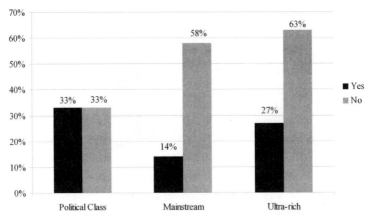

Figure 3.7.   Does the federal government today have the consent of the governed?

Views on Government

The debt-ceiling battle of summer 2011 illustrated the estrangement between the Washington political class and the American people. As Scott Rasmussen's polling showed, **mainstream** Americans faulted both parties for the fiasco: 58 percent of likely U.S. voters at least somewhat disapproved of the way President Obama and congressional Democrats handled the battle over the debt ceiling—but 53 percent also disapproved of how congressional Republicans conducted themselves.

In a battle with such high stakes, the American people had no one to root for.[5]

By strong majorities, both the **mainstream** and the **ultrarich** say that the federal government does not have the consent of the governed. Interestingly, the **political class** is split over this question—33 percent to 33 percent—indicating serious doubt even among those who wield power about whether our system remains democratic.

Both the **mainstream** (89 percent) and the **ultrarich** (71 percent) believe that the federal government has become a special-interest group, while the **political class** disagrees by an overwhelming 88 percent to 10 percent margin.

A March 2011 Gallup poll asked Americans to rank the power of various U.S. institutions and professions by whether they have too much power, not enough, or just the right amount. The top three with too much power? Lobbyists, major corporations, and financial institutions—the very entities that staff, serve in, or manipulate the political class.[6] In May 2011, Gallup found the lowest-ever approval rating for Congress, at just 12 percent, placing it dead last on a long list of institutions in American life—just ahead of HMOs, big business, organized labor, and banks.[7]

Thus it shouldn't be surprising that, when asked who they trust on important national issues—elected leaders or ordinary American people—both the **mainstream** (86 percent to 3 percent) and **ultrarich** (72

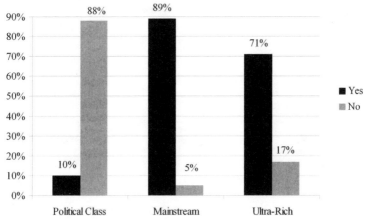

Figure 3.8. Has the federal government become a special interest group?

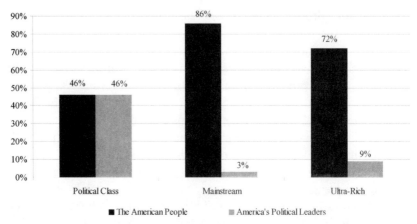

Figure 3.9. When it comes to important national issues, whose judgment do you trust more: the American people or America's political leaders?

percent to 9 percent) overwhelmingly chose the American people. The **political class** divided evenly on the question (46 percent to 46 percent).

An overwhelming majority of **mainstream** Americans (87 percent to 11 percent) say that the government works for ordinary people only some of the time, or never. The **ultrarich** agree, 78 percent to 22 per-

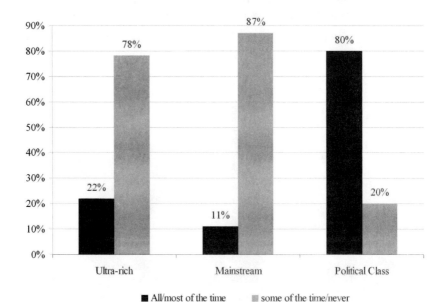

Figure 3.10. When does the government work for ordinary people?

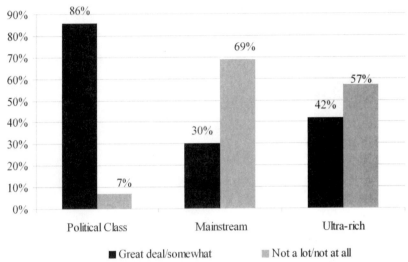

Figure 3.11. **How often do you trust that the government will do what is best for the country?**

cent. The **political class** response was almost a mirror image—80 percent answered that government works for the people all or most of the time.

A related question, phrased differently, reveals the same gulf in attitudes: the **political class** says almost unanimously that it trusts the federal government and our political leaders to do what's best for the country a great deal of the time, or at least somewhat (86 percent). The majority of both the **mainstream** (69 percent) and the **ultrarich** (57 percent) trust the government and our leaders either not a lot or not at all.

Given the responses to the two previous questions, it should not be surprising that the groups disagree about how government spends the taxpayers' money. By a 63 percent to 38 percent margin, the **political class** thinks that government is spending money on the right things. Both the **mainstream** and the **ultrarich** believe the opposite.

Moreover, there is a clear perception among both the **mainstream** and the **ultrarich** that government and big business are self-serving and collude in ways that hurt consumers and investors. The **political class** rejects this view, 71 percent to 19 percent.

The **mainstream** (60 percent to 20 percent) also believes that the federal government is more concerned with keeping Wall Street profitable than with making the financial system work for all Americans; the **political class** disagrees, 71 percent to 20 percent.

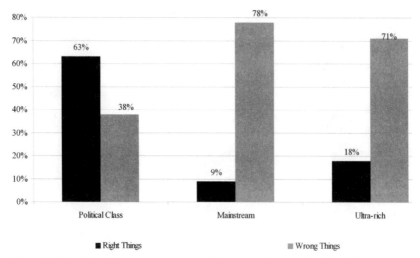

Figure 3.12.   Does the government spend taxpayers' money for the right or wrong things?

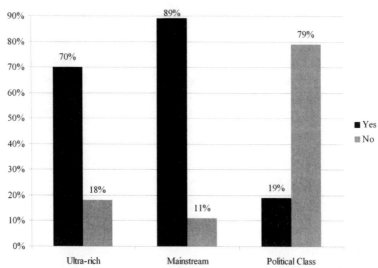

Figure 3.13.   Is the government more concerned with keeping Wall Street profitable than making the financial system work?

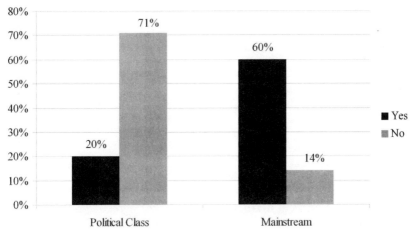

Figure 3.14. The federal government is more concerned with keeping Wall Street profitable than with making the financial system work for all Americans.

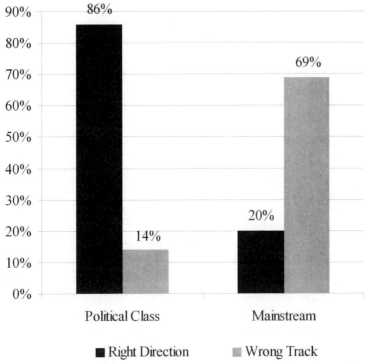

Figure 3.15. Is the economy headed in the right direction or is it on the wrong track?

State of the Economy and Economic Policy

As indicated earlier, on economic policy, mainstream Americans and the political class tend to agree on the general state of the economy and the impact of the downturn on ordinary Americans. When it comes to policy preferences and ideology, the mainstream and the political class agree on little:

- **Political class** voters narrowly prefer a government-managed economy over free markets by a 44 percent to 37 percent margin.[8] However, among **mainstream** voters, 90 percent prefer the free market.[9]
- Some 79 percent of **mainstream** voters think they're overtaxed; 87 percent of the **political class** disagrees.[10]
- About 68 percent of **mainstream** voters would be happy with an economy of fewer services and lower taxes; just 26 percent of the **political class** saw it that way.[11]
- While 65 percent of **mainstream** voters believe cutting spending is more important, 72 percent of the **political class** says the primary emphasis should be on deficit reduction.[12]
- Some 67 percent of **mainstream** Americans either "strongly" or "somewhat" favor repeal of the Obama health-care law; by contrast, just 27 percent of the **political class** favors repeal.[13]

While the groups agree that the downturn has been harsh, the **political class** believes that the economy is at least headed in the right direction, 86 percent to 14 percent; **mainstream** voters say it is still on the wrong track, 69 percent to 20 percent.

Similarly, by a 57 percent to 29 percent margin, the **political class** thinks that the government *is* solving our economic problems. Both the **mainstream** and the **ultrarich** strongly disagree.

Though the **political class** feels that the basic macroeconomic policy the nation is following is the correct one—as shown by its response above—it does agree with the **mainstream** that the economy has yet to show real improvement. Just 17 percent of the **political class** and 19 percent of the **mainstream** said that the economy was currently improving. Still, even here, the **mainstream** takes a harsher view, with nearly half (45 percent) saying that the economy is actually getting *worse* (45 percent), while half of the **political class** (50 percent) says it is staying the same.

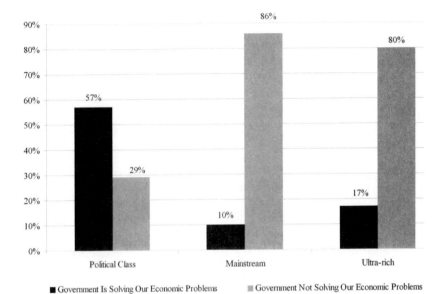

■ Government Is Solving Our Economic Problems   ▤ Government Not Solving Our Economic Problems

Figure 3.16.   Is the government solving our economic issues?

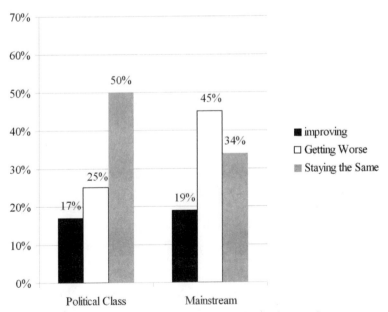

■ improving
☐ Getting Worse
▤ Staying the Same

Figure 3.17.   Do you think that the economy is improving, getting worse, or staying the same?

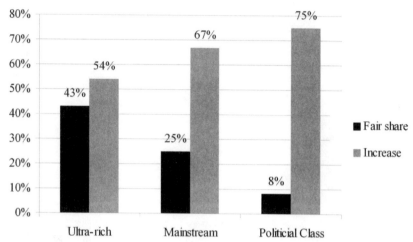

Figure 3.18. Are the rich paying their fair share of taxes or should their taxes be increased?

All three groups agree, at least, on a fundamental objective fact about today's economy: that it is *not* delivering jobs. And both the **political class** (67 percent) and **mainstream** Americans (68 percent) agree that it is primarily up to the private sector, not the government, to create jobs.

One of the few specific points of policy on which the groups agree is that the rich should pay higher taxes. Three-quarters of the **political class** say that we should increase taxes on the wealthiest Americans (75 percent), while only 8 percent say that the wealthiest Americans are paying their fair share. One-quarter of the **mainstream** says that the wealthiest Americans are paying their fair share, while two-thirds support tax increases (67 percent). Less than half of the **ultrarich** believe that the wealthiest Americans are paying their fair share of taxes, and they support tax increases by a slight majority (54 percent).

That position grows out of another conviction that all three groups share. A majority of both the **political class** and the **ultrarich** acknowledge that America has become a country where the rich get richer and the poor get poorer. **Mainstream** voters overwhelmingly agree with that assertion (84 percent to 12 percent).

Perhaps due to the severity of the downturn and the role of financial institutions in the crisis of 2008, both the **political class** and **mainstream** Americans agree that the federal government should take

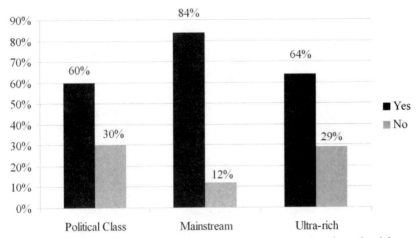

Figure 3.19. Do you believe that America has become a country where the rich get richer and the poor get poorer?

greater oversight of the Federal Reserve (**political class** 86 percent favor, **mainstream** 80 percent favor).

Wealth, Power, and Special Interests

A majority of both the **ultrarich** and the **mainstream** agree that a group of extraordinarily wealthy people in the United States have *too much*

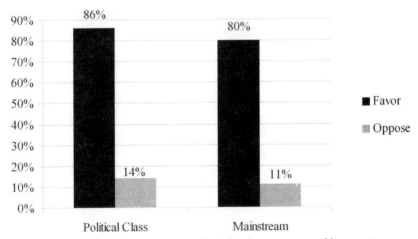

Figure 3.20. Do you favor or oppose the federal government taking greater oversight in the Federal Reserve?

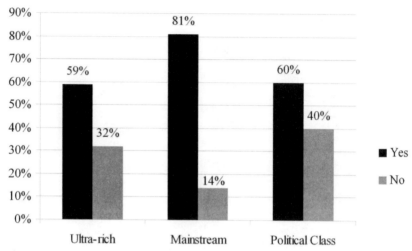

Figure 3.21. An economic elite—what some have called a super class, or the super rich—are thriving in the current economy.

influence on politics. The **political class** is divided on the question, with 38 percent saying yes and 38 percent saying no, but there is a clear consensus among all three groups that government benefits the rich and powerful over ordinary people. The **political class** (60 percent) and **ultrarich** (59 percent), and to a much greater degree, the **mainstream** (81 percent), all acknowledge that an economic elite—what some have called a Super Class or the super-rich—are thriving in the current economy.

In the most general sense, the **political class** (80 percent), **mainstream** (85 percent), and **ultrarich** (86 percent) all agree that special interests in Washington have too much power and influence on government. (But a significant minority [29 percent] of the **political class** says that special interests have the *right amount* of power on Main Street.) When the question was put more specifically, however, the familiar divergence between the groups once again surfaced.

Both the **ultrarich** (84 percent) and the **mainstream** (91 percent) believe that the government benefits special interests in Washington over the interests of ordinary people. Just 38 percent of the **political class** agreed, while 63 percent disagreed.

Similarly, when asked if special interests have too much power and influence on decisions made on Wall Street, only 20 percent of the **political class** thought so—while 83 percent of the **mainstream** and 68 percent of the **ultrarich** answered in the affirmative.

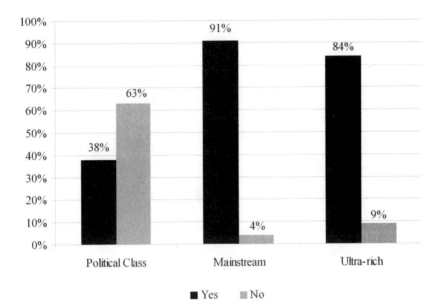

Figure 3.22.   Does government benefit the special interests in Washington over the interests of ordinary people?

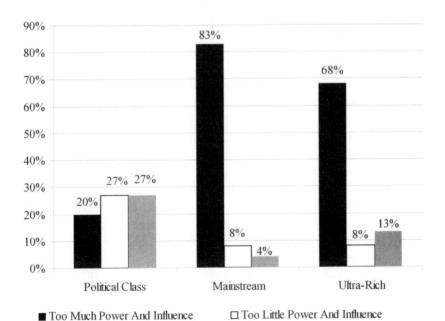

Figure 3.23.   Does special interest have too much power and influence on decisions made on Wall Street?

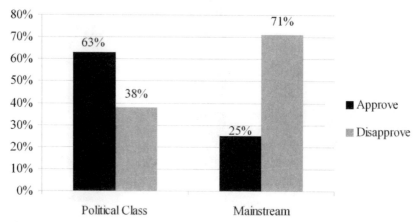

Figure 3.24. Do you approve or dissapprove of the financial industry bailouts in 2008 and 2009?

The Bailouts

Washington's rescues of financial firms in 2008 and 2009 are a special flashpoint of discord between the mainstream and the political class, and have been since the beginning. For example, according to Rasmussen polling:

- Some 68 percent of adults believe that most of the federal bailout money for the financial sector went to the same people who caused the financial and economic crisis.[14]
- About 80 percent of all Americans in 2009 believed that Wall Street benefited more from the bailout of the financial industry than the average U.S. taxpayer.[15]
- Two-out-of-three **mainstream** voters (67 percent) said that the bailouts were bad for the country, while 60 percent of those in the **political class** said that they were a good thing.[16]

In my own, more recent polling, the same divisions persist. By a 71 to 25 percent margin, the **mainstream** disapproves of the financial-industry bailouts in 2008 and 2009. By contrast, the **political class** approves, 63 percent to 38 percent.

Interestingly, however, the **political class** largely agrees (60 percent) with the **ultrarich** (78 percent) and the **mainstream** (88 percent) that the bank bailouts benefited Wall Street over the American taxpayer.

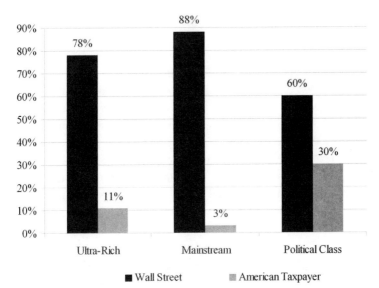

Figure 3.25.   Who did the bailouts benefit?

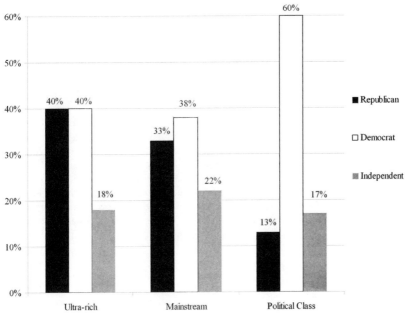

Figure 3.26.   Political party identification.

CONCLUDING THOUGHTS

Clearly, a stark divide is present between the nation's political and financial elites and the rest of the population—a population that, to substantial degree, includes those of considerable personal wealth who might be expected, in ordinary times, to side with the elites. As we've seen, this is not the case. The fact that many Americans possessing personal wealth in excess of $1 million agree with Americans of much more modest income means that the system has failed and indicates a deep-seated, pervasive sense of crisis and loss of legitimacy. That loss of legitimacy underpins what I call the Great Divide, and one of its consequences is the rebirth of American populism.

POLITICAL AND DEMOGRAPHIC TRAITS OF THE THREE GROUPS

Overall, the political class is younger, more liberal, more educated, and wealthier than the mainstream. The two groups are comparable in terms of racial and religious diversity, as well as region, though a slightly larger proportion of the political class is from the Northeast. The starkest contrast between the two can be found in their voting behavior. An extraordinary 69 percent of the political class voted for Barack Obama in 2008, while the mainstream was divided between Obama (47 percent) and John McCain (38 percent). Support for the Democratic Party dropped slightly but remained strong among the political class during the 2010 midterm elections—with 62 percent of the political class voting for the Democratic congressional candidate in their district—while the mainstream voted for the GOP, 64 percent to 36 percent, in 2010.

One-third of **mainstream** voters are registered Republicans, 38 percent are registered Democrats, and 22 percent are Independents. Only 13 percent of the **political class** are registered Republicans, while an overwhelming 60 percent are registered Democrats and 17 percent are Independents. The **ultrarich** are divided between the Democratic and Republican parties (40 percent to 40 percent), with 18 percent registered as Independents.

I also asked **political class** and **mainstream** respondents about their views of the Tea Party. One-quarter (25 percent) of **mainstream** voters say that they are either part of or supporters of the Tea Party, compared to just 15 percent of the **political class**.

4

THE GREAT DIVIDE AND THE POPULIST UPSURGE

The political brinksmanship of recent months highlights what we see as America's governance and policymaking becoming less stable, less effective, and less predictable than what we previously believed. . . . The outlook on the long-term rating is negative. As our downside alternate fiscal scenario illustrates, a higher public debt trajectory than we currently assume could lead us to lower the long-term rating again.

—From S&P decision announcing downgrade of
United States' credit rating[1]

Both parties are basically the same . . . I do not think they are in touch with the common man. They are out of touch and don't live the way most of us live . . . I think there is massive corruption. They're so removed from the ordinary working people that they become insulated.

—Evelyn H., age 61, retired, Ohio

As I write this, the United States has just seen its credit rating down-graded from Triple-A for the first time in modern history. On Friday, August 5, 2011, the ratings agency Standard & Poor's announced that U.S. Treasury bonds—the gold standard of the world's currency—would be rated AA+, at least for the foreseeable future. The agency's decision came at the end of a week in which the federal government had narrowly averted a default on its debt, finally agreeing to a deal that President Obama signed just hours before the August 2 deadline.

On the heels of the debt-ceiling standoff, Standard and Poor's downgrade was the most powerful illustration yet of a government that has simply stopped working. While commentators across the political spectrum rushed to assign blame either to the president, the Tea Party, or both, the larger point was missed: the real cause of the downgrade, the debt, the deficits, and our economic woes is not one politician or political party—it is the failure of our governing system.

Put simply, the American system of representative democracy is collapsing, and the political order as we know it is disintegrating. We might even be, as my colleague Pat Caddell believes, in a "pre-revolutionary moment."

The failure of our democracy to devise remedies for the challenges that we face—especially the suffering of tens of millions of unemployed middle-class and poor Americans—and the near-death struggles it enacts merely to secure agreements on fundamental needs such as debt-limit extensions and deficit reduction, has eroded public faith in our governing institutions and driven the polarization that we see today both in Washington and among the electorate.

Our political system in large measure has lost its credibility with the American people. A Rasmussen poll conducted after the debt-ceiling battle showed that just 17 percent of respondents believed that the U.S. government has the consent of the governed.[2] That's the lowest measure ever recorded. Just 21 percent of respondents told a *Washington Post* poll that they were satisfied with the country's political system.[3] Over half told the same poll that the S&P downgrade was a fair assessment of the nation's finances.

The political elite of both parties offer little in the way of leadership and provide no sense of a direction that might lead us out of our difficulties. Their rhetoric aside, most of their actions are motivated by the goal of preserving their political power and individual privileges. Never before have we seen such a disconnect between policy makers in Washington and those whom they were elected to represent. If nothing is done to begin bridging the gap between the electorate and their political leaders, or we might face a range of previously unimaginable scenarios—even civil disorder.

In the meantime, we can see the effects of our failed system in the resurgence of American populism among a substantial portion of the electorate. Some say the populists, left or right, are extremists. In some cases they may be, but they are reacting to an extreme situation the only way they know.

FAILURE AND POLARIZATION

When a democratic government loses touch with its constituents to this extent, a sense of public betrayal is inevitable. The way mainstream Americans see it, the political elite is engaged in an active effort to close off opportunities and advancement to all but those who belong to the exclusive ranks of that same elite. As their resentment grows, so does the divide between them and their political representatives.

As I've described in the previous chapter, both my own polling and that of others consistently shows just how angry and nervous Americans are about the economic and fiscal issues facing the country. They definitely feel that neither President Obama nor the Republicans are adequately addressing these issues. And they no longer feel confident in the future to the extent that Americans usually have.

Americans recognize that something is fundamentally broken in our politics. That's why they voted against the party in power in 2006, 2008, and 2010. Barack Obama became the third straight president to lose a congressional majority while in office. Before George W. Bush, this hadn't even happened for *two* consecutive presidents.

In Washington, left and right wage a continual war against one another for the spoils of power, and their battle goes on at the expense of the American people. The dysfunctional partisanship in Washington is a central cause of the Great Divide between mainstream Americans and the political class. It lies behind the elite's failure to solve important problems like the growing economic hardship and income inequality in the country.

Showing a widespread disdain for both political parties, Americans yearn for a leader who speaks for the American majority and stands outside the political class—someone who embodies our common interest and sense of national purpose. No such leader appears ready to emerge, however, and the system itself seems unchangeable, unfixable.

The Great Divide is, itself, the cause of another schism: the intense and growing political polarization of the American electorate.

While for some Americans, the divide has led to increased cynicism and disengagement from politics, it has driven millions of others to mobilize themselves politically, many for the first time—but not in the conventional way. Ordinary Americans have reached out for solutions that seem to make sense in the vacuum of leadership, adopting ideological positions well outside what has traditionally been seen as the centrist mainstream—whether from the extreme left or the extreme right. We often hear that the American people are polarized, and that's true—just look at the last decade's presidential maps—but our popular divisions have been driven and exacerbated by the divisiveness in Washington.

Americans' mounting frustrations with chronic problems that go unsolved and their disgust at a self-serving political class drives them to seek solutions of their own—and these solutions vary. In short, they can be broken down into left-wing and right-wing populism: one side that calls for wealth redistribution and increased government oversight of the private sector while the other calls for a much smaller government across the board. Both sides want an end to Washington's symbiotic relationship with big business and financial elites.

And so we have a resurgence of political populism in the United States that hasn't been seen in at least a generation. It's a potent and unpredictable response to the broken promise of representative democracy.

A COMMON DIAGNOSIS

While left populists and right populists have profoundly different visions of what the country needs to go forward, they begin with a remarkably broad agreement about the failures of the political class.

They share a contempt for out-of-touch Washington elites who seem completely insulated from the real-world effects of their policies; they believe that interest groups and powerful lobbies are, in large part, controlling political initiatives in Washington contrary to the public interest; both loathed TARP and in a different way were suspicious of other company and industry bailouts, seeing powerful companies and wealthy elites as the primary beneficiaries of Washington policies. Both fear for our future and sense that the nation they've known is slipping away.

They also broadly agree that government and big business are far too closely connected and have too much power. A 2009 Harris poll showed that 85 percent of Americans believe that big companies have too much influence on politicians and policy makers.[4] In May 2010, 71 percent told an NBC News/*Wall Street Journal* survey that Republicans in Congress were more concerned with the interests of big corporations than with those of ordinary Americans—up from 55 percent in 2002. As for Democrats, 53 percent felt they were more concerned with big corporations than with ordinary Americans—nearly double the 29 percent who felt that way in 2002.

And 68 *percent of all voters* across partisan, demographic, and ideological lines said that Washington and big business worked together against the interests of consumers and investors.

So left and right populists agree on the diagnosis: the political class is corrupt and inept, while the political system they have created is dysfunctional and possibly beyond repair.

Their conclusions and prescriptions, however, couldn't be more different. One group has adopted a much sharper left-wing, progressive agenda, while the other has revived some of the most traditional right-wing positions in American politics.

DIFFERENT PRESCRIPTIONS, DIFFERENT DYNAMICS

Whereas conservative populists see government as the enemy of free enterprise and personal autonomy, left-wing populists allege that government has collaborated with financial elites, especially on Wall Street, allowing them to accumulate massive wealth at the expense of working people. Their solution is not less government, but *more* government, more redistribution, and a more activist government to redress economic inequality. Their view is that government should pursue wealth redistribution through a more steeply progressive tax system, along with public-sector job programs, infrastructure programs, and new entitlements such as health-care reform. Doing this, they believe, will drive economic growth and boost employment. They believe that deficits matter far less than rectifying the injustices of a system that works against ordinary people.

Left-wing populism has gotten stronger since the 2010 midterm elections because voters have come to see that the Republicans have no answers, except to propose the elimination of core entitlement programs such as Medicare and Medicaid and across-the-board cuts in spending.

Liberal populism has also gotten stronger because of the Occupy Wall Street movement. Whatever its flaws it has focused attention on income disparity between the richest 1 percent and everyone else. Also it has sharpened awareness of the failure of the system to provide opportunity for ordinary people as well as the perceived special interest deals the wealthy and powerful have been able to garner—particularly those on Wall Street.

Left-leaning voters are increasingly disenfranchised and disillusioned as they begin to question why business and government elites remain secure—indeed, in stronger positions than ever—while their own position becomes increasingly tenuous. They find that they are no longer able to pay for their children's education, save for their retirement, or take care of their elderly parents. And their solution is higher taxes and an absolute unwillingness to adopt any policies that would jeopardize entitlement programs or social welfare programs.

Right-wing populists hold considerably more power over the GOP than left-wing populists enjoy within the Democratic Party—although that too may be changing with the defeat of the Blue Dogs in 2010 and the ascendency of the Occupy Wall Street movement in late 2011.

Establishment-oriented Republicans don't vote at nearly the same rates as right-wing populists do,[5] and they certainly haven't taken to the streets in the manner of the Tea Party movement. Indeed, what's happened is that establishment Republicans—while maintaining their clear differences with the populist Tea Party as well as a smaller libertarian cohort—have moved ideologically to the right, blurring the differences that exist between the groups. As a result, the right-wing populist impulse, both philosophically and practically, is the driving force within the GOP today.

On the Democratic side, while there are many more progressives in the party than there are centrists, progressive populism exists more as a worldview than as a mobilized, activist force—save for rare exceptions, as when people in Wisconsin took to the streets to protest a Republican governor's plan to do away with collective-bargaining rights.

Recently the balance of power has shifted—with Occupy Wall Street sweeping the nation, with progressives in the streets demonstrating against government, against concentration of power and influence on Wall Street, and with an explicit demand to redistribute wealth and power.

Labor unions have tried to align themselves with the Occupy Wall Street movement with some but not total success.

It is clear that left-wing populists are seeking to do what the Tea Party did on the right: to use Occupy Wall Street as a counterforce to traditional liberal/establishment impulses inside the Democratic Party. Indeed, it is also clear that from the President on down, Democrats have struggled to both embrace and to distance themselves from the movement.

President Obama thus has to perform a continual balancing act between his progressive base and the political center. Obama cannot win reelection if progressives don't turn out. He also can't win if moderates see him as captive to the left. A Democratic president must court the left strongly enough to ensure its support—hence the President's tentative embrace of Occupy Wall Street. But he must also be willing to push it away, lest he alienate the American center—hence the selling of his American Jobs Act as a bipartisan initiative with as many Republican-inspired as Democratic-inspired ideas. Bill Clinton mastered this technique, but he presided over much better economic times, when it was far easier to dismiss progressive economic appeals.

Things are simpler on the right. No Republican candidate can afford to go against the right-wing "base"—and in fact, as George W. Bush proved in 2004, candidates can even win elections by running almost entirely *to* their base. This reality is even more in evidence on the right today, thanks to the Tea Party. The right wing is effectively driving the bus in the Republican Party; it holds a veto power that left populists do not possess, largely because the Tea Party proved in 2010 that virtually any GOP candidate or incumbent could be beaten in a primary or party-nominating process.

Without endorsing either the right-wing or left-wing populist visions, I think it's important to acknowledge their power. Many commentators simply explain this by citing economic distress and the emotional appeal of populism, but they miss an important point: both populisms, in theory anyway, *would* do something to break the stranglehold of the elites. The right-wing, antigovernment approach would weaken the grip of the political class, the permanent campaign, and special-interest groups. The left-wing, wealth-redistributionist approach would marginalize the role of the financial elite and the professional political class, diminishing their influence and putting at least some small measure of control back in the hands of those with more modest incomes. Both approaches would undermine the Wall Street/Washington nexus and erode the influence of political and financial insiders.

CONCLUSION

After decades of a fairly moderate consensus, which reached its apex in the Clinton presidency, the United States' political landscape has been fundamentally transformed. Heading into the 2012 election, both political parties have so marginalized their centrist wings that moderates have become essentially irrelevant. Both parties are driven by populist energy, both within their Beltway caucus and in the larger electorate. Both parties have proven more than willing to practice scorched-earth policy if it means they can "win" in the end—especially since activists and ideologues have more power than ever before. Both parties are in survival mode: they feel that it's better to hide what's really going on in Washington than to acknowledge it and risk losing.

This is the landscape that to a significant extent Barack Obama inherited, but he has also contributed to it. He's driven the right further rightward with his embrace of massive new government programs such as the Affordable Care Act (Obamacare) and through his spending on economic stimulus. He's inflamed the populist left by failing to deliver on their dream of progressive renewal—disappointing them so acutely that some now regret their support for him in 2008. Lately he has embraced left-wing populism as his basic approach to political dialogue—trying to ameliorate some of the disappointment that led many to call him a betrayer of his cause and to say explicitly that they regretted having supported him in 2008.

The Republican and Democratic parties, to differing degrees, retain an establishment core that clashes with the new populism. Traditional Republicans are adamant about spending cuts, but they're willing to compromise on tax increases, grudgingly, if there is good reason to do so. Traditional Democrats are willing to compromise, to some degree, on spending cuts, preferably offset by increases in tax revenue.

Populist movements, however, remain uncompromising on both positions. Left populists refuse to consider spending cuts; right populists rule out any tax hikes. This is the process we saw play out to such disastrous effects during the debt-ceiling standoff, and it remains the operative reality in Washington—one that might endure well into the future.

We can justifiably say that the revival of left- and right-wing populism is the most politically consequential result of the mainstream/political class divide. It arose out of a vacuum of political leadership that has left millions of Americans without confidence in their own and the nation's future. As it has been in previous historical eras, populism is a cry of anger and despair from citizens desperate for answers—and for change.

In the next four chapters, I'll examine left- and right-wing populism in depth: how they developed, what their role is within both parties today, and how they're reshaping our politics.

5

LEFT POPULISM
Principles and Resurgence

There is probably no better way to sum up the essence of left-wing populism than to begin with the movement that emerged in fall of 2011 with virtually no warning—Occupy Wall Street.

Occupy Wall Street represents everything that the left has been seeking for years. It was an apparently authentic populist movement that had as its central organizing principal: opposition to the concentration of wealth, income inequality, and, most of all, the perceived favoritism that Wall Street and senior corporate executives receive.

To be sure, there was and is much to this argument substantively, even if Occupy Wall Street—as my own research has shown—is not representative either of the left wing of the Democratic Party or of broad-based populist sentiment.

Notwithstanding that, the Democratic leadership's initial reaction was to underscore that they understand the underlying motivations driving the protests.

President Obama referred to Occupy Wall Street as being the manifestation of "broad-based frustration about how our financial system works."

Nancy Pelosi said that her fellow Democrats "support the message to the establishment, whether it's Wall Street or the political establishment, that things have to change."

Senior Obama White House Advisor David Plouffe took steps to publicly align the Democratic Party with the values harbored by Occupy Wall Street protesters during an appearance on *Good Morning America* in early October 2011, stating: "The protests you're seeing are the same conversations people are having in living rooms and kitchens all across America. . . . People are frustrated by an economy that does not reward hard work and responsibility, where Wall Street and Main Street don't seem to play by the same set of rules."

To be sure, the association was and has been not complete and total.

There had been hopes on the left that the Occupy Wall Street movement would become like the Tea Party movement. Indeed, as Eugene Slaven writes in *The American Thinker:*

> As the Occupy Wall Street movement attempts to establish a firm foothold in American society, veterans of left-wing organizing, including former Obama administration czar Van Jones, are urging this fledgling movement to run candidates for office, following the Tea Party model of transforming a grassroots movement into a powerful electoral force. After all, what good is storming local bank branches and blocking Americans from going to work if you don't send representatives to Congress who share your core values and goals?"[1]

Results to polling I have conducted, which found that one-third (35%) of Occupy Wall Street protesters would like to see the movement influence the Democratic Party the way the Tea Party has influenced the GOP, affirm this argument.

While that clearly has not happened, Occupy Wall Street is probably the best representative of what the left is and has been seeking.

Occupy Wall Street could turn out to be nothing more than a flash in the pan, albeit a highly visible one that—at the time of this writing—has garnered an extraordinary amount of attention in the few months it has been in existence.

Beyond Occupy Wall Street lie labor unions and their supporters—who have argued compellingly for policies similar to those that are championed by Occupy Wall Street. These groups have indeed done their best to align themselves with the movement.

Probably the most visible and passionate advocate of these policies is filmmaker and activist Michael Moore.

In March of 2011, Moore joined the thousands of supporters of public-employee unions who had taken to the streets in Madison, Wisconsin, to argue against legislation to limit collective bargaining rights—something that Moore and the tens of thousands who congregated at the state capitol view as a fundamental American right.

The movement that Moore spoke about that day morphed into a better than $40 million dollar campaign to repeal a similar, and arguably more draconian bill passed earlier in 2011 by Governor Kasich and the Republican-dominated state legislature in Ohio. The bill that stripped public employees of their rights to collectively bargain—Senate Bill 5—by a nearly two-to-one vote in the 2011 election.

The 2011 referendum vote represented a seminal victory to those in the Democratic Party who believe that the key to victory in 2012 is the advocacy of populism and the firm, direct association with the interests of working people.

Standing on the steps of the capitol as he addressed a crowd of over fifty thousand, Moore argued that for years, Washington has been ruled by big corporations and financial institutions that operate with impunity and with complete disregard of the interests of the American worker.

The essence of what needed to be done, Moore argued, is to protect ordinary people from a predatory, rapacious system where "the moneyed elite" along with "Wall Street, the banks and the Fortune 500" sought to exploit them—for the benefit of corporate interests.

Moore developed this argument in his film *Capitalism: A Love Story*, where he maintained that throughout both the Democratic and the Republican presidencies of Reagan, Bush I, Clinton, and Bush II, the financial industry had staged what he refers to as a "coup d'etat."

Moore suggests in the film that both Democrats and Republicans are responsible for allowing the financial industry to maximize its power and profit. Indeed, congressional Democratic leaders, such as Nancy Pelosi and Harry Reid, are scrutinized in the film for holding closed-door meetings with the major players on Wall Street following the initial House vote against the bank bailouts in 2008. Moore argues persuasively that members of Congress ultimately put the interests of the banks first—rewarding those who had engaged in irresponsible, predatory, and risky behavior, despite the staunch opposition to the bailouts expressed by constituents.

Meanwhile, during the three decades in which income taxes for the richest were slashed and the principles of free-market capitalism reigned, the country's manufacturing sector disintegrated—leaving cities like Flint, Michigan, virtual ghost towns. Moreover, during this time, Moore shows, corporate America had managed to profit at the expense of working people through aggressive and virtually unregulated lending practices.

Homeowners were told that they could "be their own banks," and if they ever needed money, all they needed to do was refinance their homes.

Moore's message was clear: it's a crime that, while these banks were bailed out using taxpayer dollars, those very same taxpayers—people who dedicated their entire lives to their employers and companies—are facing home foreclosures and being laid off without pensions.

Moore is not the only prominent filmmaker to become a vocal advocate of this core liberal populist argument.

Equally compelling was Charles Ferguson's documentary *Inside Job*.

To be sure, *Inside Job* was a less dramatic film in terms of arresting images, but Ferguson's analysis of the ills of American society captured the public consciousness in a way that few have.

Inside Job guides the viewer through thirty years of financial industry deregulation—which began during the Reagan administration and continued through the economic collapse of 2008—telling the story of how our financial industry, in the quest for higher returns, spent decades taking increasingly substantial risks. This behavior ultimately led to one of the most devastating financial crises in history.

From Ferguson's perspective, the greatest injustice of all is that even after the crash, the very same Wall Street executives and institutions responsible for gambling away the U.S. economy escaped criminal prosecution, got richer, and continued to collect record bonuses, while ordinary people lost their jobs and were evicted from their homes.

"I must start by pointing out that three years after our horrific financial crisis caused by massive fraud, not a single financial executive has gone to jail, and that's wrong," declared Ferguson as he took the podium to accept an Oscar for Best Documentary at the 2011 Academy Awards.

Inside Job opens with a grand aerial tour of financial capitals, especially New York and London. We get panoramic views of the rivers and bridges and astonishing indoor shots of executive suites, five-star hotels, and government ministries.

"What do you think of Wall Street incomes these days?"

The question, asked by Ferguson off camera, is directed to an imposing elderly gentleman who looks vaguely familiar to us old enough to remember the Reagan years. A caption on screen ends our suspense: It's Paul Volcker, now eighty-three, former chairman of the Fed during the 1980s. He is sitting, looking over what looks to be financial reports, and holding what seems to be a glass of Scotch. Volcker doesn't hesitate for a moment before definitively answering with a single word: "Excessive," shaking his head.

"Would you support legal controls on executive pay?" This question is directed to a fairly young man identified as David McCormick, Under Secretary of the Treasury in the George W. Bush administration. McCormick fidgets for a moment before saying: "Uh, I, I would not."

More aerial shots, including one of a fleet of corporate jets, and then another familiar face: Eliot Spitzer, former governor and attorney general of New York.

"The regulators didn't do their job," he says. "They had the power to do every case that I made when I was state attorney general. They just didn't want to."

"Why should a financial engineer be paid four times to 100 times more than a real engineer?" asks Andrew Sheng, Chief Advisor to the China Banking Regulatory Commission later in the film. "A real engineer build bridges. A financial engineer build dreams. And, you know, when those dreams turn out to be nightmares, other people pay for it."

But make no mistake, the liberal populist argument has not only been dramatized and elaborated in the movies.

It has come to real life in the streets of Wisconsin and Ohio and more generally in New York City, Los Angeles, Chicago, Oakland, and Seattle. Indeed, associated Occupy Wall Street chapters have emerged in European capitals as well.

On Oct. 10 and 11, a senior researcher at my polling firm interviewed nearly 200 protesters in New York's Zuccotti Park. The research—published in the *Wall Street Journal* on October 17, 2011—represented the first systematic random sample of Occupy Wall Street opinion.

The polling I have done shows that among those who have taken to the streets as part of the Occupy Wall Street movement, virtually all (98%) say they would support civil disobedience to achieve their goals, and nearly one third (31%) would support violence to advance their agenda.

But beyond that, Occupy Wall Street represents the purest form of liberal populism.

Our findings showed that solid majorities of Occupy Wall Street protesters share a deep commitment to left-wing policies: opposition to free-market capitalism and support for radical redistribution of wealth.

Sixty-five percent say that government has a moral responsibility to guarantee all citizens access to affordable health care, a college education, and a secure retirement—no matter the cost.

They are strong supporters of protectionist policies to protect American jobs and industries from going overseas as well as increased regulation of the private sector—and particularly the financial sector.

Seventy percent say we need to increase regulation of the private sector, while seventy-three percent believe we need protective trade legislation.

By a large margin (77%–22%) they support raising taxes on the wealthiest Americans, but 58 percent oppose raising taxes for everybody, with only 36 percent in favor.

A number of the groups allied with Occupy Wall Street—MoveOn.org, SEIU, the AFL-CIO, and the Working Families Party among others—have been taking to the streets to rally—and in some instances to partake in civil disobedience—to protest the vast inequities of income and wealth in America since the economic downturn.

Recently laid-off workers at a steel mill, to Fairfield, Connecticut, where two AIG executives, Douglas Poling and James Haas, resided in palatial mansions.

The protesters had planned to deliver letters to the executives about their personal hardships since the financial crisis—in which AIG was so deeply involved—and to call upon the executives to return their lucrative bonuses, which had recently made the news. The company had paid its executives over $165 million in bonuses, despite having been bailed out by the federal government for $180 billion.

"It's been one outrage after another," said protester Aaron Goode, a twenty-six-year-old archivist at Yale University. "AIG is a symptom but not the only source of the problem."

The Lifestyles of the Rich and the Infamous Bus Tour, as they called it, demonstrated the clear desire, from many on the left, to see for themselves how these executives lived and where they lived and to demonstrate their palpable frustration with the enormous income inequality that exists in America.

"There's really justifiable outrage at this growing gap between people who remain insulated from the meltdown of the economy and the ones who are struggling to save their home and avoid foreclosure," explained Jon Green, the director of the Connecticut Working Families Party.

For these protesters, it didn't matter that Poling and Haas were among the AIG executives who had already voluntarily chosen to disgorge, and in some cases, donate their bonus money to charity. That simply was not good enough. As one organizer, Mary Huguley, wrote in a personal letter to Mr. Poling, which the protesters read on his front lawn: "It has been reported that you intend to return your bonus. . . . This is a good start, and we applaud this step. Most of us will never know what it feels like to turn down millions of dollars."

Indeed, the protesters didn't plan on letting the executives off the hook so easily. Pleased that the executives had returned their bonuses, they had come anyway to ask for the executives' support for anti-home foreclosure and antipoverty measures.

As they marched down Fairfield's residential streets, surrounded by sprawling estates and gilded cul de sacs, waving signs with slogans such as **TAXPAYERS WANT THEIR MONEY BACK, LIFESTYLES OF THE RICH AND THE SHAMELESS**, and **MILLIONARE'S TAX: THEY CAN AFFORD IT**, the protesters, who resembled sightseers in an exotic land rather than fellow residents of Connecticut, dramatically brought to life just how vast the disparity has become between Wall Street's "haves" and Main Street's "have-nots."

At a congressional hearing shortly before the protests, AIG CEO Edward Liddy expressed concern that some AIG executives had received death threats. He worried about his employees' safety, he said. There were no incidents at the Connecticut protest, but both AIG mansions were closely watched by private security teams. The event was peaceful, but the AIG executives, and their neighbors, had to feel somewhat under siege—and they had to wonder, if only to themselves, if their front lawns were destined to become rallying places for a nation in crisis.

What do these scenes tell us? Among other things, they indicate the enduring power of the left-wing populist critique of American society and government, which has become more powerful and relevant today than in a generation. It is a critique with multiple components, each reinforcing the other and based around a central idea: that politics is a battle between good and evil, right and wrong, and that government stands as the great—and indeed, only—defender of ordinary people against wealthy individuals and corporate interests.

It is this final point that distinguishes left populists from right populists—who believe that the key challenge is to remove government ownership and control and to devolve power back to local communities, rather than adding more layers of regulation and oversight. Indeed, right populists argue that their constitutional rights and the American principles of freedom, liberty, and free-market capitalism are under siege by government "takeovers" of the financial and auto industries and the imminent "socialization" of the health-care system under President Obama's reforms.

Like their right-wing opposites, left-wing populists are suspicious of compromise, which they view as selling out—whether it's a president who compromises with the Republicans on issues such as tax cuts and the debt ceiling or a lawmaker who receives donations from corporations that are seen as predatory and rapacious.

Take, for example, the following scene that took place at an anti-private insurance protest rally held outside of the Bristol-Myers Squibb headquarters in midtown Manhattan in the fall of 2009, during the height of the battle over Obamacare.

One hundred liberal activists, supporters, and members of the Private Health Insurance Must Go! Coalition rallied outside of the Bristol-Myers Squibb headquarters on Park Avenue and 51st Street before marching ten blocks south down Park Avenue to the Aetna headquarters.

It was outside of Bristol-Myers Squibb that my researcher, Arielle Alter Confino, met Eva-Lee Baird, an enthusiastic elderly woman. Baird was representing both CodePink NYC—which describes itself as "a women-initiated grassroots peace and social justice movement working to end the wars in Iraq and Afghanistan, stop new wars, and redirect our resources into healthcare, education, green jobs and other life-affirming activities"—and The Granny Peace Brigade, an antiwar organization founded by a group of women who went to the Times Square recruitment center on October 17, 2005, to ask to enlist in place of young people being deployed in Iraq unnecessarily. Baird put it bluntly:

If you say corporate greed and Washington in one sentence, you have to make the connection. Everybody in Congress is desperate to get a fund together for the next election campaign. And who has the most money to contribute? I think they listen more to their big donors than they do to me.

These examples are illustrative of left-wing populism, the mind-set behind it, and how it manifests itself in action. And indeed, while the left-populist impulse often engenders great passion and vehemence, there are, at root, a series of core principles that form its foundation.

PRINCIPLES OF LEFT POPULISM

How, then, can we summarize the views of left-wing populism?

For left populists, politics is a battle between right and wrong, with the hardworking American worker pitted against wealthy, malevolent, and greedy corporate interests that need to be restrained, regulated, and overseen at every juncture.

At core, left populists believe that American society is just plain unfair and that corporations dominate the political and economic scene. They have effective control of the politicians who ultimately serve their interests, and unless the United States has an active political insurgency—ever vigilant in insisting that government restrain banks, Wall Street, and corporate interests on a day-to-day basis—society will not be fair and ordinary people will be hurt, perhaps irrevocably. Fairness only comes from government intervention, which needs to be continuous, consistent, and all-encompassing.

Left populists are united by five core principles.

1. Government intervention is crucial to protect the American people from corporate greed. According to left populists, the only way ordinary people can achieve the American Dream, maintain well-paying jobs, avoid eviction from their homes, and guarantee a secure retirement is if the government regulates consumer behavior, corporate activity, and most of all, the activities of banks and Wall Street.

And indeed, the above represents the worldview of Occupy Wall Street, which if anything is more extreme—given the agenda put forward by their group in late October.

The core essence of their proposals involve $1.5 trillion in new revenue to create 25 million public sector jobs paying union wages, free public transportation, free university education, a single-payer health-care system, and other initiatives.

They also favor "reappropriating our business structures and culture, putting people and the earth before profit."

Further, they want to end free trade, spend a trillion additional dollars on environmental programs, and forgive all debt.

One of the central advocates of this point of view is the Service Employees International Union (SEIU), a national union of 2.1 million members focused on organizing workers in three sectors: health care, public services, and property services. According to the SEIU Mission Statement, the union's members are:

> United by the belief in the dignity and worth of workers and the services they provide and dedicated to improving the lives of workers and their families and creating a more just and humane society.

Hector Figueroa, secretary/treasurer for the 32BJ chapter of the SEIU, articulated this belief to my researcher on Tuesday, September 22, 2009, at a Big Insurance: Sick of It! rally held outside of the UnitedHealthcare Headquarters at One Penn Plaza in New York City. The rally, which drew a crowd of nearly one thousand to the streets around Pennsylvania Station, was one of the one hundred rallies held that day nationwide in support of the public option for health-care reform (an idea that the Obama administration would abandon).

As he adjusted his wire-rimmed glasses, Figueroa stated simply: "It is very necessary for government to step in and fix what should have been put in place much earlier in our history to alleviate some of these imbalances, protect the powerless, and ensure some measure of equal justice economically, socially, and politically."

From the perspective of left populists, the free-market system has failed the mainstream American worker. Their conclusion is that government intervention is necessary to regulate Wall Street, protect the rights of workers, rein in the excessive greed of private insurance companies, and prevent corporations and their factories from polluting the environment.

Left populists focus principally and fundamentally on corporate greed and excess and believe we need more regulation to ensure a just and equitable society.

This Us versus Them mentality is certainly what drives Josh Starcher, a young, sandy-haired Volunteer Coordinator for Healthcare-NOW! NYC, who has remained a die-hard advocate for universal, single-payer health care since I met him over two years ago.

Starcher, who sports impressively long sideburns that reach the end of his jaw, was protesting outside of Bristol-Myers Squibb at the Private Health Insurance Must Go! rally on September 29, 2009. Without substantial government intervention, he explained, ordinary Americans will continue to be marginalized. Thus, the fight to pressure state and federal lawmakers to regulate Wall Street and private corporations had become his *civic duty*:

> I think the Wall Street debacle shows us that we can't trust corporations. We can't trust them with money, why should we trust them with care. I think that they've shown that they're irresponsible. And they're not going to stop, they're not going to change. There's no middle ground with them.

Like Starcher, liberal populists believe that government has failed to rein in Wall Street and that we need more regulation in addition to redistribution of wealth.

This focus on fairness also applies to the institutions, especially the private institutions, that operate in the U.S. economy. Left populists believe so strongly that our economic arrangements are fundamentally unjust, that they consistently argue for expanded government oversight of the private economy. Nowhere is this focus more acute than in the financial sector, where the Obama administration's Dodd-Frank Law of 2010 represented the most sweeping regulation of Wall Street since the Great Depression. Yet progressives call for more, alleging that the law is largely inoperative in practice, with inadequate enforcement mechanisms.

Specifically, they point to the decision to exclude car dealers from regulation by the new Consumer Financial Products Bureau. They also lament that Senator Blanche Lincoln's original derivatives-reform proposal—stipulating that banks be required to spin off all their derivatives trading operations—and the Volcker Rule—which limits the amount of proprietary trading banks can do on their own behalf—were both "significantly watered down," to quote Salon.com's Andrew Leonard.

Moreover, the Dodd-Frank Law, they argue, is filled with loopholes. One example is that foreign exchange swaps are only regulated to the extent that they're not excepted from regulation by order of the Secretary of the Treasury . . . who, in fact, has excepted them from regulation.

The need to protect individuals from the abuses of large companies and corporations also sparked the creation of the Consumer Financial Protection Board, a massive new federal agency that would regulate consumers' dealings with banks, credit unions, payday lenders, mortgage providers, debt collectors, and other financial companies. Republicans fought the board's creation, but Democrats succeeded in voting it into law.

For left populists, such a board is a no-brainer: the imbalance between individual Americans and corporate power is so great that government must serve as an intermediary to protect against abuse and ensure fairness. Government, in the view of left-wing populists, has a *moral* duty to protect ordinary people from being exploited or abused by private-sector power. They seek to give the government unprecedented influence and control over private-sector economic and financial activity.

2. The expansion of the social safety net. The role of government to the left-wing populists is broad and expansive. They believe that there is a lot that government should do to guarantee retirement security, education, and employment opportunities.

Health care, they believe, is a human right, on par with freedom of speech and the press, the right to a fair trial, and the right to vote. To the left, allowing a free-market capitalist system to operate unregulated produces a deeply unjust society.

Why, they ask, should the health and well-being of Americans, many with barely enough money to cover their rent every month, be subject to market forces? Why should the fundamental needs of children, of any social class, be subject to market forces? What is society for, if not to create and support decent living conditions for all its members?

For progressives, then, the most transformative pieces of social legislation in the United States—Medicare, Medicaid, and Social Security—

are simply inviolate. These government-provided health and welfare programs, they argue, have saved millions of seniors and the poor from abject poverty. Rather than discuss curtailing their scope and funding, or making eligibility requirements more onerous, progressives believe these programs should be expanded.

Health coverage is provided to the elderly through Medicare and to the poor through Medicaid. But for decades, the progressive left has fought to extend both programs more broadly so that all Americans would be covered by either or both of the programs.

When the Obama administration *did* in fact pass an historic law in 2010 mandating that private insurers provide coverage to uninsured Americans—the most transformative piece of social legislation since the 1960s—it wasn't enough for the populist left. As they see it, the struggle for health-care justice continues until the day we enact a "single-payer" plan of universal health coverage in the United States, the single payer being the federal government. They argue that Medicare for all is the only comprehensive way to reform the health-care system to expand coverage and make health care more affordable, and they're convinced that nothing will change so long as private insurance companies continue to exist.

Indeed, they believe that President Obama has let his desire to appease those on the right drive him to abandon the single-payer model, which they believe is essential. Expansion of Medicare for all Americans, they believe, is the ONLY reform that could really make universal health care a reality.

From their perspective, the health-care-reform debate was usurped by big insurance lobbyists who sabotaged real reform. Far more concerned with acquiescing to the demands of Republicans and Blue Dog Democrats in order to secure votes for the legislation, congressional Democrats and President Obama abandoned the more progressive demands.

Some on the left—feeling betrayed by their president, disgusted with Congress, and ignored by the media—have concluded that civil disobedience is the only way that they can make their voice heard. These acts of civil disobedience got far less media attention than the Tea Parties on the right, but they should not be underestimated in their importance.

In the spring of 2009, thirteen single-payer advocates, who became known as the "Baucus Raucous Caucus," were arrested for interrupting Senator Baucus's May 5 Senate hearing because it failed to include a single-payer option. The "Baucus Raucous Caucus" inspired a national mobilization to end what they see as private insurance abuse and build support for single-payer health-care reform.

In October of 2009, a series of sit-ins were held across the country.

"Like many people who are passionate about health care reform, I felt revitalized when I saw blasted all over the media that 13 people had put themselves on the line to resist the forces of the medical-industrial complex that are systematically dismembering the health care reform initiative taken up by Congress and President Obama," explained one liberal populist, Marilena Marchetti, a twenty-nine-year-old resident of Chicago and one of the seven members of the Chicago Single-Payer Action Network (ChiSPAN) who came to be known as the CIGNA 7.

In October 2009, having grown frustrated with the seemingly endless health-care deliberations then going on in Congress, the seven activists entered the CIGNA headquarters in downtown Chicago and demanded to speak with CIGNA executives, calling on the company to approve all doctor-recommended treatments. When they were denied a meeting, they sat down on the lobby floor and were arrested.

"I knew getting arrested was going to be scary, but I was willing to risk it because I'm so sick of health care being treated like a pair of Air Jordans. It's not a commodity. It's something all people need . . . . Hundreds of people die each day because insurance companies deny them lifesaving care that they need," Marchetti said.

Marchetti was expressing a fundamental article of faith among progressives: that quality, affordable health care is a human right and ought to be legally guaranteed in the United States for all citizens.

We had a chance to speak with Marchetti and the rest of the CIGNA 7 five days later, when my researcher dropped in on a ChiSPAN meeting at the Access Living Center in downtown Chicago. There were about twenty members in attendance, ranging in age from late twenties to midsixties. While ChiSPAN meetings had originally been held on a bimonthly basis, they had begun meeting weekly in the fall of 2009 as the congressional stalemate over health-care reform dragged on.

"Private insurance companies," Timi Papas, another member of the CIGNA 7 told us, "are dictating the debate. As a matter of fact right now, in the past few months, they have given Congress $380 million in campaign contributions and lobbying. They are definitely I guess you can say bribing every legislator. They have six lobbyists for each legislator right now, and these lobbyists are working on the legislators. So yes, we are very much concerned about them. The insurance companies have been writing the bills."

Liberal populists are just as suspicious of private insurance companies as they are of Wall Street. They believe that private insurance companies control politicians through campaign contributions, and those politicians in turn serve their interests.

Another fundamental aspect of the social-safety net is retirement security, a goal that, to a substantial extent, the progressive left achieved in the twentieth century with Franklin Roosevelt's creation of Social Security, which kept millions of senior citizens out of the poverty that was once common to old age. But as the decades passed, it became clear that the program faced serious solvency challenges, which could only be met through a combination of benefit cuts, increased taxation, or an extension of the eligibility age. Some reasonable, if difficult, proposals have been put forth for doing that, but progressives are united in their opposition to any curtailing of retirement security benefits. They vehemently oppose the conservative vision of privatizing Social Security by allowing younger citizens to invest their funds in the stock market. President Bush's plan to do this went down in flames in 2005—a significant victory for progressives.

Still, the defeat of the radical privatization plan for Social Security hasn't solved the program's long-term cost issues. The option that left populists prefer for sustaining Social Security is increased taxation, especially on the wealthy. Rather than limiting benefits for people who need them, they believe that the rich, who don't need Social Security, should pay more to sustain the program for the millions who do.

3. The redistribution of wealth. Another core principle of left-wing populism is that government exists principally to promote equity and fairness by any means necessary.

For progressives, fairness means more redistributive policies. They believe that a steeply progressive tax system is necessary to pay for the level of regulation needed to help rein in corporate excess and preserve the social safety net for poor and middle-class people who are struggling to make ends meet.

Indeed, this focus on taxation of those with more means is another fundamental aspect of the left-populist vision. Some left populists argue for higher taxation rates on *all* income groups; others believe rates should be raised only on the wealthy. But they agree unanimously that the wealthy, at minimum, simply must pay more to provide retirement security and health care for all. Taxation on the wealthy would also support broader economic goals, such as macroeconomic stimulus and job creation.

For progressives, higher taxes and wealth redistribution are both an economic argument and a principle of fairness. Listen to Robert Reich, a revered progressive and former Labor Secretary under Bill Clinton:

> We need a new WPA to put the unemployed back to work. And an infrastructure bank to create jobs repairing the nation's crumbling roads, bridges, and water and sewer systems. Exempt the first $20,000 of income from payroll taxes, and apply payroll taxes to incomes more than $250,000. Extend the Earned Income Tax Credit wage subsidy all the way up through the middle class.
>
> Pay for this by raising marginal income taxes on millionaires. Under President Dwight Eisenhower, the top marginal rate was 91 percent. I'm not advocating this, but a millionaire marginal tax of even 70 percent would also go a long way toward reducing the nation's future budget deficit.[2]

While Reich's argument clearly points to a practical economic justification for higher taxes, it's important to understand that progressives see taxation of the wealthy as a good in itself, for several reasons. For one thing, they argue, higher taxes on the wealthy will reduce income inequality, which in the United States stands at record levels. For another, higher taxes on the wealthy (and on business) will reduce, however slightly, their economic dominance over others and create a somewhat more level playing field. And finally, higher taxes on those of means are simply morally right—those with more economic wealth *should* pay more to support a just, stable society.

It is, in the end, an issue of justice. Think of it as a variation on the old biblical injunction: "For everyone to whom much is given, of him shall much be required."

Given the events of recent years, it should be easy to understand the rationale of such a view, whatever one thinks of its merits.

4. Job creation and protection. Another major component of the left-wing populist agenda is the need for huge public works programs both to rebuild infrastructure and to generate centrally planned economic activity.

Seeing a broken society—a broken world, really—progressives believe in government planning on a large scale. Where conservatives argue that free markets and the "invisible hand" of market forces will produce a thriving economy and broad, if uneven, prosperity, progressives urge "fair markets"—which are essentially regulated markets where the government determines how wealth will be distributed. Rather than leave it to the private sector to create, and eliminate, jobs when it sees fit, the government should strive to ensure full employment, protecting jobs when necessary and creating jobs through infrastructure projects and public works programs.

In the Obama years, progressives argued for a much larger federal stimulus than the $800 billion package that the government passed in February 2009—and they have even called for a second round of economic stimulus from Washington.

"Creating jobs in a depressed economy is something government could and should be doing," writes Paul Krugman of the *New York Times*. Krugman, one of the leading voices of progressive economics, speaks for many when he laments that the Obama administration has abandoned serious attempts at job creation.

"Our failure to create jobs is a choice, not a necessity," he argues, "a choice rationalized by an ever-shifting set of excuses."[3] What's needed, Krugman and others argue, is *more* economic stimulus from Washington and more FDR-style public-sector jobs programs.

"Where are the big public works projects?" he asks.

He's referring to progressive calls for a range of federally funded employment initiatives, the most popular of which would include the creation of an "infrastructure bank" to fund massive infrastructure creation and repair projects around the country—projects that would, undeniably, employ many, whatever their price tags might be.

Progressives see the government as a key player, perhaps *the* key player, in sparking economic activity and creating jobs. They see deficit reduction and fiscal austerity, which would reduce government's role in the economy, as precisely the wrong approach to our problems.

Left populists are strongly devoted to labor and our domestic manufacturing industries, including some of the hardest-hit sectors of our economy. As beleaguered as they are, private-sector labor unions have tried to revive union activism and rally Americans to manufacturing jobs in the United States.

In May 2009, United Steelworkers (USW), a union of 1.2 million American workers, launched the "Keep It Made in America Tour." As posted on the USW website:

> Our union is embarking on an 11-state, 30-plus city bus tour with the Alliance for American Manufacturing to deliver an important message: that our domestic auto industry matters to all of us and all of us need to be in the fight to save it . . . In our union, in the U.S. and Canada, more than 350,000 of our members' jobs depend on the auto industry—from rubber, steel and glass workers to those who manufacture computer chips, paper used for auto catalogs and boxes, and auto parts. We also have members who make chemical brighteners used in cars, bank tellers who deal with auto loans, bus drivers who work for schools and health care workers whose jobs are in communities that would be hurt by the loss of auto jobs and the tax base they provide.[4]

It stands to reason, then, that progressive populists also want to protect American workers through protective tariffs and legislation to keep immigrants out.

In a letter to the *New York Times,* Alan Hassenfeld observes:

> As an international businessman and retired leader of a major toy company, I have spent the last four months travelling the world. I have never before seen such intense, widespread populist pressure to increase tariffs and domestic subsidies and tighten import standards.[5]

America's labor unions have rallied behind a platform that free trade is un-American. They laud the viewpoint expressed by economist Dean Baker that free trade essentially helps America's elite class while it victimizes America's working class. "'Free traders' could not care less about free trade. They don't like policies that favor ordinary workers, like those in the steel industry. On the other hand, they are very happy when the government intervenes to help the rich, as was the case with the Wall Street bailout. And that's un-American."[6]

In the eyes of labor unions, big business has used free-trade policies to marginalize America's working class. According to policy director and chief international economist of the AFL-CIO, Thea Lea:

> Globalization has been used by American corporations to bargain down workers' benefits and wages and to bust unions . . . And so we've had

the wrong kind of globalization. It's been a corporate-dominated globalization, which has not really served working people here or in our trading partners very well. And so the impact has been that we've seen this long-term—decades-long stagnation of wages and growth of wage inequality in the United States. . . . So to the extent that the benefits haven't gotten down to the average worker, to the typical worker, of course there's going to be a backlash against globalization and of course we need to do our trade policy differently, not just throw a few crumbs to the losers.[7]

5. Antimilitarism. Finally, the left-populist vision has important implications for the U.S. role in the world. The populist left overwhelmingly opposed the U.S. invasion of Iraq—and many opposed the attack on Afghanistan as well—out of an antimilitarist, anti-interventionist philosophy.

There is an economic component to this outlook that argues that money is better spent at home than overseas unless we are directly threatened.

Thus, those who subscribe to this school of thought not only view most U.S. foreign policy initiatives as driven by corrupt goals—whether of superpower hegemony or economic exploitation of vulnerable populations—but also see U.S. military interventions in the twenty-first century as financial luxuries the nation can no longer afford.

Moreover, there is also a civil liberties component that vehemently opposes a number of policies associated with the "War on Terror," including "roving" wiretaps for domestic intelligence gathering, torture, the Guantanamo Bay Detainee Center and secret prisons, and the CIA's rendition program.

In this view American exceptionalism, which holds that the United States is unique among nations by virtue of its history and principles, is a convenient excuse for seemingly endless military adventurism. The proper American focus in 2011, progressives believe, should be on the needs of its citizens at home. And U.S. interventions, on balance, have done more harm than good, anyway.

As George McGovern said famously in his disastrous 1972 presidential campaign: *Come home, America.*

Clearly, the principles of the populist left are grounded in a long and deep experience of political struggle and national history. How did left populists develop their vision?

A BRIEF HISTORY OF LEFT POPULISM

Certainly political progressivism and liberal populism have a long history in the United States, dating back as far as Thomas Jefferson himself and his warnings about "concentrations" of power, whether governmental or private. Jefferson's Democratic-Republican Party, which eventually became today's Democratic Party, pledged itself to popular representation, states' rights, and limits on federal power. It also took exception to Treasury Secretary Alexander Hamilton's insistence on a commercial, industrial society, which it feared would empower financial and commercial forces at the expense of yeoman farmers and free laborers. These concerns, adjusted for today's realities, have never really changed.

Policies advocating the redistribution of wealth, the institution of a safety net, and government intervention in the private sector were key components in late nineteenth- to mid-twentieth-century political movements—from William Jennings Bryan and the People's Party in the 1890s, to Teddy Roosevelt's progressivism, to Franklin Delano Roosevelt and Huey Long in the Depression/New Deal Era. In 1873, American farmers, odd men out of the Industrial Revolution, were furious when the federal government failed to recognize the silver dollar—the currency of the masses. Thus began the Free Silver Movement, which found common cause with the growing agrarian movement of farmers upset with economic conditions and the growing power of a political and business elite.

This populist uprising culminated in the creation of the People's Party, also known as the Populist Party, in the 1890s. The party's Omaha Platform called for the expansion of the federal government's authority to act on behalf of the marginalized workers—both rural and urban—and protect them from "oppression, injustice, and poverty," language immediately recognizable over one hundred years later.

"The fruits of the toil of millions," the platform argued, "are boldly stolen to build up colossal fortunes for a few, unprecedented in the history of mankind; and the possessors of those, in turn, despise the republic and endanger liberty."

William Jennings Bryan, the great populist crusader, was nominated as the People's Party candidate for president in 1896. The Democratic Party, seeing the populist writing on the wall, nominated Bryan as well. Though Bryan lost the election of 1896 to Republican William

McKinley, the Populist Party's influence resonated for decades, and the Roosevelt and Wilson administrations adopted many of its reforms.

Like the contemporary populist left, Teddy Roosevelt believed that government had a responsibility to be the "steward of the people." As president, Roosevelt expanded government's role in the private sector in an attempt to benefit working Americans. He further regulated interstate commerce, monitored the safety of food and drugs, and fostered land conservation. He was an ally of labor unions and took on Wall Street, filing public "trust-busting" suits against firms such as J. P. Morgan. Though his foreign policy and his demeanor would be anathema to later progressives, Teddy Roosevelt's domestic policies were a template for a century of progressive change.

Modern left populism in America traces its true antecedents to Franklin Delano Roosevelt. During the Great Depression, FDR became the warrior of the working class. He championed the empowerment of ordinary Americans and railed against the corporate and government co-conspirators who derailed the U.S. economy.

FDR and his huge Democratic majority in Congress enacted landmark legislation that transformed American life, altering forever the relationship between American citizens and their government. Roosevelt's New Deal legislation remains the foundation of America's limited welfare state as well as the high-water mark of progressive achievement in the twentieth century: Social Security provided a guaranteed income to the elderly, the Fair Labor Standards Act established a minimum wage and largely prohibited the hiring of children, and the National Labor Relations Act made it illegal to fire employees for trying to unionize a workplace.

Three-quarters of a century later, these laws are so fundamentally embedded in American life that it is impossible to imagine a time when they did not exist.

FDR's populist vision continued to evolve. Eventually, he declared that government had an obligation to "assure us equality in the pursuit of happiness," as he put it in a 1944 State of the Union address calling for a second Bill of Rights. Acknowledging the liberties guaranteed by the first Bill of Rights, FDR described what remained to be done, in words that are still strikingly contemporary for left populists today:

> We have come to a clear realization of the fact that true individual freedom cannot exist without economic security and independence.

"Necessitous men are not free men." People who are hungry and out of a job are the stuff of which dictatorships are made.

In our day these economic truths have become accepted as self-evident. We have accepted, so to speak, a second Bill of Rights under which a new basis of security and prosperity can be established for all—regardless of station, race, or creed.

For FDR, those rights included public education; remunerative work; freedom from "unfair" competition in business; decent housing, food, clothing, and recreation; medical care; care for the elderly; and other rights. To that list, today's left populists would add retirement security, mortgage assistance, access to credit, consumer protection, unemployment relief—and equal marriage rights, and strong environmental protections, and equality in public school funding . . . and on and on. Their vision, always, is of a society transforming itself continually, evolving toward a more humanistic perfection, and with government as the instrument of this process.

In the 1960s, Lyndon Johnson's Great Society gave them their last great shot at it.

Before it became engulfed in the Vietnam War that would destroy its legacy, the Johnson administration advanced more progressive legislation than any other but for FDR's—and no one else is even close. The LBJ programs had two key focal points: the landmark Civil Rights and Voting Rights acts of 1964 and 1965; and the War on Poverty programs that included Head Start for early-childhood education, food stamps, the Jobs Corps, Community Action programs—and Medicaid, a guaranteed health program for the poor. For the middle class, LBJ created Medicare and instituted significant expansions of benefits to Social Security.

In a speech at the University of Michigan in 1964, Johnson set out the Great Society agenda, as ambitious a vision as any American statesman has ever advanced:

The Great Society is a place where every child can find knowledge to enrich his mind and to enlarge his talents. It is a place where leisure is a welcome chance to build and reflect, not a feared cause of boredom and restlessness. It is a place where the city of man serves not only the needs of the body and the demands of commerce but the desire for beauty and the hunger for community.[8]

Of course, the Great Society's center couldn't hold. While some of the programs, like Medicare and Medicaid, have survived and generally work well today, others—particularly the War on Poverty programs—either failed to work effectively or, arguably, did more harm than good. This became central to a growing conservative critique of the American welfare state as the 1960s wound on, and it provided a spark for the right-wing populist movements that would eventually erupt.

The Nixon administration did not seek to roll back any of the Great Society's populist policies—implementing environmental protection, desegregation, wage and price controls, and consolidating the programs initiated under FDR and LBJ. Nixon established a broad consensus for government's expanded role in society as well as expansive social-welfare programs.

The Vietnam War, rampant social unrest and spiraling crime, especially in the cities, and the end of the long American economic boom in the early 1970s brought a close to an era of unparalleled hope and energy on the populist left. What would follow would be a generation spent largely in the shadows of the nation's political history.

Before Barack Obama's victory in 2008, the Democratic Party elected just two presidents in forty-four years—Jimmy Carter, who served one traumatic term in the 1970s, and Bill Clinton, whose two-term presidency in the 1990s, though controversial, was much more successful. Carter managed his narrow victory over Gerald Ford in 1976 by casting himself as a conservative Democrat. The populist left never embraced him, and his failures launched the rise to political power of the American conservative movement in the person of Ronald Reagan. In just sixteen years, the nation had gone from the most expansive social-welfare programs in history to the most restrictive government role in the private economy since the 1920s.

The Reagan years were dark ones for the progressive left, and the marginalization continued during the moderate presidency of Bill Clinton, who presided over the longest economic boom in American history. It seemed that progressivism's historical moment had come and gone. Clinton's championing of a balanced budget, welfare reform, a federal crime bill, and free-trade agreements effectively represented a tacit acceptance of much of the critique of liberal society that the Goldwater, Proposition 13, Reagan, and Gingrich revolutions stood for.

But Clinton's presidency planted the seeds for the next left-populist revival. This was partly due to trade policies and NAFTA, partly in reaction to Clinton's use of "triangulation"—positioning himself as the moderate alternative between resolute liberals and hard-core, antigovernment insurgents like Newt Gingrich, leaving left populists out in the cold—and also the result of several key events that played out at the end of the twentieth century.

A decade and a half after the passage of NAFTA, many on the left felt vindicated in opposing the bill. While free trade brought increased economic prosperity on a macro level, improving corporate bottom lines and enriching the coffers of Wall Street firms and investors, its record in the broader economic sector was much more uneven. The manufacturing economy, already in decline since the 1960s, continued to hemorrhage jobs and displaced blue-collar workers struggled to learn new skills.

Along with economic decline, two key events created a pretext for a revival of left-wing populism: Clinton's impeachment in 1998 and the 2000 Florida recount.

Democrats, from centrists to liberals to progressives, saw the Republican impeachment effort against President Clinton as an outrage against democracy, the Constitution, and basic political decency. Democrats and the broader left were pushed back into alliance because of it; in fact, Clinton's persecution had the effect of shoring up his support among progressives, who had usually complained about his policies. Now, seeing a far worse enemy in right-wing Republicans, they doubled down on their support for a Democratic president.

A married couple, Joan Blades and Wes Boyd, cofounders of a computer company called Berkeley Systems, started a website to circulate a petition calling on Congress to put an end to the impeachment drama:

September 22, 1998

Disgusted Citizens Organize on the Internet: Urge Congress to *Censure and Move On*

Across the United States today, a diverse group of online Americans launched an Internet political campaign and petition drive called *Censure and Move On*. Angry and disgusted by the behavior of our representatives in the nation's capital, we are using email and the world-wide web to crystallize public opinion.

Censure and Move On is a bipartisan group of concerned citizens that organized around a single issue: speedy resolution of the Lewinsky scandal. The petition web page simply states the Congress must "Immediately Censure President Clinton and Move On to pressing issues facing the country."

Blades and Boyd had launched what would become one of the most powerful online left-wing activist groups: MoveOn.org. They would eventually link up with others, like Daily Kos, to form the bedrock of the left's Netroots Nation.

The incredible divisiveness of the 2000 election recount in Florida—which featured huge demonstrations and even an infamous "Brooks Brothers riot" by Republicans in Miami—and George W. Bush's contested victory, decided only when the Supreme Court voted 5–4 to halt the recount, seemed to foreshadow an era of division. On the left, the Battle of Florida would not be forgotten, and it seemed to be the trigger for a generation of young, left-wing activists. Blogger Jerome Armstrong and Markos Moulitsas (who would found the influential Daily Kos website) saw the recount, and its result, as a defining event in the forging of a new left-wing populist movement:

> Five years ago, the Republicans took over the government through non-democratic means. Establishment Democrats, for the most part, stood back and watched as a partisan judicial body halted the counting of presidential votes. While conservative activists led the charge on behalf of their party, there was nothing happening on our side. That was the spark. Fed-up progressive activists began organizing online. Fueled by the new technologies—the web, blogging tools, internet search engines—this new generation of activists challenged the moribund Democratic Party establishment.[9]

Moulitsas, Armstrong, and a new progressive generation watched with mounting rage as George W. Bush aggressively pursued a right-wing agenda. Bush's policies, from taxes and energy to the environment, education, and social issues, rallied the left wing of the Democratic Party to impassioned opposition. By midway through Bush's second term, the impact of two wars, an uneven economy, and Bush's divisive effort to privatize Social Security finally shattered Americans' trust in him. The 2006 midterm election saw an anti-GOP backlash that led to the Democratic recapture of both houses of Congress.

WAR, PATRIOTISM, AND LIBERTY

On September 20, 2001, eight in ten Americans watched Bush's address to Congress, nine days after the September 11 attacks. Fires at the World Trade Center were still burning and would continue burning for months; the death toll from the attacks on New York and Washington was estimated at six thousand (it would, fortunately, come down); and Americans were entering high-rise buildings, and boarding planes, trains, and buses, with a fear they had never known.

Bush's speech that night soared with eloquence and moral passion. The "war on terror," he said, "will not end until every terrorist group of global reach has been found, stopped and defeated." The next morning, a poll found that 91 percent of Americans agreed with his approach. Democrats appeared to feel the same way, more or less.

"I think the president spoke for all of us," said the Senate Democratic leader, Tom Daschle of South Dakota. "He spoke eloquently. He spoke passionately. And he spoke in a way that I think unified all of America."[10]

For at least six months after the attacks, Bush enjoyed the broad approval of Americans, Republicans and Democrats, in his efforts to prevent future terrorist attacks at home and defeat terrorist networks abroad, particularly in Afghanistan.

That support was short-lived, however, for two principal reasons: first, Bush initiated a detainee policy that would immediately arouse opposition from left-wing civil liberties advocates, and second, Bush would soon begin arguing for an invasion of Iraq as the next theater in the war on terror. Both sparked enormous left-wing opposition. The administration's detention of thousands of terrorist suspects without charge, and with no formal legal plan for dealing with their cases, was mostly accepted on the right as a necessary "wartime" measure. But it sent the left into an uproar.

In the face of large-scale public fear, Bush was able to identify his political opponents with procedural niceties—legal and bureaucratic detail—while vowing that he would do whatever it took to prevent another attack. He accused Democrats of excessive concern with international opinion, of seeking a "permission slip" before they would defend America. His approach was powerful and simple, devoid of moral ambiguity—and in a time of fear and uncertainty, it resonated with the American people.

Bush's war policies had a galvanizing effect on a long-dormant wing of the Democratic Party—anti-interventionists, as well as a broad base of left-populist activists more generally. These activists saw the war as the work of an administration that, to their minds, had committed serial offenses against American laws and decency.

"War criminal, take her to the Hague!" a protester memorably shouted in October 2007, holding up her bloody hands to Secretary of State Condoleezza Rice at a Capitol Hill hearing in 2007. Such incidents were common during the Bush years. Raw, disturbing spectacles, they offered graphic evidence of left-populist rage.

ANTIWAR DEMOCRATS AND THE RISE OF THE NETROOTS

The surprise presidential candidacy of former Vermont governor Howard Dean in 2004 marked the first time many Americans heard of a phenomenon called "Netroots." The term was coined by Jerome Armstrong in 2002 to denote the new left-wing political activism and commentary through blogs and other online media (which eventually included social media such as Facebook and Twitter). But more than technology, what distinguished Netroots was a return to a much harder edged, combative political style that had long been out of fashion in established Democratic circles. It was a full embrace of politics as combat, with definitive winners and losers, and it disdained bipartisanship and compromise. Netroots loyalists saw Democratic moderates as sellouts captured by Beltway thinking after spending too much time in Washington.

In that last respect, Netroots had something in common with rightwing activists, and in fact, as Jonathan Chait wrote in a 2007 essay about the movement, Netroots pioneers like Moulitsas and Armstrong modeled their own effort after the conservative movement. They both saw, in the history of the conservative movement from the candidacy of Barry Goldwater, through the 1970s and the Reagan era, a movement of unwavering political unity and discipline, one that ruthlessly enforced ideological orthodoxy.

As Chait wrote: "The netroots' dream is of a liberal army of grass-roots activists, pundits, policy wonks, and politicians all marching more or less in lockstep."[11]

This new movement would not seek conciliation, but victory; not compromise, but purity; and it valued ideas not for their own sake, but for their effectiveness in achieving political outcomes. It wanted to take on the Bush-led right at its own game—political polarization—and win.

As Markos Moulitsas put it aptly: "They want to make me into the latest Jesse Jackson, but I'm not ideological at all. I'm just all about winning."

But they were ideological; they hoped to win victories for largely progressive causes, causes well to the left of the Democratic Party establishment, which saw its political power waning after 2004 for its accommodation of Bush's foreign policies. As those policies increasingly looked like failures, the growing ranks of the Netroots stepped to the forefront of Democratic politics.

Moulitsas, in creating Daily Kos, has become a representative figure among the new populist left. Born to a Salvadoran mother and Greek father in Chicago, Moulitsas served in the U.S. Army after graduating high school, and by his own account, "missed deploying to the Gulf War by a hair." His military background—he described the army as "perhaps the ideal society"—distinguishes him from more typical progressive activists, who wouldn't go near a military recruiting station.

It also helps explain his combativeness, and his fury. In April 2004, after the ambush and killing of four American contractors for Blackwater USA, Moulitsas raged in the comments section of a blog post:

> Let the people see what war is like. This isn't an Xbox game. There are real repercussions to Bush's folly. That said, I feel nothing over the death of merceneries [sic]. They aren't in Iraq because of orders, or because they are there trying to help the people make Iraq a better place. They are there to wage war for profit. Screw them.[12]

Before the emergence of the Tea Party, Netroots had good claim to the status Chait gave them: "The most significant mass movement in U.S. politics since the rise of the Christian right more than two decades ago."[13] Netroots became a significant force in Democratic campaign fund-raising and activist recruitment, as well as political conventioneering.

Its annual convention, Netroots Nation, is attended by prominent Democrats from Howard Dean and Nancy Pelosi to Al Franken and Bill Clinton. Most important, the movement pushed the Democratic Party inexorably to the left, forcing it to make tougher, more partisan critiques of Bush and the GOP and raising the stakes of the debate. Netroots sharpened the contrasts between the two parties, bringing an unabashed ideological edge—a populist edge—to Democratic arguments.

Both the failure to find weapons of mass destruction (WMDs) in Iraq and the failure of the initial invasion to produce immediate political stability further polarized the electorate, further demonized President Bush, and gave further moral certitude for those on the left.

The populist groundswell of opposition to the Iraq War put Washington Democrats in a bind. Most of the party's leading presidential contenders, in both 2004 and 2008, had voted to authorize force in Iraq or had openly advocated the invasion itself. As the war teetered toward calamity, they slowly ramped up their criticism of Bush, insisting that they weren't changing their position—though they were—while also stressing their support for the troops. These efforts didn't convince the American people, who tended to see Bush as a man of principle, whatever his faults, and Democrats like John Kerry as opportunists and flip-floppers who lacked the courage of their convictions.

TRICKLE-DOWN ECONOMICS, REVISITED

For left populists who felt spurned in the Clinton years, George W. Bush's championing of a $1.35 trillion tax cut in 2001 was an outrage. The left already saw the American economy as favoring the wealthy; the Bush tax cuts would only accentuate that tendency.[14]

The Bush tax cuts did not stimulate the economy, at least not in proportion to the enormous cost they exacted on the federal budget. GDP and employment growth both lagged after the Bush cuts were phased in, at rates below that of other postwar expansions. Nor did Bush's cuts have much impact on small business growth. Indeed, like many of their critics alleged, the Bush tax cuts in 2001 seemed mostly to benefit the wealthy. Nor did the Bush tax cuts narrow the federal budget deficit, as predicted—a common argument of "supply-side" conservative economists, who believed that lower tax rates drive increased federal revenue because they spark economic activity.

Overall, Bush's economic policies fostered inequality, stagnating incomes, and lost economic ground. About one-quarter of Bush's tax cuts in 2001 and 2003 went to the top 1 percent of earners. As Nobel laureate economist Joseph Stiglitz documented, the Bush years exacerbated American income inequality and left millions of middle-class and lower-middle-class Americans behind economically.

"A young male in his 30s today," Stiglitz wrote, "has an income, adjusted for inflation, that is 12 percent less than what his father was making 30 years ago." Over five million more Americans were living in poverty when Bush left office than when he entered.[15]

Moreover, the beneficiaries of those tax cuts often opposed them. Take Mike Teahan, a fifty-two-year-old owner of an espresso equipment importer. Though Teahan, who clears about $250,000 a year, was seeing an extra $12,000 or so from the tax cut, he saw no uptick in his business, since his customers' economic situations hadn't changed.

"What we do in business, how we spend our money, how we allocate our resources—that has very little to do with tax policy," Teahan says. "I map my business based on my customers, and what my customers want to buy, and what they can afford to buy."

Rick Poore, owner of DesignWear, Inc., a screen-printing business based in Lincoln, Nebraska, agrees. "We are fed by our consumers, not by our tax breaks," he says. "If you drive more people to my business, I will hire more people. It's as simple as that. If you give me a tax break, I'll just take the wife to the Bahamas."[16]

Repealing the Bush tax cuts has been a central goal of the populist left almost since they were instituted. Barack Obama's election in 2008 offered hope for achieving this goal, but in December 2010, Obama dealt progressives a harsh blow. As part of a budget deal with the Republicans that included GOP agreement to extend unemployment insurance, Obama agreed to extend the Bush tax cuts. The populist left was furious.

HOPE, CHANGE, AND FRUSTRATION

The December 2010 budget deal underscored the stark difference between left populists and President Obama. Populists believed the president had betrayed all those who had worked so hard to elect him by compromising on one of their core principles: that higher taxes for the rich are necessary.

Five major progressive groups—MoveOn, Democracy for America, TrueMajority, Credo Action, and the Progressive Campaign Change Committee—urged the Senate not to ratify the deal. DFA chair Jim Dean issued a clear ultimatum to Democrats: "As for any Democratic members of Congress who are going along with extending the tax cuts for high income earners—*this is the stuff that primaries are made of.*"[17]

That remains to be seen. But the deal passed.

The reaction to the budget deal was a microcosm of the way Obama's presidency has served, more often than not, to frustrate the lofty hopes of the populist left. Here was a president elected with enormous progressive support, a historical figure in the nation's history, a symbol of racial healing and social progress. Surely his presidency would herald a new progressive dawn, wouldn't it?

Not quite.

6

HOPES DASHED

Obama and the Left

"For a lot of the folks who have been in New York and all across the country in the Occupy movement, there is a profound sense of frustration . . . about the fact that the essence of the American dream—which is if you work hard, if you stick to it, that you can make it—feels like that's slipping away. And its not the way things are supposed to be. Not here. Not in America."

—President Barack Obama[1]

It's time for the president to realize that sometimes populism, especially populism that makes bankers angry, is exactly what the economy needs.

—Paul Krugman[2]

What we're trying to do is save the world from the Republican budget. . . . we're trying to save life on this planet as we know it today.

—Nancy Pelosi[3]

In 2008, as the economic bubble burst, left-wing populists saw the rise of a presidential candidate who talked like one of them. Barack Obama entered the White House with enormous expectations from the progressive left.

As an outsider candidate, Barack Obama offered the promise of hope and change, and the left was confident that once elected, he would do their bidding. Indeed, as senator, Obama had opposed the war in Iraq, and his history as a community organizer gave organized labor the impression that he would put their interests front and center.

But three years into his presidency, he has become for many on the left a symbol of hopes dashed for failing to live up to the core progressive principles which they believed that he once stood for yet has systematically abandoned. While this disillusionment may have been inevitable, the nature of the disappointment illustrates the dynamic today between Obama and his left-wing base.

And indeed, probably the most important element from the Occupy Wall Street movement specifically and left populism generally is a countervailing pressure on the President and the Democratic Party to avoid moving to the center at any point.

The President—having failed to achieve any compromise with the Republicans on fiscal issues—seems to have made his peace with the notion that there will be no Grand Bargains, no compromise with the GOP, and that a moderated and diluted populist worldview will be the most effective way for him to win the 2012 election.

Put another way, liberal populism provides the answer for why there continues to be economic uncertainty and income inequality in America. If only there were redistribution, if only there were an equitable tax system, if only the favoritism of Wall Street and moneyed interests disappeared—America would be a much healthier country.

"I think a lot of us came in here without a lot of faith in elected politicians to introduce truly progressive legislation. We're here to push for what we think is the right thing," explained Eric, a young press liaison for the Chicago Single-Payer Action Network when I approached him after a meeting that he moderated in October 2009. "We're basically here to make Obama live up to his rhetoric," he added.

The left's frustration with President Obama is all the more striking when considering what Obama has already achieved.

Despite the fact that he has expanded the role of government in American life to a level not seen since the Great Depression, all of President Obama's policy achievements—from his sweeping health-care reform and major financial-reform legislation, to his consumer-protection and Environmental Protection agencies, to his $800 billion stimulus package—are seen by the populist left as inadequate and as having failed to achieve their goals.

The problem for Obama is that he must perform a continual balancing act with his left flank: it is something like a good cop, bad cop relationship. For each populist push he makes, he seems bound to attempt a counterweight that is more centrist leaning.

"Unfortunately," lamented HealthCare-NOW! volunteer Josh Starcher while protesting outside of Bristol-Myers Squibb, "Barack started to compromise, instead of supporting single payer and then negotiating to find a middle ground. Instead, he started at the middle ground, so we're only going to get a quarter of what we want. Basically Barack and Rangel and Baucus—the key players in the government— have been paid off with campaign contributions from the insurance industry. They basically got elected through the insurance industry."

Such is the nature of Obama's predicament that he often seems to alternate populist and centrist themes about the same issue.

This dynamic played itself out repeatedly during the 2011 debt-ceiling showdown, which went from a minor issue to a defining episode of the Obama presidency. Democrats argued that the over $14 trillion debt couldn't be narrowed without "revenue increases," meaning tax hikes, primarily on the wealthy; Republicans argued that only spending cuts, including to entitlement programs, were acceptable, and that tax hikes would hurt any chance of economic recovery.

In a late June 2011 press conference, while arguing for tax hikes on the corporate jets of the super-rich, Obama sounded the progressive theme of human needs:

"If we do not have revenues, that means there are a bunch of kids out there who do not have college scholarships," Obama said. "[It] might compromise the National Weather Services. It means we might not be funding critical medical research. It means food inspection might be compromised. I've said to Republican leaders, 'You go talk to your constituents and ask them, Are you willing to compromise your kids' safety so some corporate-jet owner can get a tax break?'"[4]

Two weeks later, Obama was tacking to the center again, arguing for shared pain in making a budget deal: "I continue to push congressional leaders for the largest possible deal," he said from the White House. "It is possible for us to construct a package that would be balanced, would share sacrifice [and] would involve both parties taking on their sacred cows."[5]

Indeed, during the long and drawn-out debt-ceiling battle, Obama sounded increasingly like a moderate Republican in his willingness to cut entitlements. While astute political observers saw the president's positioning as logical and politically shrewd, the populist left was not pleased.

"The president's proposing cuts to Social Security and Medicare has the potential to sap the energy of the Democratic base—among older voters because of Medicare and Medicaid and younger voters because of the lack of jobs," said Damon A. Silvers, policy director of the AFL-CIO. Furthermore, Silvers argued, "All these fiscal austerity proposals on the table will make the economy worse."[6]

Ultimately, the president's rhetorical balancing act throughout the debt-ceiling episode—as he switched back and forth between liberal populist and fiscally conservative centrist rhetoric in the effort to appease both his independent and left-wing constituencies—backfired. The result was what liberal populist John Quiggin refers to as a "Mordor-inspired debt ceiling deal."

From an economic perspective, the deal was an abject failure, wrote liberal economist Robert Reich:

> The deal does not raise taxes on America's wealthy and most fortunate—who are now taking home a larger share of total income and wealth, and whose tax rates are already lower than they have been, in eighty years. Yet it puts the nation's most important safety nets and public investments on the chopping block.
>
> It also hobbles the capacity of the government to respond to the jobs and growth crisis. Added to the cuts already underway by state and local governments, the deal's spending cuts increase the odds of a double-dip recession. And the deal strengthens the political hand of the radical right.[7]

In today's polarized political environment, Obama's perpetual straddling of populism and centrism has put him at odds with both the hard left and hard right—both of whom are convinced that he's hostile to their interests—while doing him little good with the political center.

As the 2012 election approaches, Obama is hearing urgent calls from the left to take up a populist message—and angry condemnations of his increasingly rightward political tilt, especially on fiscal issues like the national debt and entitlement spending.

To be sure, President Obama knows that he cannot win the 2012 election running entirely as a populist. Hence, he has tried to sell his jobs bill as a compilation of Democratic and Republican ideas—particularly the payroll tax cut which is quintessentially a Republican idea.

Indeed, if there were a formula, it would be two parts populist and one part centrist to try to emphasize to financial elites and the media that he hasn't completely abandoned a more mainstream approach than the one he has taken.

But it is an awkward process.

The president typically couples his proposals for tax cuts for working people with invariable proposals to raise $1.5 trillion in new tax revenue mostly on the backs of wealthier Americans.

But while raising taxes on the rich is popular in the polls, it is not the sort of issue that will win swing voters over—something the White House undoubtedly knows.

Rather, the cost of advocacy for tax cuts for working people is consistent advocacy of repeal of the Bush tax cuts—something the President compromised on in December of 2010 only to suffer near unanimous criticism from the left for selling out to Republicans.

The tension plays itself out on most major issues.

FINANCIAL CRISIS AND REFORM

The 2008 presidential campaign unfolded during a time of nearly unprecedented fiscal distress, as Americans consistently opposed the Bush bailouts offered to firms such as Citigroup and AIG. Left-wing populists were clearly emboldened by the public mood, which meshed well with their ideology. Their arguments that corporate executives, who were responsible for so much corruption and irresponsibility, had not been adequately punished, took hold in the political culture. Three years later, the public still largely feels this way.

To left-populist thinking, only a Democratic presidential victory could have begun to unravel the Bush economic and financial legacy. But Obama would disappoint them here almost immediately. His inner circle, including Treasury Secretary Tim Geithner and economic advisor Lawrence Summers, urged him to support the stability of the banks through capital infusions and "stress tests," putting most of their energies to work on behalf of a Wall Street–centered recovery.

"What haunts the Obama administration," writes Frank Rich, "is what still haunts the country: the stunning lack of accountability for the greed and misdeeds that brought America to its gravest financial crisis since the Great Depression. There has been no legal, moral, or financial reckoning for the most powerful wrongdoers. Nor have there been meaningful reforms that might prevent a repeat catastrophe. Time may heal most wounds, but not these."[8]

Rich is undoubtedly right. Not only the members of Occupy Wall Street but the American people in general look at what has happened with financial crimes and see that save for a few insider trading prosecutions no one in the financial sector or on Wall Street has been prosecuted or severely sanctioned for any of the abuses that took place before 2008.

Whether or not sanctions or criminal prosecutions are justified, it was outrageous to those on the left that a quarter of America had mortgages underwater, mortgages that could not be restructured, but people who profited from the packaging of mortgages that went into foreclosure continued to earn record profits and receive record bonuses.

While the right opposed the Bush administration's TARP bailout package on free-market grounds, the left opposed the bailout not because of the dollar amounts but because of where the money went: banks, at the expense of ordinary people (an oversimplification, to be sure). They also objected to the way the bailouts propped up and perpetuated a system that made them necessary. For the left, the instigation of the financial crisis and the bailout to save its lead actors amounted exactly to an *Inside Job*, as the documentary a few years later would call it. As Jim Hightower, the populist political commentator, wrote:

> Both parties tell us that AIG, Citigroup, Bank of America, and the rest are "too big to fail," so taxpayers simply "must" rescue them to save the system. Populists, on the other hand, note that it is this very system that has caused the failure—so structural reform is required. Let's reorganize the failed giants by ousting their top execs, splitting the behemoths into their component parts (banking, investment, and insurance), and reducing them to decentralized, manageable-sized financial institutions.[9]

Obama understood that Americans' views of Wall Street had shifted. After nearly a generation in which Wall Streeters were viewed as financial adventurers and even heroes, most ordinary Americans now regard Wall Street with suspicion or outright hostility. So Obama pursued some safe reforms: promising to "take the air out of golden parachutes," he announced in February 2009 that executives of companies that had taken federal money would see their annual pay capped at $500,000. He called Wall Street's $18 billion in 2008 bonuses "shameful,"[10] saying that the beneficiaries showed "exactly the kind of disregard for the costs and consequences of their actions that brought about this crisis: a culture of narrow self-interest and short-term gain at the expense of everything else."[11] The administration also appointed a pay czar, Kenneth Feinberg, who would announce in late 2009 major pay cuts of up to 50 percent for the highest-paid executives at a host of leading companies that had taken federal cash to stay afloat: Citibank, Bank of America, Chrysler, and General Motors among them.

One of the principal rallying cries for left-wing populists was the opposition to the bailout of AIG.

On March 13, 2009, AIG announced that it had used federal bailout money (dispensed the previous fall by the Bush administration) to distribute $165 million in retention bonuses to employees in the company's Financial Products Unit. The initial reaction of the Obama administration and congressional leaders was to "claw back" the bonuses through legislation. President Obama publicly chastised AIG for "recklessness and greed," vowing to "pursue every single legal avenue" to block the bonuses. Cooler heads in Washington prevailed, however, and the Obama administration backed down amid arguments from Washington insiders that this "claw back" could have a cataclysmic impact on the financial system.

The public outrage against AIG, like the rise of the Tea Party, demonstrated that a broad cross segment of Americans—of all ideologies—felt that their government had neglected the needs of mainstream Americans. Progressive voices repeatedly urged Obama to act more boldly. As Paul Krugman wrote in September 2009: "The administration has suffered more than it seems to realize from the perception that it's giving taxpayers' hard-earned money away to Wall Street . . . in this case populism is good economics. Indeed, you can make the case that reforming bankers' compensation is the single best thing we can do to prevent another financial crisis a few years down the road."[12]

Obama has tried to send signals that he shares public anger at the financial industry. "I did not run for office to be helping out a bunch of fat cat bankers on Wall Street," he told *60 Minutes* in December 2009. But from the left's perspective, his policies have proven more accommodating than his words.

This is especially true given a climate charged with more antibanker hostility than at any time since the Great Depression. As Michigan congressman John Dingell told *Newsweek*, Americans' anger at the financial sector reminds him of when, as a boy in 1933, he listened to men like his father rail against Wall Street interests. "Americans all hated the damn bankers, they hated Wall Street," Dingell said. "We had more communists in this country than there were in the Soviet Union" because of rage against the banks.[13]

What angered the populist left most was Obama's refusal to pursue punishment for the perpetrators of the crisis. Obama's Justice Department gave its blessing to a plan suggested by the Iowa attorney general, Tom Miller, to persuade the other forty-eight states to sign on to a financial settlement that would end all investigations of the biggest mortgage lenders. It turned out that Miller's reelection campaign had received generous financial support from lawyers for some big banks.[14]

Obama did promise to pass financial reform legislation, and in summer 2010, he signed the Dodd-Frank bill into law—the most sweeping change to U.S. financial regulation since the Great Depression in the 1930s. The law promises to set up strong protections for consumers of financial products; end "too big to fail" bailouts of financial institutions; create an advance warning system for systemic risk; impose transparency and accountability for exotic financial instruments; provide shareholders with a say on pay and corporate affairs, including executive compensation and golden parachutes; provide tough new rules for transparency and accountability for credit-rating agencies to protect investors and businesses; and strengthen oversight and empower regulators to aggressively pursue financial fraud and conflicts of interest.[15]

From the standpoint of those on the right, or even the center, Dodd-Frank was a huge imposition of financial regulation on par with Obama's health-care reform legislation. But for many on the left, it didn't go far enough.

Rich speaks for many when he laments the administration's unwillingness to confront the problem of financial fraud and impose meaningful checks on Wall Street power:

> Obama had taken office at a true populist moment that demanded more than this. People were gagging over their looted 401(k)s and underwater homes, the AIG bonuses, and the bailouts. Howard Dean rage has never

been Obama's style—hope-and-change was an elegant oratorical substitute—and had he given full voice to the public mood, he would have been pilloried as an "angry black man." But Obama didn't have to play Huey Long. He could have pursued a sober but determined execution of justice and an explicit, major jobs initiative—of which there have been exactly none, the too-small stimulus included, to the present day.[16]

On the issue of financial reform and the financial crisis more generally, the dynamics of left-wing populism put Obama in an almost impossible position. He has achieved a major legislative victory with Dodd-Frank, but the bill is not even popular on the left, which finds it inadequate and toothless. Those on the right believe that the law overreaches and overregulates. Most mainstream Americans don't understand the law and doubt that it will do much good. On the issue of Wall Street regulation and culpability for the financial crisis, Obama, for all of his efforts, has managed to please no one.

OBAMA AND WEALTH REDISTRIBUTION

As described earlier, Obama pledged to repeal the Bush tax cuts during his presidential campaign, but once in office, he compromised with Republicans to preserve the upper-income tax cuts in exchange for Republican agreement to extend unemployment insurance. Though the move provoked outrage on the progressive left, it was from Obama's perspective another instance where his political fortunes lay in the center, and not on the populist left.

This political calculus is what progressives object to in Obama's economic policies. They see him as timid in pursuing the welfare of ordinary Americans. Most progressives don't doubt that Obama's sentiment is with them, but for whatever reason, he has not pursued the kind of economic agenda they would have hoped for.

In summer 2011, a staggeringly bleak jobs report was released showing job growth of just eighteen thousand jobs created in June. The depressing news renewed calls from many on the progressive left for another economic stimulus plan, investment in public-sector jobs programs, and attempts to address the nation's burgeoning income inequality.

"You can't fundamentally break this cycle," wrote Robert Creamer, "without addressing the root cause—the increased concentration of wealth that is strangling economic growth and destroying the American middle class upon which long-term economic growth completely depends."[17] Progressives like Creamer believe that Obama must reduce income inequality and boost middle-class incomes by shoring up entitlements and other social spending—funded through higher taxes on the wealthy.

Citing the last decade's GDP growth, which primarily benefited the top 2 percent of income earners, Creamer points back to the period from 1929 to 1947, when income for manufacturing workers rose 67 percent and income for the richest 1 percent dropped 17 percent. Those gains, he argues, were owed to the power of labor unions and the social programs of FDR's New Deal. What followed was a long postwar boom, but since then, the middle class has slowly seen its income gains dry up, while the rich have gotten much richer.

In short, the economic left sees Obama's track record as woefully inadequate to the task of resuscitating the middle class. The pressure they exert on the president makes a difference in what policies he pursues, at least to an extent; but the problem for Obama is that left-populist approaches on economics, even during a recession, are not broadly popular with the electorate. Reich's proposed 70 percent top income-tax rate may have progressive support, but politically, it's a pipe dream.

OBAMA AND THE UNIONS

Obama won the presidency with strong union support, and he has repeatedly sent signals of his support for unions. At an Iowa town hall in April 2010, Obama made probably his most eloquent prounion statement:

> I've said this before publicly and I'll say it again, I make no apologies for it. I am a pro-union guy . . . Our unions helped build our middle class. We take for granted so much stuff—minimum wage laws, 40-hour work week, overtime, child labor laws. Those things wouldn't have happened if it hadn't been for unions fighting for those rights. So even if you're not a member of a union, you've got to be appreciative of what unions have done.[18]

After years of adverse policies and difficult relationships with presidents, organized labor seemed to revive with Obama's presidential campaign, in which he promised support for the Employee Free Choice Act ("card check"), the Lily Ledbetter Fair Pay Act, and other progressive-friendly legislation. The union movement also rallied in the midst of adversity, as battles in Wisconsin for collective-bargaining rights for public-sector workers sparked a wave of union activism—and Obama spoke out in their favor. Poll data showed an uptick in popular support for unions. As Richard Trumka, AFL-CIO president, said in March 2011: "We've never seen the incredible solidarity that we're seeing right now. People are giving us another look. They're saying, 'We support collective bargaining.'"[19]

In truth, though, unions have much less popular support than Trumka suggests, even in the Democratic Party, where a recent study of registered Democrats found just 10 percent identifying themselves as union members.[20] Today's unions are less a broad-based movement than a powerful special interest, one that can influence, and distort, policy outcomes when its influence is strong. When it isn't, labor becomes mostly a marginalized segment of the Democratic base.

Unions have played a central role in the populist pressure on Obama. The Clinton years marginalized organized labor perhaps more than any other liberal constituency; some progressive labor supporters even argued for a primary challenge to Clinton in 1996 in response to the president's championing of NAFTA legislation. Under George W. Bush, labor's rage built steadily.

As AFL-CIO president John Sweeney said in 2004, "George W. Bush has done everything he can to put us down and keep us on the bottom." Worn out by battles with the administration on safety rules, overtime pay, and privatization of government jobs—all of which the unions lost—Sweeney said, "I don't even want to think about what another four years would be like." Labor was out in full force against Bush in 2004 in a massive push to defeat the president, but to no avail.

In Bush's final year, the administration awarded a lucrative contract for air force refueling tankers, valued at somewhere between $40 billion and $100 billion, to Northrop Grumman and the European firm EADs, bypassing a Boeing bid. The administration claimed that the contract would create twenty-five thousand new jobs in Alabama and other southern states, but Boeing claimed that far more jobs—higher-paying, unionized jobs, to boot—would have been created had the company won the deal. The Northrop/EADs jobs would not be unionized. As an AFL-CIO blog summarized:

> At a time when American jobs are disappearing and our manufacturing base is being decimated, working people are outraged that Republican presidential nominee John McCain played a key role in the Bush Defense Department's decision to award one of our largest military contracts to a foreign company.
>
> . . .
>
> Defense expenditures are supposed to comply with federal Buy American Law provisions, which require purchasing certain products from American companies when possible. But this administration has granted more waivers of the Buy American provisions than any administration in history.[21]

The tanker-contract battle of 2008 provides the essential backdrop to another Boeing story—this one involving President Obama. Boeing built a $750 million airplane factory in North Charleston, South Carolina, to manufacture 787 Dreamliners, the company's largest-ever investment in that state. The company expected to employ one thousand workers at the outset. South Carolinians cheered the jobs boost the new factory would bring, citing the ripple employment effects of a BMW plant that opened in Spartanburg in the 1990s: opening with 1,200 workers, it now employs 7,000.[22]

But Obama's National Labor Relations Board stepped in, alleging that the company was moving the Dreamliner manufacturing operation to South Carolina to avoid the labor strikes that had plagued its operations in Seattle. (Companies are barred by law from moving their production plants in response to unions' exercising their rights to organize or strike.) Boeing reportedly cited issues with its unions as a rationale for the move to South Carolina, a right-to-work state. Boeing couldn't afford "to have a work stoppage every three years," one company official told the *Seattle Times*.

The Board—at the behest of Boeing's union—asked a federal judge to order the company to move Dreamliner production back to Washington State.[23] The issue quickly became a political cause, as GOP presidential candidates attacked Obama and his NLRB, whose officials he had appointed. It was fair to conclude, then, that the president supported the NLRB's position, but the issue was far from a guaranteed winner for the president beyond his union base. With jobs scarce, the administration's attempt to shutter the Boeing plant will antagonize centrists.

Obama's stance on the Boeing plant is consistent with his generally prounion orientation. In his stimulus package, he successfully inserted a "Buy American" clause that made it illegal for public funds to go to projects that did not use materials manufactured in the United States. Some exceptions were provided, but the clause was fairly comprehensive.[24]

Obama also fought for the Employee Free Choice Act, a hugely controversial bill dear to unions, which would have abolished the secret ballot in elections that determine whether unions are organized in workplaces. If the bill passed, workplaces could have been unionized if a majority of workers merely signed cards indicating that preference.[25] The bill was killed in the Senate by a Republican filibuster.

Often, however, the labor movement seems disappointed with the president, though he has generally been supportive of their causes, including speaking out on their behalf in the battles in Wisconsin and Ohio between state governments and public employees. Yet the pervading sense among hard-core labor loyalists is that Obama talks the talk, but doesn't walk the walk—especially on issues such as free trade and job flight.

As Rose Ann DeMoro, executive director of National Nurses United, said of the president: "He's basically trying to be everything to everybody . . . Until you look at the policies, and then it's clear he's there for the corporate sector."[26]

Politically, Obama can afford neither full-scale support nor desertion of the union movement. He can only appease labor so far before he starts losing the center.

OBAMA AND HEALTH CARE

No issue of Obama's presidency has illustrated the difficult balance he must strike with left populists and progressives more than health-care reform. The idea that the government should take care of its citizens, to shield them from being taken advantage of, is the core of left-wing populist ideology. It applies equally to health care, in their view, as it does to jobs and the economy—probably more so.

Progressives see health care not as a commodity, but as a fundamental right to which all Americans deserve equal access. This core belief is the driving force behind the populist movement for single-payer health insurance—that is, government as the sole provider of insurance. Yet the president they had invested their hopes in never even tried for single payer.

The most progressive plan Obama sought was one that included a "public option," a government-run health insurance agency that would compete with private insurers. If Americans could not afford coverage on the health-care exchanges the bill would create, they would always have a government alternative to fall back on.

Even the public option did not survive into the final bill. For many on the populist left, the Affordable Care Act of 2010 was a watered-down, hopelessly compromised, "corporate" health-care reform that would not address the unfairness of a system that failed to guarantee universal coverage. Obama, seeking broader Senate support for the bill from centrists like Joe Lieberman, agreed to kill the public option.

"One of my strongest hopes is that everyone in the media, especially on the left, can simply stop pretending the new health reform law is some great progressive victory. It is not. It is a conservative, pro-corporate piece of legislation," wrote Jon Hunter of the progressive Firedoglake blog.

The tensions within the Democratic Party between Obama and his Beltway Democrats and the populist left were probably best illustrated by the intense opposition of Howard Dean, former chairman of the Democratic National Committee and a 2004 presidential primary candidate.[27] In a highly unusual move for such a prominent party figure, Dean took to the airwaves to assail the administration for abandoning the public option, and he announced that he opposed passage of the bill, which he said was not worth passing.

The bill, Dean said in December 2009, represented "a bigger bailout for the insurance industry than AIG." He claimed that 27 percent of what people paid for health-insurance premiums under the new bill would go straight into CEOs' pockets.[28] Dean also scoffed at the administration's claims that the bill would cover thirty million uninsured Americans, suggesting that that figure was too high.

Many left populists feel that Obama starts most policy debates determinedly in the center, giving occasional lip service to the progressive position but little else when the chips are down. According to the progressive critique, since the right never budges, this leaves most policy compromises well to the right of the spectrum. They want to see Obama fight harder for genuinely progressive positions, but while Obama seems determined to retain their support, he is also eager to reclaim the mantle of centrism that he represented in 2008. The result on the left is a lack of trust.

And yet, no sooner does the populist left rail against the president than he does something clearly calculated to win their approval. During the health-care negotiations, Obama voiced support for a "Cadillac Tax" on high-cost, high-end health insurance policies. But at union insistence, he and Democrats exempted union contracts from the tax until 2018, five years beyond the start date for other workers. Unions had, over the years, negotiated generous health-care packages for their members, and they were eager to protect these packages from the Cadillac Tax.

OBAMA AND WAR POLICY

By 2008, among Democrats, opposition to the war had become so dominant that Barack Obama was able to turn his stance against the war in 2002—though only a state senator at the time—into a crucial strategic advantage over his rival, Hillary Clinton, in the Democratic presidential primaries. Obama was a remarkable candidate, but without his opposition to the war—and the passionate support of Netroots—it's unlikely that he could have won the 2008 nomination.

But on war policy, President Obama has proven a major disappointment to his left-wing supporters.

Bottom line: three years into his presidency, President Obama has not gotten us out of Iraq or Afghanistan, he has not closed down Guantanamo Bay, he has not done enough to protect civil liberties by outlawing "roving" wiretaps, and he has not discontinued the use of rendition as a counterterrorism policy.

While he has never admitted that the 2007 troop surge in Iraq was a success, his actions make clear that he understands that it achieved its goals.

He's proceeded with a troop drawdown that had begun under Bush, but only as conditions warrant. Meanwhile, in Afghanistan, to the bitter disappointment of progressives, he has added fifty thousand troops, even as he pledged to begin bringing them home in summer 2011. Obama escalated enormously the use of Predator drone strikes to kill terrorists in the Pakistan tribal areas, exceeding Bush's total sorties early in his first term. He has extended these strikes to Yemen as well, prompting questions about international law and national sovereignty—the kinds that Obama himself once raised as a candidate.

Though he signed an executive order on his first day in office outlawing torture, Obama has more or less preserved the Bush detention regime—most notoriously, by breaking his promise to close the detention camp at Guantanamo Bay.

Obama's national security policies have been bitter pills for the populist left to swallow. On foreign policy and national security, the American people might be more conservative than on any other issue. So the populist left is likely to endure one disappointment after another under Commander in Chief Obama, because their support in this area is far from vital—in fact, their opposition can be politically useful.

THE POPULIST SHADOW

In the aftermath of the debt deal, the left felt abandoned by a president who caved on entitlement reform, failed to protect core programs, and was unable to negotiate a compromise on revenue enhancement to reach a budget deal—a deal that failed to achieve anything else but extend the debt limit through the 2012 election.

But, demonstrating yet again the push-pull dynamic with the left, Obama in late September 2011 announced that, as part of a plan to reduce the budget deficit by $3 trillion over ten years, he would propose $1.5 trillion in tax increases on the wealthy—which would be raised by letting the Bush tax cuts on top-bracket earners expire, along with closing some loopholes and limiting deductions. Here it was, at last, after three years: finally, a proposal to *raise* taxes on the rich. And Obama sounded like he meant it; anticipating GOP objections, he said: "That's not class warfare. I'm not attacking anybody. It's simple math."

Backed up against the wall in the wake of the debt-ceiling debacle and seeing his approval ratings plummet, Obama had finally thrown in—at least for now—with the populist left's desire to raise taxes. But the long struggle to reach this point only underscored how warily progressives have now come to regard him.

"Nobody loves Obama," Peggy Noonan wrote in the *Wall Street Journal* in July 2011, describing how progressives' love affair with the candidate had devolved into a cold, distant relationship with a politician they didn't really understand.[29] As Noonan wrote, even if Bill Clinton disappointed them most of the time, progressives understood him—he was such an engaging personality, such a consummate politician, that one *knew* him, even when disagreeing. By contrast, Obama seems unknowable, and his remoteness makes his diversions from populist goals more difficult to absorb.

"This is the time when Barack Obama has to care," said Jane Hamsher, founder and publisher of the progressive blog Firedoglake, at the annual Netroots National Convention. "This is the time when he needs your vote. So don't give yourself away cheaply."[30]

"It's like the president's not our boyfriend anymore," said Joan McCarter, an editor at the Daily Kos website, at Netroots. McCarter spoke as part of a panel discussion called, "What to Do When the President's Just Not That into You."[31]

From now until Election Day, Obama will feel pressure from the populist left—and not just from activists like Hamsher.

In July 2011, upset about the president's willingness to discuss cuts to entitlement programs as part of a debt-ceiling extension agreement with Republicans, the Progressive Change Campaign Committee threatened to withhold financial support from the Obama reelection campaign. The committee delivered two million pledges from people saying they won't volunteer or donate if Obama cuts the programs.

"It's not a question of who they're going to support for president, they're going to vote for Barack Obama. It's a question of where their time and money is going to go," spokesman T. Neil Sroka said.[32] And Obama's wealthy 2008 donors feel similarly—while still planning on supporting Obama, they're not sure how deep into their pockets they're willing to go.

They are exemplified by figures like Guy Saperstein, a lawyer and former president of the Sierra Club Foundation, who says that the 2012 election will be a "plebiscite" on Obama. "I think there is almost universal disappointment" with the president, he says, pointing to Obama's "weak stewardship" of the environment, his escalation of the Afghan war, and his extension of the Bush tax cuts. Another donor, also citing Obama's extension of the Bush tax cuts, said simply of the president: "I have my concerns about what I would call a lack of fiber."[33]

Populist energy on the left is not likely to dissipate anytime soon. After a long period in the wilderness, populists have more sway within the Democratic Party than they have had in a generation. Yet left-populist influence exists in perpetual tension with the centrist instincts of the American electorate. As a result, the Democratic Party, even if many of its members in principle agree with the populists, often disappoints them when it comes to actual policy. Obama slams the Republicans with class-warfare rhetoric one week, but then, with the time for a debt agreement nearing, positions himself as the reasonable centrist between ideological factions.

This is a posture left-wing populists are all too familiar with. Populism is a strong tendency within Democratic liberalism, but it is not as strong as right-wing populism is within today's Republican Party. The left has not been able to mobilize, for instance, the unemployed or the working class as it once did. In fact, it has watched in dismay as the Tea Party has seemingly become the political movement that speaks for these people. For the most part, the left can no longer put people in the streets. Its influence on the Democratic Party establishment, while important, is far from absolute.

"The activist liberal base will support Obama because they're terrified of the right wing," said Robert L. Borosage, codirector of the liberal group Campaign for America's Future. He also believes that "the voting base of the Democratic Party—young people, single women, African-Americans, Latinos—are going to be so discouraged by this economy and so dismayed unless the president starts to champion a jobs program and take on the Republican Congress that the ability of labor to turn out its vote, the ability of activists to mobilize that vote, is going to be dramatically reduced."[34]

Left-wing populists may not achieve most of their goals, but they might yet succeed—unintentionally—in defeating a Democratic president in 2012.

RIGHT-WING
POPULISM

Principles and Resurgence

When the vice president of the United States talks about terrorism in our midst, it tends to get people's attention. So when Joe Biden mentioned terrorists in July 2011, it made people sit up and take notice.

Except that Biden wasn't talking about al Qaeda. He was talking about the Tea Party.

As the debt-ceiling showdown in Washington reached its climax last summer, gloom and despair on Capitol Hill comingled with a mounting sense of panic and rage. By the last weekend of July, the United States was just days away from defaulting on its sovereign debt obligations before the mandated August 2 deadline. As party leaders in both chambers scrambled to put together the package that would eventually spare the nation a default, Biden met for a closed-door meeting of the Democratic caucus. He listened as members vented their frustrations with Republicans.

Democratic congressman Mike Doyle of Pennsylvania complained that in dealing with the Tea Party–led GOP, "we have negotiated with terrorists." Biden reportedly concurred, saying, "They have acted like terrorists."[1]

Biden later denied using the term, but several sources confirmed it. His description marked the climactic moment of weeks of angry political rhetoric on both sides. For those who opposed the Tea Party, one dominant theme had emerged: the movement, and its role within the Republican Party, resembled that of a terrorist group.

On MSNBC's *Morning Joe*, one analyst likened the Tea Party to a guy "strapped with dynamite standing in the middle of Times Square at rush hour and saying, 'Either you do it my way, or we're going to blow ourselves up and the whole country with us.'" Another called Tea Party members "suicide bombers."

On *Hardball*, Chris Matthews declared, "The GOP has become the Wahhabis of American government—willing to risk bringing down the whole country in the service of their anti-tax ideology."[2]

The onslaught continued in print media. "If sane Republicans do not stand up to this Hezbollah faction in their midst, the Tea Party will take the G.O.P. on a suicide mission," wrote Tom Friedman in the *New York Times*.[3]

"The same Republicans who have so eagerly prosecuted the war on terror, running up huge deficits in the process, are now behaving like the enemies on which they have squandered so much blood and treasure: They are acting like terrorists. Yes, terrorists," wrote Huffington Post business columnist Peter S. Goodman (who later revised the column to remove the offending words).[4]

"You know what they say," wrote *Times* columnist Joe Nocera. "Never negotiate with terrorists. It only encourages them."[5]

What led to this kind of extreme hyperbole—so extreme that it wasn't meant as hyperbole, but as literal description? Clearly, by summer 2011 the Tea Party had driven many in the political class to his or her own breaking point. In being willing to face down the possibility of an historic default of the United States' sovereign debt obligations, the Tea Party sent a message about how far it was willing to go to stand for its principles of spending restraint, balanced budgets, and small government.

In doing so, they broke the rules of the political class: they rejected compromise, deal making, and standard political back scratching. The Washington establishment couldn't follow that script, and it reacted with some extreme behavior of its own. It was hard not to see the commentators' sputtering as evidence of their own disconnect from reality.

The truth is, comparing the Tea Party to terrorists was baseless and wrong—and irresponsible, a word Beltway pundits usually reserve for describing the Tea Party.

Are Tea Party supporters and leaders zealots? Absolutely. Have their actions been politically extreme, ideologically reckless, with perhaps damaging consequences down the line? There's a solid basis for that argument. But the point is this: the Tea Party is a legitimate, if angry, political movement that expresses the sentiments of millions of Americans. The political class continues to dismiss and deride the movement, but the Tea Party has become effectively an independent and equal force in American politics alongside the Democrats and Republicans.

The intensity of the Tea Party's political passion has stunned seasoned political observers since the movement's inception three years ago—as has its ability, in such a short time, to become the ideological driving force behind not just the Republican Party, but most of the debate in Washington. The movement's critique of a Washington leadership culture insulated from the problems of ordinary people, spending tax dollars with no restraint or accountability and failing to confront the nation's most important problems, resonated with millions of Americans. Moreover, the Tea Party gave voice to the anger many Americans felt about a federal government that seemed to play by two sets of rules: one for itself and its political allies on Wall Street, the other for everyone else. They called for an end to federal bailouts of private companies and demanded that the government begin living within its means the way most Americans do by simple necessity. That it chose to name itself after the famous act of economic sabotage perpetrated by American colonists in Boston in 1773 made plain the sense of rebellion at the heart of the movement: enough is enough, they've said again and again, since 2009.

The movement's passion, of course, partly explains its power: politics abhors a vacuum, and the establishment Republican Party offered no compelling leadership whatsoever in the aftermath of the fall 2008 presidential campaign. The post-Bush Republican Party had seen its brand deeply tarnished by runaway spending, ineffective or incompetent leadership in running two wars, a failed economic policy, and finally, the financial crisis and the bailouts. Its presidential candidate was routed at the polls in 2008, and both houses of Congress were turned over to the Democrats. It was a clean sweep; the GOP was shut out.

Voters seemed to have little use for the mainstream Republican Party in 2008, and in the years since, they haven't changed their minds. A Rasmussen Reports survey conducted during the week following the midterm 2010 elections showed that only 19 percent of likely Republican primary voters believe Republicans in Congress have done a good job representing the party's values over the past several years, while 72 percent say GOP members of Congress instead have lost touch with Republican Party members throughout the nation in recent years.

The Tea Party stepped into this breach of leadership, not only by calling out Washington on its waste, abuse, and hypocrisy but also by arguing for a rebirth of America's oldest principles of individual liberty and a small, but responsive, federal government. And in doing this, the movement connected itself to time-honored philosophical principles of conservatism, especially those of the populist right.

What are those principles, and why do so many Americans find them compelling?

PRINCIPLES OF RIGHT-WING POPULISM

One major advantage conservatives have over liberals is that it generally seems easier—and shorter—to define what conservatives believe than what liberals believe. Liberals have struggled with this problem for many years. It's difficult to compete with the clarity and simplicity of committed conservatism. I doubt many Tea Party supporters would quibble with these core principles of the American right: smaller government, lower taxes, free-market capitalism, constitutionalism, and American exceptionalism.

1. Smaller government. The right-wing view of government is diametrically opposed to that espoused by left populists. Whereas progressives believe that a powerful and activist government is essential to protecting vulnerable people from economic distress and corporate greed, right-wing populists maintain that government itself is, at best, a necessary evil and at worst, a tyranny.

They see government predominantly as a distorting or destructive influence in a whole range of private activities: from private-sector economic transactions to the nation's energy, environmental, and educational policies. Government regulates where noninterference would create better results, driven by market outcomes and the individual choices of free, independent forces acting in what Adam Smith called their "rational self interest." When government enters the picture, it distorts incentives—by favoring, say, one source of energy production over another via the tax code—and suppresses the market's natural efficiency in finding effective solutions. As for the vulnerable whom left populists seek to protect through government action, they end up being hurt more, not less, by government: government regulations, such as the mandated minimum wage, discourage employers from offering the kinds of jobs less-skilled people can do.

Though most right-wing populists, including those in the Tea Party, would not identify themselves as strict Libertarians, the Libertarian Party platform is an eloquent statement of principles in favor of small government and individual autonomy:

> We hold that all individuals have the right to exercise sole dominion over their own lives, and have the right to live in whatever manner they choose, so long as they do not forcibly interfere with the equal right of others to live in whatever manner they choose.
>
> Governments throughout history have regularly operated on the opposite principle, that the State has the right to dispose of the lives of individuals and the fruits of their labor. Even within the United States, all political parties other than our own grant to government the right to regulate the lives of individuals and seize the fruits of their labor without their consent.
>
> We, on the contrary, deny the right of any government to do these things . . .
>
> Since governments, when instituted, must not violate individual rights, we oppose all interference by government in the areas of voluntary and contractual relations among individuals. People should not be forced to sacrifice their lives and property for the benefit of others. They should be left free by government to deal with one another as free traders; and the resultant economic system, the only one compatible with the protection of individual rights, is the free market.[6]

The Tea Party is not libertarian, but its fundamental governing philosophy is libertarian in spirit. It supports fewer regulations and regulators, fewer social programs, fewer departments and bureaucracies. Only the most essential of these should be maintained. The rest—including such cabinet-level departments as the Department of Education—should be abolished and their functions returned to states and localities, which are closer to the people they serve and already invested in providing government services to their constituents. In short, right-wing populists believe that the government in Washington should be pared back dramatically; they don't always agree on every specific, but most target the kinds of social-welfare, environmental, and even consumer protections that are cherished by liberals and progressives.

The only way to get a smaller government is to spend less, of course. Thus fiscal conservatism is the hallmark of the small-government philosophy, the virtue that makes the vision possible. Only when government gets its books in order and begins spending less than it takes in can it even begin the arduous process of downsizing.

Naturally, President Obama's lavish spending, from his $800 billion stimulus package to his massive, trillion-dollar health-care reform legislation, alarm and infuriate small-government advocates.

Obama's stimulus package—dubbed the "Porkulus" because of all the goodies it held for democratic special-interest groups—finally prompted Tea Party events in early 2009. The Porkulus sparked a grassroots rebellion around the nation, driven by anger and fear of the implications of Obama's excessive government spending. It's worth remembering this: government spending, plain and simple, was *the* issue creating the Tea Party phenomenon.

Spending—this time, an Obama plan to bail out homeowners—prompted a spontaneous outburst on the air from CNBC financial analyst Rick Santelli on February 19, 2010. Delivered on the floor of the Chicago Mercantile Exchange, Santelli's rant became an instant YouTube classic. After voicing his opposition to the "proposed $275 billion deficit-financed homeowner bailout plan and other massive spending measures," Santelli called upon like-minded Americans to make their voices heard with a twenty-first-century revival of the Boston Tea Party.

"This is America!" Santelli raged. "How many of you people want to pay for your neighbor's mortgage that has an extra bathroom and can't pay their bills?" Behind him, the traders on the exchange floor roared their approval of his words. It was one of the iconic media moments of our political era.

It wasn't just the size of the government spending; it was where those dollars were being directed. Many Americans felt the money was being given to the undeserving—such as homeowners who had purchased homes on credit that they should have known they couldn't afford. And in bailing out Wall Street firms, the government was showering money not just on the undeserving, but on the culpable—on companies whose practices had caused the bubble and the eventual crisis. Santelli's rant spoke for millions of Americans already deeply concerned about the government's runaway spending before Obama and now were even more worried by Washington's apparent intention to spend regardless of deficits.

Those worries only grew worse with the president's health-care reform plan, which would represent another massive, and permanent, federal expenditure. Obama's plan, in which uninsured Americans would have to purchase health insurance or face penalties, soon became another focal point of the Tea Party movement. Not only was the health-care plan fiscally unsustainable but also it violated small-government principles and perhaps even the Constitution, which contained no clause empowering Congress to force American citizens to buy anything. The movement saw the proposed legislation as more evidence of Obama's supposed socialism, as a government takeover of one-sixth of the economy that would tax and fine Americans, curtailing their individual rights and taking control of the most intimate aspects of their lives. The raucous health-care town halls of summer 2009, which I chronicled in my previous book, *Mad as Hell*, became the inevitable result.

Still, for all of their focus on Obama's out-of-control spending, small-government conservatives, and especially those in the Tea Party, don't see great progress from the Republicans, either.

As Sally Oljar of Seattle, a member of the national coordinating team for the Tea Party Patriots, told the *New York Times*:

> The mood here is that we're a little disappointed in the Republicans in the House in not living up to their pledge . . . We realize we have to keep the pressure on these guys all the time. If you leave them alone they revert back to their own ways . . . We're not an appendage of anyone . . . If someone is not a real fiscal conservative, they will be outed very quickly. There are politicians who have taken on the Tea Party mantle. That's fine. But we care about the issues, and we're watching them all.[7]

Carter Brough, a retiree from Whitney, Texas, echoed that view. "If these politicians don't get the message, they had better step aside. Right now, I can't tell the difference between the parties. I've chopped my credit cards. I'm watching my spending. This country needs to do the same."[8]

Watching our spending would mean, ultimately, a balanced budget amendment, and this goal is in fact a crucial one for Tea Party members in Congress. Polls show broad public support for the BBA, as it is sometimes called, which would make it unconstitutional for the Congress to spend beyond its means. The BBA would represent a tangible, major reform of Washington's big-spending ways by elevating spending restraint to a constitutional principle. For that reason, no doubt, it has strong opponents, including Obama—and so far, the quest for the BBA remains unfulfilled.

2. Lower taxes. A government that plays a smaller role in our everyday lives would also need to collect less in taxes. What conservatives have often called Leviathan—the massive, all-pervasive presence of government in our lives—would have less fuel to keep it going with diminished tax burdens across all incomes and at the federal, state, and local level. Government would be forced to focus its resources on core services—police, fire, courts—and let go of the rest. Some conservatives have referred to this philosophy as "starving the beast," meaning that the government would have less to subsist on and would thus be forced into efficiency.

On the other hand, some right-wing thinkers still believe in supply side economics, which maintains that lower taxes will bring in *more* government revenue in the long run—because the lower rates will spark more consumer spending and greater investment returns, which will in turn throw off greater tax revenue. If supply side is true, then lower tax rates might end up presenting more of a problem to the project of government austerity, since the government would remain flush with cash.

But regardless of where conservatives stand on the debate over supply side economics, the right is united in a conviction that lower taxes *are* good for the economy. Lower taxes mean greater disposable income, more money for investment, and more economic activity all around. Greater consumer spending in turn drives higher employment, as companies experiencing more demand for their goods and services will hire more workers. Lower taxes are a win/win all around; if they starve the beast in the bargain, then all to the better.

Moreover, and in a parallel way to how progressives see higher taxes as an issue of fairness, conservatives see lower taxes as a fundamental matter of justice and individual liberty. The government ought not to have the right to tax more than it needs, and it should always err on the side of frugality and respect for the effort and value created by hardworking, individual Americans. In its essence, taxation coerces: Americans who don't pay what they owe are, of course, violating the law. But the coercive power of governments to tax ought not be abused with higher rates than are necessary, or just.

Crucially, this antitax concern for justice also applies to those in the highest income brackets—the wealthy and super-wealthy. The right rejects the formulation often voiced by liberals and progressives that the wealthy should pay a much higher rate of taxes. The rich, in fact, are easily scapegoated for problems in society and often are blamed for not paying their fair share—even though statistics consistently show that the top 10 to 20 percent of American earners pay most taxes already. Targeting these people, the most successful in our society, will discourage them from starting businesses or otherwise using their talents in ways that can employ or benefit others.

3. Free-market capitalism. At the heart of ideas about smaller government and lower taxes is the idea of freedom—freedom of the individual, to be sure, but also economic freedom in its broadest sense. Right-wing populists and conservatives urge a diminished role for government and fewer taxes because, fundamentally, they champion the operations of the free-market system. They believe that companies and individuals acting with a minimum of government interference can create a wealthy, innovative, and successful society. For proof of their argument, they cite the United States itself, which became the richest country in the world by embracing capitalism and free markets and allowing innovation to flourish.

It's important to understand this latter point: conservatives don't support free markets because they don't care about the people for whom the left is concerned but because they honestly believe that those people will do better, too, in a free-market system that offers maximum economic opportunity for all. They *are* comfortable, however, with uneven outcomes—such as the widening income inequality in the United States over the last several decades.

Free-market advocates argue that focusing on income inequality is wrongheaded, because in a free system, the most talented and gifted will always outpace the rest of us. What matters is that the vast majority of able and willing Americans have access to employment opportunities and a chance to better their economic prospects and quality of life. If an economy delivers in this way, why should it matter if some of us are billionaires? Conservatives see this focus as fostering class envy and resentment—an unproductive and socially divisive outlook.

At the macro level, free-market advocates take the same approach to companies, industries, and economic competition. They supported the landmark free-trade agreements of the 1980s and 1990s that opened up the global economy, reduced corporate expenditures through access to cheaper labor, and resulted in an explosion of innovative, affordable consumer products. These changes, they argue—from the high-tech goods that permeate our wired existence to cheaper clothing, household items, and gourmet or organic foods—have made life better for millions.

Moreover, the open global market forces companies to make better and cheaper products for increasingly knowledgeable, demanding consumers—and if companies can't keep up, they will fail. This should be allowed, conservatives argue, even if those companies are venerable ones with connections to an older America—such as the Detroit auto companies. Conservative free-market advocates opposed the auto bailouts, which they saw as another instance of Washington both interfering with a natural economic process of winnowing and playing favorites within an industry.

Why not allow the Detroit auto giants to fail, they ask, and let the U.S. auto business be run from the South, where foreign manufacturers operate thriving plants with nonunionized labor? If the Detroit firms want to compete, they can change their ways—restructure their crippling union expenses, for example, and start producing more efficient, more affordable cars. This would be a win for everyone concerned—companies, consumers, and taxpayers. The only thing holding it back is Washington's insistence on interfering with the free market, which made clear some time ago—actually, a generation ago—that the Detroit auto giants were no longer competitive.

Conservative advocates concede that the free market is not perfect. Without question, its more volatile processes can lead to considerable economic hardship—especially, laid-off workers—and social decline. But innovation and progress, or what economist Joseph Schumpeter called "creative destruction," have always presented challenges and downsides. The upsides, free marketers argue, far outweigh them.

4. Constitutionalism. At the opening of the 112th Congress in January 2011, House members took turns reading from the Constitution of the United States—the first time, remarkably, that this had ever been done in the chamber. The new Republican majority imposed a requirement that every bill submitted must justify its constitutional grounding.

From its very name, the Tea Party invokes the American Revolution. One of its principal themes is that the America given to us by the Founding Fathers is being lost through the actions of an overgrown, intrusive, incompetent, and corrupt federal government—and through a court system that has, for decades, misinterpreted and abused the

Constitution's authority. Hand in hand with the Tea Party's focus on reconnecting to the principles of the revolution is its belief in constitutionalism.

The new focus on constitutionalism was sparked by President Obama's excessive overreach of federal power, especially in health care. While Obama's predecessor, George W. Bush, aroused some constitutional objections on the right, most of his violations concerned civil liberties in wartime—which for the most part aroused the objections of the populist left, not the right (with the exception of Libertarians). The main focus of the new constitutional movement is on the Obama administration's flouting of Article 1, Section 8, of the Constitution, which identifies the "enumerated powers." They claim that the Constitution does not explicitly grant the federal government power to require the purchase of a good or service. Their concerns are provoked by the progressive left's seeming contempt for the issue itself.

This was best embodied in Nancy Pelosi's infamous response when a reporter asked her where the Constitution provided authority for the health-care bill's individual mandate:

"Are you serious?" she asked. "Are you serious?"[9]

The constitutionalists' concerns extend beyond the current White House occupant, however. What Charles Krauthammer calls the "new constitutionalism" is at heart an extension of the conservative idea of originalism, which mandates that the Constitution be interpreted strictly, bound by understandings of what the text meant at the time it was written. Originalism, the judicial philosophy practiced by Supreme Court justices Antonin Scalia and Clarence Thomas, contrasts with the idea of the "living Constitution," an approach favored by liberals that advocates much broader interpretive powers to justices based on the contemporary context in which the document is read.

As Krauthammer points out, the movement toward constitutionalism, as favored by those in the Tea Party, represents potentially a new governing model:

> What originalism is to jurisprudence, constitutionalism is to governance: a call for restraint rooted in constitutional text. Constitutionalism as a *political* philosophy represents a reformed, self-regulating conservatism that bases its call for minimalist government—for reining in the willfulness of presidents and legislatures—in the words and meaning of the Constitution.[10]

The sense on the right is that we have never moved so far from constitutional principles of governing restraint as we have during the three years of Obama's term. Again, the health-care bill was the leading offender here, representing a government takeover of one-sixth of the economy. The Supreme Court may well strike down the health-care law, where it seems headed for a hearing. If it passes legal muster, however, the implications for government power over other sectors of economic and personal life will be enormous. What's next? conservatives ask.

As Krauthammer writes, the right's renewed focus on the Constitution provides not just a philosophy of governance but also a grounding in enduring principle: "In choosing to focus on a majestic document that bears both study and recitation, the reformed conservatism of the Obama era has found itself not just a symbol but an anchor."

5. American exceptionalism. For over half a century, the idea of American exceptionalism has driven foreign policy and national security for the right. American exceptionalism can be defined as the belief that America is a unique city on a hill, the best and most just nation that has ever arisen, far superior to any other society on Earth.

For some on the right, this idea has led to isolationism, emphasizing the need to avoid foreign entanglements and for prudence and caution in foreign policy—especially in an age of budget austerity. For others, however, it means that America in its greatness has a unique burden to spread its ideas and practices of liberty and freedom. What unites the approach to foreign policy and national security for all those on the right is a sense of vision and purpose that makes America a great nation and a commitment to standing up forthrightly for America and its core principles.

During the 1950s, although the Republican Party became tarnished owing to its association with the witch hunts of Senator Joseph Mc-Carthy, it was also associated with the strong, wise, and pragmatic foreign policy leadership of President Dwight Eisenhower. Eisenhower's approach contrasted with that of Democratic leaders, who for many Americans seemed not to grasp the magnitude of the Soviet threat then engulfing the world. The association of Republicans, and the right more generally, with military strength grew exponentially during Ronald Reagan's presidency. Reagan spoke in a bold, confrontational way about Soviet Communism that no president before him had ever attempted; and as Americans and Soviets soon learned, he meant what he said. When the Berlin Wall came down in 1989, a year after Reagan left the White House, the right was quick to claim credit for him in this revolutionary development. Ever since, the notion of "peace through strength"—a Reagan motto calling for an aggressive, bold, and unapologetic pursuit of American interests around the globe—has defined foreign policy and national security for the right.

Under George W. Bush, the right's ownership of national security issues reached its zenith. After 9/11 and for years to come, Bush and the right defined what it meant to be tough on terrorism and devoted to the nation's safety and survival. The marginalization of Democrats, and indeed critics of any kind, intensified, reminding many of the darkest days of the Cold War.

The fundamental element that unites this disposition on the right across the decades is this: not just a conviction that they know how to defend American freedom and security, but that those who reject this approach are deluded or, worse, disloyal. This is the foundation for the bitterness of the Bush years—not just the difficulties of the events themselves, from 9/11 to Iraq, but the willful fostering of division, tarring of critics, and the creation of an Us versus Them mentality—not just overseas, but at home.

For right-wing populists, even today, the George W. Bush approach to foreign policy, counterterrorism, and national security remains fundamentally sound and just. One of the must surprising qualities about the post-Bush right is the near-lockstep foreign-policy defense of the president's record in Iraq, Afghanistan, and counterterrorism. If anything, some GOP presidential candidates in 2012 are to the right of Bush. No one in the presidential field has even taken the step of condemning the administration's most contentious policies on detainees, rendition, and torture.

Although right-wing populists have attacked Barack Obama for his deviations from Bush national security policy, the irony is that Obama's breaks from Bush in many respects have been fairly mild—especially as regards aggressive targeting of terrorists in Pakistan, Yemen, and elsewhere, measures that Obama has in fact accelerated beyond the rate of his predecessor. Barring a national security calamity between now and November 2012, the right doesn't figure to make a lot of headway against Obama on this core principle of their philosophy. For all of the more extreme attacks on the president as a somehow alien figure in American politics, Obama turns out to be a fairly hawkish national-security liberal. He is, after all, the president who took out Osama bin Laden and presided, however wanly, over the demise of Moammar Gaddafi's terroristic regime.

Still, the right's approach to national security remains the dominant one in Washington today, give or take some deviations. It is influential and enduring because it articulates a worldview of unabashed American exceptionalism and because it refuses to rule out measures that might be necessary in the defense of the country. It makes no apologies for wanting America to come out on top—a priority more nuanced critics are not always so able or willing to convey. Mainstream Americans understand it instinctively. We have always been a nation of pragmatists, not theorists.

These core conservative principles—along with a commitment to traditional values, both religious and cultural, which I have omitted here since they don't seem to play a key role in the current climate—form the foundation of right-wing populist ideals and principles. None are new: like the Tea Party itself, they reflect a tendency that goes back a half century or more, within the Republican Party and in the electorate at large.

A BRIEF HISTORY OF RIGHT-WING POPULISM

The rise of the conservative movement to power in American politics has been much documented over the last few decades, and there is no need to rehearse that history again here. However, the component of the right that has relied on populist appeals is important to understand, both because of its prominence today and because of its centrality to the conservative vision.

"Sometimes I think this country would be better off if we could just saw off the Eastern Seaboard and let it float out to sea," Barry Goldwater said in 1961.

That's the kind of statement you could imagine hearing from a Tea Party member today, but back then, such words shocked the Washington establishment. Goldwater would spark the revival of modern right-wing populism with his 1964 presidential campaign. Rejecting the legacy of FDR's New Deal and President Johnson's expansive vision for a Great Society of social-welfare programs, Goldwater argued against federal government intrusion in state affairs—even to the point of opposing the landmark Civil Rights Act. That stance earned him plenty of condemnation, but Goldwater had supported civil rights bills before and genuinely objected to what he felt were the law's violations of individual and local liberties.

Nearly fifty years later, Goldwater's warnings about excessive government are still relevant, and in a different context, the Tea Party has often resounded his themes. The United States did not have the specter of debt default and crippling budget deficits back then, but otherwise, Goldwater's messages have proved remarkably durable over the decades.

While Goldwater suffered one of the worst defeats in presidential history, his campaign launched the modern conservative movement in politics. Working for Goldwater that fall were legions of young, idealistic conservatives—like Pat Buchanan—who would go on to help shape the arguments and communication styles of the movement. The campaign also launched Ronald Reagan, who gave a classic televised address, "A Time for Choosing," in support of Goldwater. Reagan's words that night also sound like they could be spoken today:

> This is the issue of this election: Whether we believe in our capacity for self-government or whether we abandon the American revolution and confess that a little intellectual elite in a far-distant capitol can plan our lives for us better than we can plan them ourselves.[11]

Two years later, Reagan was elected governor of California.

That a candidate as conservative as Reagan could be elected governor of the nation's most populous state shocked many seasoned political observers, who had long argued that the nation had arrived at a "liberal consensus." In fact, that liberal consensus was crumbling. (A generation later, seasoned political observers would just as smugly, and erroneously, dismiss the Tea Party's power and significance.)

As Rick Perlstein has written, Reagan was a powerful candidate because he provided "a political outlet for the outrages that, until he came along to articulate them, hadn't seemed like voting issues at all." Reagan's speeches included topical issues of the time—he hammered away at campus unrest, urban crime, and welfare—but they also expressed a broader unease, a sense that the nation was slipping away from its core principles and becoming unrecognizable to an older generation. This is a timeless populist theme, on both left and right, but on the right it generally encompasses a vigorous attack on government itself and the myopia of political "elites."

Those themes took stronger hold as the tumults of the 1960s spiraled out of control, by the end of the decade helping to spawn Richard Nixon's "Silent Majority"—the middle-class Americans who, he said, wanted nothing more than the peace and quiet they had once taken for granted. Nixon helped deliver some measure of that peace by bringing an end to the war in Vietnam; by the mid-1970s, the 1960s counterculture and antiwar movements were pretty much played out. The radicals of just a few years earlier now began planning their careers. As Todd Gitlin put it, "The zeitgeist settled down."

But if the antiwar movement was over, the antitax movement was just beginning. "Death and taxes may be inevitable, but being taxed to death is not inevitable," said California businessman and antitax activist Howard Jarvis.

In what would soon become known as "taxpayer revolts," California in the late 1970s passed the landmark Proposition 13. The proposition decreased property taxes by restricting annual increases of assessed value of real property to an inflation factor, not to exceed 2 percent per year. It required a two-thirds majority in both legislative houses for future increases of any state tax rates or amounts of revenue collected, including income tax.

Jarvis, "a burly and profane spud of a man,"[12] was the lead sponsor of Prop 13, collecting tens of thousands of signatures to get the initiative on the ballot—after which it passed with nearly two-thirds of the vote and survived a Supreme Court challenge. Proposition 13 was a foundational moment, revealing a conservative populism capable of taking effective political action. Jarvis and his supporters brilliantly used the state initiative process, originally championed by progressives, to bring about major conservative reform. Since Proposition 13, right-wing populists have proved as adept at using initiatives—passing everything from Taxpayer Bills of Rights to bans on gay marriage—as their adversaries on the left.

By the 1980s, many longtime, middle-class Democrats had become Reaganites, whether over frustration with liberal policies or their own growing economic prosperity and a conviction that Republicans were more likely to protect it. The 1980s saw one of the great economic booms in American history, but its unevenness was felt later in the decade, especially in the working class, as manufacturing jobs began their long flight from the United States. Deficit spending and stock-market volatility, too, eventually led to a painful recession in the early 1990s.

These tougher times set the stage for the end of Republican presidential rule, but they also brought a political surprise: the Perot movement. Billionaire Texas businessman Ross Perot's 1992 campaign was part of a budding populist movement, one often compared with the Tea Party. Perot supporters, like the candidate himself, were much less ideological than the Tea Party, sometimes to a fault—it wasn't always clear what Perot would actually *do* should he become president. But it was clear what he and his cohorts were angry about: spiraling deficits and debt; an economy that was beginning to serve only the wealthy and powerful while the middle class struggled to stay afloat; and a culture of irresponsibility and blame shifting from a government in Washington that had stopped serving the people.

Perot appealed to Americans with commonsense, folksy sayings that evoked a simpler time in the country when Americans were masters of their fate. "The activist is not the man who says the river is dirty," he said once. "The activist is the man who cleans up the river." If he got to Washington, he promised, he would "clean out the barn."

Perot won 19 percent of the vote in 1992, the best performance by a third-party presidential candidate since 1912. If he hadn't been such a volatile personality—pulling out of the race in the summer, then coming back in, making bizarre conspiratorial accusations—he might have done even better. Even as flawed a candidate as he was, though, his appeal is obvious. Like any good political candidate, he articulated powerful and enduring themes. Nearly twenty years later, the issues Perot raised have changed in only one sense: they have all gotten much, much worse.

Between Perot and the Tea Party, the most effective burst of right-wing populism occurred in 1994, when Republicans, led by Newt Gingrich, took control of both houses of Congress for the first time since the early Eisenhower years. Gingrich, too, sounded the tried-and-true themes: the need for responsiveness and accountability from public servants; the importance of keeping government as small as practically possible; the justice of returning to citizens as many of their hard-earned dollars as possible. The soon-to-be-House Speaker's platform, The Contract with America, was mocked mercilessly during the 1994 campaign—but it carried the GOP caucus to victory against a legion of Democratic legislators, like then-Speaker Thomas Foley, who had lost touch with their constituents.

Gingrich, being a politician who relished battle, soon overstepped, both practically and rhetorically. He branded the Democrats, and liberalism more broadly, as responsible for most of the ills besetting American society. That kind of broad-brush rhetoric—and a government shutdown in 1995 triggered by GOP intransigence—helped alienate Americans from Gingrich's leadership. But the former Speaker's hard-core style of politics has now become the norm. Indeed, the Tea Party cites the 1995 government shutdown not as a cautionary tale about excessive ideology but as an example of a conservative backing down in a fight. They resolved to stand their ground during the debt-ceiling fight of 2011.

What seemed extreme in 1995 has become typical a decade and a half later, in an era driven by populism, ideology, and widespread public anger. By 2011, it had become routine to hear leaders of both parties speak of the other as something just short of political villains. That habit became especially prevalent during the tumultuous presidency of George W. Bush, whose policies, as we've seen, managed to revive the left-wing populist movement.

Much less recognized today is that the right-wing populist revival, culminating in the Tea Party, also has its roots in the disappointments of the Bush years and their aftermath.

8

GEORGE W. BUSH AND THE RIGHT-WING IMPLOSION

My friends in the mainstream Republican Party no longer have a home unless they embrace Tea Party values.

—Chris Redfern, Ohio Democratic Party Chairman[1]

Like many of my colleagues in the freshman class, I came down here to get our fiscal house in order and take care of the threat to national security that we see in the federal debt. We came here not to have long careers. We came here to do something. We don't care about re-election.

—Representative Tim Reed (R-N.Y.)[2]

For most of the administration of George W. Bush, right-wing populism lay dormant. Conservatives had one of their own in the White House, and right-wing critics of the administration mostly kept their powder dry.

In December 2003, Bush broke with traditional conservative ideology when he signed into law an extension of Medicare, the Medicare Prescription Drug Modernization Act, which subsidized the purchase of prescription drugs for seniors covered by Medicare. On the right, criticism was relatively muted, although early estimates put the law's cost at $20 trillion for twenty years.[3] In December 2003, the terror attacks of 9/11 still weighed on Americans' minds, and the Iraq war was in its first year. Shortly before Christmas, American troops would capture

Saddam Hussein and ignite hopes that the Iraqi insurgency would be stopped in its tracks. Bush simply had the support of the right at this time, and more libertarian voices—which would eventually be heard over the din—were mostly drowned out. Only years later did voices on the right begin to speak out with real force about this massive new entitlement. Now, even Bush's home-state ally, Texas governor Rick Perry, criticizes the program.[4] In 2011 alone, Medicare Part D, as the prescription-drug program is known, will contribute $55 billion to the federal deficit.

Bush would oversee the greatest rise in federal spending since the Johnson administration, increasing discretionary outlays in his second term by an estimated 48.6 percent.[5] These increases were not just staggering for a purported fiscal conservative—they dwarfed the spending hikes of Bush's Democratic predecessor, Bill Clinton. Clinton's inflation-adjusted growth of the federal budget over eight years in office amounted to 11 percent. In his eight years in the White House, Bush increased the federal budget by *104 percent.*[6]

By midway through Bush's second term, a revolt was building on the right. As the war in Iraq became a national calamity, right-wing critics began assailing Bush as an ineffective commander in chief. Some even began backpedaling from their previous advocacy of Bush's "freedom agenda" and started to sound more like those in the foreign policy "realist" camp represented by James Baker and Henry Kissinger. This retreat would foreshadow what, a few years later, would become a more aggressive walk-back from the Bush policy among some GOP presidential candidates, who began sounding more isolationist, like conservatives of a generation earlier.

With Bush looking more like a failed president, right-wing critics now began excoriating the administration for its lack of fiscal restraint. Other failures, too, weighed on Bush: his lackluster leadership during Hurricane Katrina further damaged his image as an effective chief executive. As the housing bubble began to burst in late 2006 and 2007, what some right-wing partisans had taken to calling the "Bush boom" seemed increasingly artificial and transient.

The only area where Bush met with unabashed admiration on the right during his second term was in his Supreme Court picks, and even there, he briefly ran afoul of his now restless right-wing base. When Justice Sandra Day O'Connor announced her retirement in the summer of 2005, Bush finally had his chance to fill a court vacancy, and he named John Roberts, a staunch conservative and a figure of great acumen and personal character. The pick met with broad applause. Before confirmation hearings could be held for Roberts, however, Chief Justice William Rehnquist died of cancer. Bush then nominated Roberts to replace Rehnquist as Chief Justice, and the Senate confirmed him, 78–22.

But Bush still had to name a replacement for O'Connor. When he picked his White House counsel, Harriet Miers, a woman with no judicial experience and a nonexistent background in legal opinion, the conservative right revolted. Everyone from Beltway conservatives to Rush Limbaugh hammered the White House for picking someone other than a true believer.

"I'm disappointed, depressed and demoralized," said *Weekly Standard* editor and staunch Bush defender William Kristol, speaking for many on the right. But conservatives were also energized, and they fought the nomination furiously. Miers realized that she didn't have support on Capitol Hill and withdrew her nomination.

The Miers brouhaha was a clear message to Bush that the days of his rubber-stamp approval on the right were over, but he recovered strongly by picking Samuel Alito, a conservative perhaps even to the right of Roberts—and a figure who would clearly move the Court rightward because he would be replacing the moderate O'Connor. The right was thrilled, while the left vowed all-out opposition. After contentious hearings, the Senate confirmed Alito by a vote of a 58–42, the lowest margin it had given a nominee, except for Justice Clarence Thomas.

Alito and Roberts were just about the only bright spot on the president's domestic agenda, however. Although the 2007 surge in Iraq began to show genuine results by early 2008, Republicans had begun looking forward to the end of Bush's presidency almost as much as Democrats did.

Then came the final cataclysm.

The fall of 2008 was the hinge moment: The Republican Party, in the midst of a presidential campaign, asserted its independence from Bush and his spending policies. For the right, the government intervention in the financial crisis in the form of the $700 billion Troubled Assets Relief Program represented a bridge too far. Washington's intervention in the private sector on this scale clearly violated free-market principles, crisis or no crisis. On top of Bush's deviations from conservative orthodoxy on spending, it was simply too much to bear.

Members of the conservative Republican Study committee, which included more than one hundred lawmakers, sought to find a "free-market alternative to the Treasury Department's proposal" to purchase so-called toxic assets from Wall Street financial firms. As the *New York Times* reported, congressional Republicans revolted against their own White House after years of going along with rampant spending:

> After years of acceding to the White House on a variety of initiatives despite deep misgivings, House Republicans found the administration's latest proposal to be too much to swallow.
>
> Just as they were trying to reassert themselves as a party of fiscal restraint, President Bush, on his way out the White House door, was asking them to sign off of on a $700 billion bailout built on taxpayer dollars, with very few questions allowed.
>
> "You were being asked to choose between financial meltdown on the one hand and taxpayer bankruptcy and the road to socialism on the other and you were told do it in 24 hours," Representative Jeb Hensarling of Texas, head of the conservative group, said. "It was just never going to happen."[7]

What would become the Tea Party in early 2009 begins here, in a right-wing revolt against a seemingly limitless notion of federal power in Washington. No sooner had the presidential campaign ended—in which John McCain and Sarah Palin delicately tried to defend the president's response to the crisis—than most key party figures began speaking out more openly against the "bailout culture" in Washington.

THE POST-BUSH POPULIST REVIVAL

As the Great Recession decimated millions of middle-class jobs, right-wing populism reemerged in a renewed opposition to massive federal spending and determination to shrink the size of government. The return to fiscal restraint—whether in discretionary spending, deficit reduction, or taxation—became the core doctrine of a reinvigorated, post-Bush Republican Party.

The Tea Party is now the crucial player in a right-wing political spectrum that includes two other key strands: first, the establishment GOP, which strikes a difficult balance between its mainstream instincts and a full-out embrace of the Tea Party's taste for ideological warfare;

and second, Libertarians, who comprise a much smaller part of the Republican base but who have seen significant gains in support over the last four years. Allied with the establishment GOP are other generally pro-Republican groups, such as the Chamber of Commerce and the Business Roundtable, organizations that viewed a potential debt default with horror and pleaded with representatives to find a compromise. Allied with the Libertarians are such super-rich individuals as the Koch brothers, who essentially believe in an unregulated economy and who use their wealth and influence to lobby for it.

The Tea Party reconnected the GOP to its core principles: small government, low taxes, deficit reduction, and constitutional conservatism. For many, the activist approach of the new president, Barack Obama, set off the populist reaction.

The Tea Party held its first major national event on Tax Day, 2009. The bailout of AIG and the creation of TARP under Bush preceded the auto industry bailout under Obama—in effect, a bipartisan government takeover of huge segments of the economy. Obama followed the auto bailout with a $787 billion economic stimulus program that most right-wing populists considered a gift to profligate state governments and the Democratic interest groups feeding at their troughs. These policies, the right contended, would not stimulate the economy or save any private-sector jobs. All told, an estimated $2 trillion in government spending added up to record deficits.

Obama's plan to overhaul the nation's health-care system also aroused angry opposition. But for many who took to the streets, even those who considered themselves devoted conservatives, the problems began with President Bush.

"There was nothing [fiscally] conservative about the Bush administration," said Mark Williams, an organizer with the Our Country Deserves Better PAC, which was founded in 2008 but became a key player in the Tea Party phenomenon the following year. The PAC held the Tea Party Express bus tour in late summer 2009 that campaigned against the administration's health-care reform plan. But Williams suggested that the Tea Party began not so much in response to Obama as to the Republican Party betraying its core economic principles. Citing TARP, Williams said, "I think that's when conservatives truly parted company with W. . . ."

Joe Wierzbicki, a coordinator for the Tea Party PAC Our Country Deserves Better, agreed. "The problem that people have is eight years of Bush, who was supposed to stand for limited government, going into out-of-control deficit spending. In the end throwing in the towel on free market principles saying that we have to have bailouts 'for the good of capitalism' which makes no sense."

Across the country over the last two years, at Tea Party rally after rally, these same sentiments could be heard. "It started with the Bush administration spending so much money," said Cynthia J. Biegher, the founder of the Beavercreek Liberty Group, a subchapter of the Dayton (Ohio) Tea Party, in 2010. "We are spending all this money, but we're not really succeeding at anything."

By 2011, with a Republican primary process about to begin, one presidential candidate, Representative Michele Bachmann, who is immensely popular with the Tea Party, summarized the by-now standard position on federal bailouts and spending on the right:

> I was behind closed doors with Secretary Paulson when he came and made the extraordinary, never-before-made request to Congress: Give us a seven-hundred-billion-dollar blank check with no strings attached. And I fought behind closed doors against my own party on TARP. It was a wrong vote then. It's continued to be a wrong vote since then. Sometimes that's what you have to do. You have to take principle over your party.[8]

Bachmann's opposition to TARP at the time it was being considered gives her credibility with the Tea Party that few GOP figures can match. In fall 2008, even staunch conservatives conceded that the emergency measure was probably necessary to prevent a systemic crisis. Three years later, Bachmann's view is practically gospel on the populist right. "Many Tea Partiers," *City Journal*'s Nicole Gelinas writes, "consider TARP such a terrible idea that they would have chosen to brave a worse financial disaster instead."[9]

As the Tea Party's power grew in 2009 and 2010, the right, including Republicans in Washington, began taking hardened ideological positions, particularly on controlling spending and opposing any new taxes—the latter with an almost religious devotion.

This renewed focus on fiscal austerity is the central premise of today's John Boehner–led House Republicans, the GOP's second key strand. They have faced enormous pressure to move even further rightward since January 2011, and their resistance to doing so has, so far, been futile. Most, if not all, of the political energy on the right is with the Tea Party, which has already proven its capacity to defeat establishment GOP candidates in party primaries. Because the Republican Party as an institution doesn't poll well, it has little basis for resisting the Tea Party's power.

A third strand of right-wing populism is a reinvigorated Libertarian movement, whose standard bearer, Texas GOP congressman Ron Paul, is running for the Republican presidential nomination in 2012, as he did in 2008. Paul advocates the abolition of the Federal Reserve, the Department of Education, and other government departments that, in his view, are counterproductive and extraconstitutional.

Paul has his differences with the Tea Party—especially in the area of national defense—but in other ways, he was in the Tea Party before there was a Tea Party. On December 16, 2007, in Boston—the 234th anniversary of the Boston Tea Party—he led supporters from the State House to Faneuil Hall. Paul and his compatriots "re-enacted the dumping of tea in Boston Harbor, by tossing banners that read 'tyranny' and 'no taxation without representation' into boxes that were placed in front of an image of the harbor."[10]

Paul ran for the GOP presidential nomination in 2008, just as the mortgage crisis began to hit but before the financial meltdown of that fall. Many of his positions, as stated at candidate debates, put him on the fringe. He advocated abolishing the federal income tax and the Federal Reserve and repealing the 1973 War Powers Act that let the president initiate hostilities without a formal declaration of war from Congress. His main platform plank was to return America to the gold standard, the last vestige of which was ended by President Nixon in 1971. He was often the odd man out at GOP presidential debates.

But Paul was onto something, as we can see four years later, when many others on the right echo his themes—most of all, his withering criticism of runaway federal spending under presidents Bush and Obama and the resulting deficits. His son, Rand Paul, won a Kentucky Senate seat by explicitly associating himself with the Tea Party.

During the debt crisis, Ron Paul stayed true to his philosophy, suggesting that the U.S. *had to default* on its debt, one way or the other—because even if the nation did raise the debt ceiling, our crippling debt would eventually make our money worthless. The only way out, Paul consistently argues, is to cut spending. But "the reason we don't cut spending is, one side loves entitlements, the other side loves war."[11]

What links Libertarians and the Tea Party is a commitment to constitutionalism, fiscal conservatism, and states' rights. Such is the resurgent appeal of libertarianism, in fact, that Paul's 2012 presidential candidacy will have company, from the former New Mexico governor Gary Johnson—who cut taxes fourteen times in his tenure, never approved a tax hike, and left office as one of just four governors with a balanced budget.[12]

The relationships and tensions between these three right-wing strands will form a central dynamic to the 2012 race on the Republican side. While the Libertarian strand has gained significantly since 2008, libertarianism is still a minority outlook on the right. The central tension remains between the Tea Party insurgents and the GOP establishment. The challenge for the Republican Party will be how to tap into Tea Party energy and principle without destroying the party's appeal to a broader electoral base.

What *Wall Street Journal* scribe Gerald Seib wrote about the Tea Party and the GOP in 2009 remains true today: "Movements like these aren't easy to control. . . . Republicans who think they can harness Tea Party Patriots and their anger may be in for a rude surprise of their own."[13]

TEA PARTY IMPACT

The Tea Party is forcing a national conversation about fiscal responsibility, limited government, and deficit reduction. The final resolution of the debt-ceiling battle, which concluded in an agreement to make spending cuts larger than the debt-ceiling hike and with no new taxes, showed clearly that the Tea Party is driving the political agenda in Washington. It has done this by fundamentally altering the political conversation—from a debate over how much to *spend* to a debate over how much to *cut*, and how quickly.

This is a stunning, perhaps historic transformation of political priorities. In just three years, the Tea Party has become a political force with much more fuel behind it than the mainstream Republican Party—to say nothing of the Democratic Party or any equivalent political movement on the left.

"The difference is the intensity here," said David R. Mayhew, a political science professor at Yale. "The Republicans have the Tea Party, and the Democrats don't have anything of comparable animation on their side."[14]

Indeed, as the debt-ceiling battle showed, the Tea Party has become the dominant force in American politics, and the principal reason why the populist right, even after such a sound defeat in 2008, came roaring back almost immediately after President Obama took the oath of office. Since the rise of the Tea Party in 2009, the Republican Party has been transformed, both in terms of policy initiatives and leadership. The movement has greatly accelerated a tendency toward ideological purity, which was already a hallmark of the populist right during the Bush years and strained the Republican Party's reputation as a "big tent" of diverse constituencies. Moderate Republicans, as every political observer today knows, constitute an endangered species.

A January 2009 Rasmussen poll, for example, found that "the plurality of GOP voters (43%) say their party has been too moderate over the past eight years, and 55% think it should become more like Alaska Governor Sarah Palin in the future." Those numbers played out in the 2010 congressional elections, in which 67 percent of GOP voters were self-identified "conservatives."[15] In returning the House of Representatives to Republican control, conservative-minded voters swept into power eighty-seven new Republican House members, of whom nearly 40 percent had affiliations with the Tea Party.[16]

The Republicans have become a party driven by a populist core. Its House members are increasingly uninterested in compromise or building bridges, disgusted with the state of Washington politics. They are determined to "make a difference" rather than build a long career or advance in the time-honored process of climbing the party seniority ladder. They are motivated, rather, by ideology and principle—and they see all around them career politicians, including some respected conservatives, who, in their view, have surrendered principle for expedience, self-gain, or lack of political will. They reject the establishment Republican appetite for deal making.

"The tea party," writes GOP strategist Clark S. Judge, "is the first broadly based American political insurgency since California's Proposition 13 in the 1970s." The insurgent intensity of the movement continues to make GOP establishment figures uncomfortable, but as Judge and many others see it, that's all for the good:

In short, the tea party movement is Reaganism updated. A contest has been fought over and over in Washington since Republicans embraced cutting tax rates and nondefense spending under Ronald Reagan in the early '80s. When Republicans have united behind these priorities, they have won elections.[17]

Much evidence supports that assertion, and Tea Party leaders haven't been shy in acting on that basis, almost from the beginning. So the movement has been relentless in policing Republican "sellouts" and pushing GOP candidates either to accept Tea Party principles or get out of the way.

As the Tea Party Declaration of Independence put it in 2010:

We Declare ourselves INDEPENDENT of the Republican Party, which has in the past manipulated its Conservative Base to win election after election and which then betrays everything that Base fought for and believed.

We reject the idea that the electoral goals of the Republican Party are identical to the goals of the Tea Party Movement or that this Movement is an adjunct to the Republican Party.

We reject the Republican Party professionals who now seek to use the Tea Party Movement for their corrupt and narrow political purposes. . . .

We reject the scare tactics of the Republican Party, which seeks to herd us into voting for candidates who supposedly represent the "lesser of two evils" in the name of fealty to the principle of small government and then having to suffer such candidates as they betray that principle. . . .

We insist that the Tea Party Movement does NOT consider the election of Republicans in and of itself to be necessarily beneficial to our goals.

We demand the Republican Party understand that we reject its attempts to co-opt us.[18]

In November 2009, the Republican National Committee considered a so-called purity test that would deny funding and endorsements to candidates who didn't uphold core conservative principles. Members had to pass muster on eight out of the ten principles or face a cut-off of funding. The measure didn't get through in its original form, but a few months later the GOP adopted a similar version of the purity test without the binding penalties. Candidates would merely have to express "support" for that platform.

Of the many remarkable things about the Tea Party, one of the most striking is its consistent, strong sense of overarching principles—this within a movement that has hundreds of local chapters around the country. "We have our pillars," says Rob Scott, cofounder of the Dayton

Tea Party. "It's advocacy for small government, fiscal responsibility, support for free markets and small business and support for the U.S. Constitution."[19]

In Ohio, the ideological purists gained a scalp in Mike DeWine, who ran for state attorney general in 2010 after being ousted as a U.S. senator in 2006. DeWine had lost his Senate seat in 2006, somewhat bewilderingly, after voting with Democrats the year before on a judicial-appointments compromise. Before that, he'd been considered a conservative stalwart.

As Greg Gantt, chairman of a local Republican Party in Ohio, put it: "You can be a conservative and carry the banner for all these years and (with one vote) you're haunted for life."[20]

DeWine struggled to court Tea Party loyalists, somewhat pathetically announcing that he had applied for a conceal-carry gun permit. DeWine said he was only doing so to better understand the law because he would be administering it as attorney general, but critics saw his gesture as pandering.

DeWine went on to win the Ohio attorney general's race in November 2010, but with just 47.5 percent of the vote.

After the Tea Party swept eighty-seven new Republican House representatives into power in the 2010 midterm elections, it was clear that the movement had crossed a threshold. Now it held genuine political cards, and federal budget expert Stan Collender watched them being played forthwith.

In early February 2011, as another "Snowmageddon" descended on the Midwest and East Coast, Collender was sitting home—where he had already lost power and heat—when he received a cell phone call from Minnesota congresswoman Michele Bachmann. She wanted to know if Collender would address the first House of Representatives Tea Party caucus meeting. Although Collender had been considered for a post in the Obama administration's Office of Management and Budget, making him an unlikely Tea Party acolyte, Bachmann thought enough of his background to invite him. He had, after all, been the founding editor of the influential *Federal Budget Report* newsletter and had worked on House and Senate budget committees.

"Where I come from," he said, "you don't say no to a member of Congress." He accepted Bachmann's invitation. What he saw that day offers a vivid snapshot of how right-wing populism is changing the Republican Party.

After Collender spoke for about twenty-five minutes, he watched in amazement as Tea Party state chairs from Virginia, Pennsylvania, and Florida lit into their elected GOP representatives, making clear that they had the power to vote them out of office if they didn't make the right votes.

"I have never seen members of Congress treated like that," said Collender, "especially by their friends." The Tea Party's demands, he observed, were specific and uncompromising:

> The marching orders were, first, you must not vote to extend the continuing resolution [that would keep the government open through 2011] unless it, in their words, "defunds Obamacare." Number two, you must not, under any circumstances, vote for an increase in the debt ceiling. Period. No conditions. Number three, and they said this explicitly, we don't trust John Boehner or Eric Cantor. And the state party chair from Virginia was from Cantor's district. And, finally, the members themselves told me afterwards that what they thought they did wrong in 1995 and 1996 was they gave in too early to Clinton.[21]

The day after the meeting, February 28, 2011, five Tea Party–affiliated House Republicans voted against the first debt-ceiling extension sought by the Obama administration. Fifty-four Republicans nixed the second ceiling extension on March 15; by the third, on April 14, fifty-nine voted against it. Collender realized that raising the debt ceiling, which had long been a pro forma vote for Congress, had become a major struggle because of the Tea Party's "religious-like fervor" against extending the limit. At a minimum, the negotiations would go down to the wire, since the Tea Party caucus was determined not to repeat the GOP experience with Clinton.

Above all, what Collender saw that day made clear to him that the GOP leadership had hitched itself to a tiger in the Tea Party—one they might well ride to success, if they didn't get devoured first. "Boehner and Cantor," Collender realized, "were going to have a lot more trouble than anyone thought."

That's proved true. What John Boehner, Eric Cantor, and other GOP leaders are dealing with in the Tea Party caucus is a movement convinced that its hard-line positions reflect the popular will—otherwise, they reason, they wouldn't have won their seats. They're right about this, at least when it comes to most conservative voters. Thus they believe that if anyone should back down, it's the Democrats or, by extension, less ideological, establishment Republicans.

Building on the popular rejection of George W. Bush and the GOP in the 2008 elections and then the widespread public concern about the Obama administration's spending in 2009 and 2010, the Tea Party built a plausible case that it was the only force in American politics properly focused on controlling the nation's out-of-control spending and fiscal policies. Coupled with their electoral victories in 2010 and the unpopularity of the mainstream GOP in polls, the Tea Party soon became the dominant player in the Republican congressional caucus.

Thus, the most ideological and polarizing positions are now the norm for Washington Republicans. The power the Tea Party caucus exerts within today's GOP is exponentially greater than that of the reawakened populist left within the Democratic Party. When establishment figures like Boehner or Cantor show any sign of wavering, the Tea Party quickly asserts itself—forcing the party leadership to accede to its demands and withdraw from the negotiation table.

Going into the 2012 elections, the Republican Party straddles a dilemma quite different from that of Obama and the Democrats: like the Democrats, Republicans have seen a populist upsurge make demands on the party and threaten to withdraw support if its needs are not met. Unlike the Democrats and left populists, the Republicans face a movement that has demonstrated potent political force by electing dozens of new members of Congress and by defeating incumbent Republicans in party primaries. Moreover, their articulation of principled conservative themes about spending restraint and smaller government not only resonate with millions of non–Tea Party conservatives but also with Independent voters.

In short, the Republican Party's political future is now firmly hitched to the Tea Party. It is almost impossible to imagine Obama riding a left-populist wave to reelection next November; if the president is to win, he will have to retain his liberal support, but he will also need to reclaim the center. By contrast, one can imagine a scenario in which Republican congressional candidates, or even the GOP presidential nominee, ride a tide of right-wing, Tea Party–inspired populism to victory next November.

This is the fundamental difference, in political terms, between the two populist impulses: the left can only lose if its left-populist faction becomes too powerful, but the right might prevail through the burgeoning strength of the Tea Party.

Yet, the Tea Party is not an unambiguous gift for the GOP. Although its hard-line stands have reenergized the right-wing base, this confrontational, uncompromising approach could spell doom for the party with Independent and centrist voters. Already, 2010 candidates Sharron Angle, who ran for the Senate against Harry Reid in Nevada, New York's Carl Paladino, who took on Andrew Cuomo in the New York governor's race, and Christine O'Donnell, who ran against Chris Coons for a Senate seat from Delaware, demonstrated that even Tea Party populism has its limits. All three went down to crushing defeats, doomed by their extremism, ignorance, and overall lack of political viability.

If the Tea Party association becomes, as it did in these races, more liability than strength, then the Republican Party will pay dearly, because its Washington establishment has become ideologically closer to the Tea Party than ever—out of sheer political necessity. As the Declaration of Tea Party Independence puts it:

> We demand the Republican Party recognize that while the Tea Party Movement cannot guarantee their aid will help them win elections, it is very likely WE CAN MAKE THEM LOSE if they are disdainful of our goals.[22]

How close should the GOP be to the Tea Party?

THE TEA PARTY AND THE GOP ESTABLISHMENT

Without question, the emergence of the Tea Party resuscitated the Republican Party with stunning swiftness. It forced, as Peter Boyer wrote in the *New Yorker,* "in one cycle, a rebranding that otherwise might have taken the Party a generation to achieve. The channeling of the Tea Party transformed the House Republicans."[23]

It also set the stage for conflict between the reborn populist right and Beltway Republicans, a struggle that might define the soul of the Republican Party for a generation or more.

In November 2010, John Boehner, a more or less old-fashioned Republican, achieved a cherished dream when the Republican recapture of the House of Representatives made him House Speaker. But Boehner was simply not prepared for the virulence of the House freshmen swept into Congress by the right-wing populist tide. Boehner doesn't differ from them in principle on anything—he's a tax-cutting, low-spending, pro-business Republican. The distinction is a matter of degree: Boehner entered Congress in 1991, a far more congenial era. He is accustomed to making deals with Democrats. He was a friend of Ted Kennedy's and a supporter of George W. Bush's lavishly expensive education reform bill, No Child Left Behind.

At the same time, Boehner understood that he would not have become Speaker without the Tea Party. So from day one, he has had to strike a balance like that Obama must perform with his left-wing base. But the Tea Party is a far more potent political force within the GOP than left populists are in the Democratic Party, meaning that Boehner has both more to lose by spurning them and more to gain by courting them.

"There's no daylight between the freshmen and any of our members or the leadership," Boehner told Peter Boyer, trying to craft an image of party harmony. Yet Boehner spent much of the epochal debt-ceiling debate alternating between a negotiating posture with the White House and attempts to confirm his loyalty and solidarity with the right wing of the Republican Party, which is now indistinguishable from the Tea Party. Concerns from Tea Party loyalists that Boehner had moved too close to the White House negotiating positions—which called for spending cuts but also new tax revenue—caused nearly open friction with his deputy, Cantor, and protestations from both men that they were, in fact, on the same page. When Senate Minority Leader Mitch McConnell of Kentucky proposed his own plan, which would give Obama the authority to raise the debt ceiling on his own, some began to wonder who was driving the Republican agenda.

Assistant Leader James Clyburn (D-S.C.) suggested that Republican disarray left President Obama with no clear negotiating partner. "If what I saw in the media reports this morning is an indication, then we've got a real problem because it seems as if the president can't seem to figure out whether he's dealing with the Speaker or the leader. . . . There's a real problem here inside the Republican Conference, and nobody on the Democratic side should be held responsible for that." The GOP disarray during the debt crisis led *Washington Post* columnist Dana Milbank to suggest that the party was practically "leaderless."

The real question, however, is not who the leaders are, but which instinct will prevail in the party over the long run: the establishment's appetite for compromise or the Tea Party's devotion to principle above all?

As Speaker, Boehner will have a lot to say about how that question is answered, but so will several of his younger lieutenants. Three in particular—who dubbed themselves, in a 2010 book, the *Young Guns*—are Majority Leader Cantor, Republican Whip Kevin McCarthy, and Paul Ryan, the party's intellectual leader on entitlement reform. Though they're not explicitly affiliated, they enjoy strong support from the Tea Party, and they often talk and act like members. They come from a younger GOP generation, one raised on scorched-earth partisan warfare, and they didn't have Boehner's burden of having to negotiate with the White House. They took pains to distinguish themselves from older, establishment Republicans, as when they wrote in *Young Guns*: "We had a majority of people who came here to do something, and we atrophied into a majority of people who came here to be something."[24]

Even Young Guns like Cantor are not immune to the Tea Party's wrath. The Virginia Tea Party Patriot Federation attacked him in March 2011 when he voted against an amendment that would have made even deeper spending cuts than the $61 billion passed by the House. Cantor's office argued that the House had just passed "the single largest spending cuts in modern history," but it wasn't enough for Virginia's Tea Party Patriots.

"We are extremely disappointed in Eric Cantor, but not surprised," said Mark K. Lloyd, chairman of the federation, in a news release. "The will of the American people was pretty clear in November—cut, cut, cut spending. Apparently, Eric Cantor's 'conversion' to fiscal restraint was only temporary."[25]

If the Tea Party will go after Cantor, it will go after anybody, and indeed, Tea Party leaders have criticized some of their strongest supporters in Congress when they have deviated from preferred positions. They even went after congressman Allen West, a Tea Party hero, when he endorsed the final debt-ceiling bill, refusing to go along with sixty-six other House Republicans in voting against it. Just like that, the Tea Party branded West a "defector." West fought back, telling conservative radio host Laura Ingraham: "I'm going to stand with this Boehner plan and, once again, if the folks who one minute they're saying that I'm their 'Tea Party hero' and what, three or four days later 'I'm a Tea Party defector'—that kind of schizophrenia I'm not going to get involved in."[26]

That the Tea Party would accuse Allen West of disloyalty makes clear how stringent its ideological standards are and how thin the line is between staying in the movement's good graces and losing standing. One key question in the upcoming GOP presidential nomination contest is how the Tea Party will evaluate candidates. Will the movement grade them as harshly as it did West? Or will it take the long view and see victory over Obama as a goal worth pursuing, even if compromise is necessary?

Certainly Tea Party voters expect to be heard in the primaries. In March 2011, a NBC/*Wall Street Journal* poll found that more than half (53 percent) of those planning to vote in the Republican presidential primaries were self-described Tea Party voters. Around the same time, a *New York Times* poll offered fresh insight into the breadth of the Tea Party's appeal in the electorate: 30 to 40 percent of Tea Party voters identified themselves as either Independents or Democrats. Looking over those results, Jeffrey Anderson in Pajamas Media questioned how any GOP candidate could get far without Tea Party support:

> Thus, even if a candidate were to squeak out the Republican nomination without widespread Tea Party support, he or she would suffer from a two-fold disadvantage in the general election: a large number of Republicans wouldn't be very enthusiastic about their nominee, and those independents who are Tea Party voters—or who share Tea Party sympathies—wouldn't be, either.[27]

Anderson also took stock of the Tea Party Presidential Poll, conducted by the same people who wrote the Tea Party's Contract from America. Contrary to the already emerging consensus among such conservative Beltway pundits as George Will or Ross Douthat, who have argued that only a "safe" candidate like Mitt Romney or Mitch Daniels could win, the Tea Party poll has elevated politicians who articulate positions consistent with the small-government philosophy.

Topping the list, in March 2011, was Paul Ryan, author of the "Roadmap for America's Future," a radical reenvisioning of America's budget that proposed enormous spending cuts, flat-tax rates, and the conversion of Medicare, essentially, to a voucher program.

Since then, of course, the rankings have changed, and Ryan has announced that he isn't running. The top ten presidential choices in the Tea Party poll, as of August 2011, were:

1. Michele Bachmann
2. Sarah Palin
3. Tim Pawlenty
4. Rick Perry
5. Newt Gingrich
6. Herman Cain
7. Rick Santorum
8. Ron Paul
9. Gary Johnson
10. Mitt Romney

Republicans simply cannot nominate a presidential candidate in 2012 who lacks substantial Tea Party support. How stringent the ideological standards will be remains to be seen, but if the Tea Party's conduct during the most important political battle of 2011 is any indication, the movement will not be in a compromising mood.

THE GREAT DEBT-CEILING BATTLE

For those who still doubt that the Tea Party was the most powerful political force in American politics, the debt-ceiling negotiations of summer 2011 provided an unequivocal answer. The issue of extending the nation's debt limit became one of the most grueling Washington political battles in years. Driven by Tea Party energy, Republicans made the debt ceiling a rallying point for their antispending agenda and declared that they would not vote for an increase that did not also include substantial cuts to government programs—in amounts that exceeded the amount of the debt extension—and a reduction of the federal debt. Despite their focus on cutting the debt, they ruled out any new tax revenues, even the kinds that Obama was talking about, which did not involve marginal-rate increases but rather elimination of tax loopholes that would raise revenue.

Official Washington was stunned by the GOP position for two reasons. First, raising the debt ceiling had never been a political issue before. Obama's predecessors had raised it many times during the course of their presidencies. Second, failing to raise it, or even sending uncertain signals about a debt extension, could have catastrophic effects on the global economy and the financial system.

The *Washington Post*'s Ezra Klein summarized the broadly accepted view among economists and policy makers about what a default, and eventual failure to make the interest payments on the debt, would mean:

> This is too scary to consider for any serious length of time. Treasury securities sit at the base of the global financial system. They are considered so safe that the interest rate on Treasuries is called the "riskless rate of return," as the market assumes there is no chance of default under any circumstances. Almost all other types of debt—mortgages, credit card, auto loans, business loans, hospital bonds, etc.—are yoked to Treasuries. . . . If the market has to reassess the risk of Treasuries, the resulting financial crisis will be beyond anything we've ever seen in this country.[28]

Faced with those consequences, a deal on the debt limit ought to have been simple, but instead, it became an existential battle for political survival. Led by the Tea Party, Republicans decided to make raising the debt limit an issue to spotlight their concerns with government spending.

The Boehner- and Cantor-led House GOP, pushed relentlessly by right populists, resisted *any* deal that would include new tax revenues, even when that position became a central obstacle to reaching an agreement with President Obama.

"His administration has been burying our kids and grandkids in new debt and offered no plan to rein in spending," Boehner said in June 2011. The longer Obama refused to concede the reality that no deal involving new tax revenues would pass the House, Boehner said, "the more difficult he makes this process."[29]

In fact, polls showed that more than half of self-identifying Republicans didn't think that the economy would suffer if Congress failed to raise the debt ceiling by the deadline of August 2. Among those who identify with the Tea Party, 65 percent didn't see a problem with not raising the debt limit.[30]

As freshman GOP representative Todd Rokita of Indiana put it:

> The debt ceiling negotiations are a great opportunity to enact monumental reform within the federal government. In order to raise the

debt ceiling, the price for that concession must be the passage of permanent and structural reforms like the balanced budget amendment—period. There is no additional negotiation.[31]

Here is where the tension between the Tea Party and the mainstream GOP surfaced. John Boehner had made some harsh statements about Democrats and the president, but at heart, he believed in making deals and compromises for the sake of the country. He believed that the nation's interests were best served when the two parties found ways to work together. Boehner was a conservative by any standard, but he was also a deal maker.

He went to see the president, one-on-one. In early July, it looked like Obama and Boehner might be able to reach a "Grand Bargain": a $4 trillion deficit-reduction proposal comprised of $3 trillion in spending cuts and $1 trillion in new tax revenues. Three-quarters of the package, then, would have been on the GOP's terms. Boehner knew that Obama would hear it from his caucus for agreeing to steep cuts in entitlements as well as changes to these programs, such as raising eligibility ages for Medicare. These programs were the Democrats' Holy Grail; Boehner felt that, with Democratic concessions, he could get his caucus to agree to a deal whose tax component was small.

He guessed wrong. Rank-and-file House Republicans, heavily influenced by the Tea Party freshmen, balked. The new-tax revenue component, they said, was out of the question. No new taxes, said the House freshmen—*no matter what*. Boehner had no choice but to back off, and the talks went back to square one. Soon Boehner was doing his best to sound like a member of the Tea Party.

"Let me be crystal clear on this—at no time, ever, during this discussion did I agree to let taxes go up," he said, though the reports indicated that he had contemplated doing exactly that. "I haven't spent 20 years here fighting tax increases just to throw it all away in one moment."

"This debt-limit increase is his problem," Boehner went on to say of Obama, reiterating the standard right-wing populist position: any agreement must include spending cuts larger than the increase in the debt ceiling, without any new taxes. And Boehner, echoing many House freshmen, called for a balanced budget amendment, which he said would prevent such fiscal crises.

If Boehner had been negotiating in 1991—the year he entered Congress—the Grand Bargain might have become law. But it had no chance of getting past the Tea Party forces in the House. Moreover, conservative momentum had also gotten behind a group of GOP legislators who had crafted their own plan called Cut, Cap, and Balance. Their pledge was to vote against any budget measure that didn't have major budget cuts, mandatory caps on future spending, and a balanced budget amendment that would make it unconstitutional for the federal government to spend beyond its means. The House passed it. Senator Jim DeMint of South Carolina—a Cut, Cap, and Balance stalwart—tried to bring the plan before the Senate, but it was immediately tabled by Majority Leader Harry Reid. In response, Tea Party groups encouraged Americans to write to their legislators and urge them not to vote for bills containing tax increases.[32]

Boehner tried to build support for an alternative bill that would cut the debt by $1.2 trillion, with no tax increases and a pledge to submit the balanced budget amendment to a vote down the road. Boehner got a boost from the U.S. Chamber of Commerce and other business groups, who pressed GOP leaders to make a deal and extend the debt limit. The Chamber came out for Boehner's plan, playing their own brand of politics by telling Republican legislators it was "a with-us-or-against-us moment that would be remembered during the next election campaign."[33] They represented the business interests long aligned with the establishment GOP, and their misgivings illustrated the dilemma on the broader right: the Chamber and other groups had enthusiastically cheered the Tea Party's attacks on business taxes and excessive regulation, but now their own hands were being bitten by a movement they'd helped unleash.

The establishment lobbying didn't work. Boehner couldn't get his bill past the Cut, Cap and Balance Coalition, which included more than one hundred conservative groups and dozens of lawmakers. As the coalition's spokesman, Joseph Bretell, suggested, the Boehner plan merely gave lip service to Tea Party demands:

> A symbolic vote on a balanced budget amendment at some later time minimizes its importance, as it will not be tied to an increase in the debt ceiling . . . A BBA that allows a tax increase with anything less than a 2/3 supermajority is not a serious measure.[34]

Mark Meckler, cofounder of Tea Party Patriots, called the Boehner plan an "embarrassment" full of "smoke and mirrors." As for the Speaker himself, Meckler graded his performance as a "D," because he'd "give him credit for rhetoric."[35]

Less than a week before the August 2 deadline, the Tea Party helped kill Boehner's deal in the House. A sense of impending doom began to settle on Washington. The Tea Party, it seemed to some, was dead set on default; to others, the Tea Party's unwillingness to accept even legislation from its own side pointed up the movement's ideological radicalism. Tea Party adherents themselves, however, were mostly uncowed. To them, a default, or the risk of default, was the price for getting America's fiscal house in order.

Fortunately, we didn't reach that point—though the party leaderships and the White House dragged the drama out to the final few hours of August 2, when Obama finally signed compromise legislation cobbled together by Boehner and Reid.

The deal called for a two-phase increase of $2.1 trillion in the debt ceiling in exchange for at least $2.4 trillion in spending cuts over ten years and a new congressional committee to recommend a deficit-reduction proposal by Thanksgiving. The Super Committee would be tasked with navigating the second round of cuts.

Most important for those in the Tea Party, the deal contained no new tax revenues. Obama, only a month earlier, had insisted that new revenues were nonnegotiable; they had to be part of any deal. Now, looking down the barrel of a debt default, the president backed down and signed the deal. Even so, it didn't stop Standard & Poor's from downgrading the United States' credit rating for the first time a few days later.

For most observers, the debt-ceiling deal constituted a resounding victory for the Tea Party. With the highest stakes imaginable, they had succeeded in keeping new tax revenue out of the deal. They had withstood months of nearly uniform Beltway condemnation from Democrats and media pundits. They had greatly weakened Obama, forcing him to make concession after concession as he sought compromise. And they had established a precedent for using debt-ceiling increases as leverage in adjudicating other political issues.

"Never again will any president, from either party, be allowed to raise the debt ceiling without being held accountable for it by the American people and without having to engage in the kind of debate we've just come through," said Senator Mitch McConnell of Kentucky.[36]

Perhaps most important, the Tea Party had lived by the political principles they had pledged to govern on in November 2010: they had put fiscal discipline and small government on the agenda in Washington, and they hadn't backed down no matter what names they were called. When pundits argued that the Tea Party was betraying the American people, it was a classic case of projection. The Tea Party had spurned the political class but done exactly what the voters in November had told them they wanted done: Stop the spending. Get Washington's fiscal house in order. No more saying one thing and doing another. Make the hard choices. Put principles into action.

All of this they had done, and yet—one-third of House Tea Party freshmen rejected the debt bill, despite Boehner's urgent cajoling. Tea Party–affiliated presidential candidates such as Michele Bachmann voted against it. For many in the Tea Party, the defeat of Cut, Cap and Balance meant that little had changed in Washington. There was nothing to celebrate in the debt deal, they said.

Perhaps nothing better illustrates the ideological zealotry of the Tea Party movement than its refusal to recognize its own success. Yet that same restlessness drives its energy and resolve—and presents a volatile mix of opportunity and danger for the Republican Party.

THE FUTURE

At the height of the debt-ceiling battle, when the GOP freshmen were feeling heat from all sides to compromise, Sarah Palin decided to send them a timely reminder. On her Facebook page, she reposted a letter she'd written to the GOP freshmen after the November 2010 elections. Palin urged the freshmen to "remember us 'little people' who believed in them" and reminded them that "they were sent to D.C. for such a time as this." And then, after signing off—"All my best to you, GOP Freshmen, from up here in the Last Frontier"—she stuck in the knife with a P.S.:

"Everyone I talk to still believes in contested primaries."[37]

Palin's veiled threat underscores the stakes for both the GOP freshmen and Republicans generally as the 2012 elections approach. The conflict is simple but profound: How closely should the Tea Party be embraced? While talking tough about the debt-ceiling increase—and even voting against it—earns credibility with the right wing, it risks alienating the Independent voters the party will need to attract next year. During the debt-ceiling battle, those voters told most pollsters that they wanted to see more compromise and less confrontation. How will Tea Party candidates reach them?

Between now and November 2012, the Tea Party will wage other battles that will demonstrate the limits of GOP allegiance to its purist vision. The movement's next great goal, a balanced budget amendment, will provide more clues about which Republican politicians are considered members in good standing.

One key dynamic within the Tea Party is that many of the 2010 freshman class of Republicans tack farther to the right than the districts they represent. This disparity owes to a depressed Democratic turnout in 2010. In 2012, more Democrats from these districts are likely to return to the polls, as is usually the case in presidential election years. That means that some of the most ardent Republican freshmen could face a serious challenge in 2012, especially if the Tea Party is less popular by then.

So Boehner and Cantor must deal with a movement that, in the here and now, is impossible to resist—yet whose long-term impact remains uncertain. Should Boehner bow to Tea Party demands only to see the movement's appeal wane, he and many of his colleagues could face defeat themselves. Even Tea Party partisans concede that the future is uncertain, which only redoubles their resolve. As Arkansas representative Tim Griffin says: "A lot of us feel that we're here on a mission, and the mission is now, and we're not that concerned about the political consequences."[38]

Those consequences could just as easily be greater Tea Party appeal and political strength—but for Boehner and other establishment GOP figures, that scenario can also pose a threat to survival. If Boehner refuses to climb on board sufficiently, and the Tea Party continues to be the most vibrant force in American politics, he could be ousted, either from his leadership or even from his seat, for being out of step with the movement.

In the Senate, the same tensions are at work. Even such longtime GOP stalwarts as Orrin Hatch of Utah and Richard Lugar of Indiana, both of whom are seeking reelection next year, seem to be factoring the Tea Party into their calculations in different ways. Lugar has faced Tea Party attacks for voting in favor of the debt compromise, calling it a "victory for conservative fiscal responsibility." Hatch went the other way, voting against the bill—perhaps having in mind the fate of his former colleague and fellow Utah senator Bob Bennett, who was beaten by a Tea Party candidate in the 2010 primaries. So Hatch is touting "every ultraconservative vote he's ever made, and he's going around saying 'I was Tea Party before it was cool to be Tea Party,'" Bennett says.[39]

Tea Party power will also figure heavily in the presidential campaign. As we've seen, Tea Party loyalists strongly back politicians with small-government credentials and show much more skepticism about mainstream names. Potential front-runners, like Mitt Romney, have work to do to convince right-wing populists that they're on their side—Romney has a state-run health-care plan in Massachusetts to explain, for example. He also has to shake his image as a transparent, calculating politician: he was mostly silent during the month-long debt-ceiling battle before saying that he opposed the bill, after the fact. Tea Party supporters weren't impressed.

Even seemingly more palatable candidates such as Texas governor Rick Perry, who became something of a hero when he spoke at a Tea Party rally in 2009 and made vague hints about Texas seceding from the Union, have felt the displeasure of the populist right. Perry's sin is his more accommodating stance on illegal immigration.

In a time of national crisis, when political energies run to the extremes, a movement with a clear, simple vision and passion for ideological purity has built-in advantages. Such is the case with the Tea Party. In the absence of clear leadership within the GOP, the Tea Party movement, both in terms of ideology and impulse, is driving the direction and the agenda of the GOP, pushing the party further and further to the right. Is this, in the end, good for the Republican Party? Is it good for the nation?

That's why we have elections.

9

INDEPENDENT VOTERS
Angry, Volatile, and Growing

Amid the rampant partisanship in Washington and the tendency of Republicans to go harder to the right and Democrats to go harder to the left, a vast—and angry—constituency stands apart: Independent voters. How vast? Polling over the last few years makes clear that self-identified Independents are essentially the largest voting group in the U.S. electorate. A July 2011 Pew Research Center survey of voter identification found "the highest percent independent since party identification was first measured in the late 1930s": 34 percent Independent, 34 percent Democrat, and 28 percent Republican.[1] Those numbers are even more pronounced among young voters: a July 2011 CNN survey found that 45 percent of voters under the age of thirty-five were registered Independents.[2]

These trends have been unfolding for years. By 2008, registered independents outnumbered registered members of *both* parties, combined, in six states. By 2010, this held true for eleven states: Massachusetts, Connecticut, Rhode Island, New Hampshire, Maine, New Jersey, Ohio, West Virginia, Iowa, Colorado, and Alaska. That same year Pew noted an even higher rate of Independent voter identification—39 percent—which it called the largest in seventy years.

Readers of my previous books will know that, while I remain a registered Democrat, I'm a strong advocate for third parties and for opening up our political process. So the rising tide of Independent voters can only be a good thing, right? It's certainly not a bad thing. As I've said elsewhere, any trend that exerts democratic pressure on the two-party monopoly in Washington can be constructive. And without question, the growth in Independent voters represents a clear rebuke to the two parties.

But we should be careful about how we interpret the Independent bloc, and particularly about drawing definitive conclusions about its goals and direction.

Why? Because today's Independents are an intensely discouraged, angry, disaffected, and even disconnected group. Their Independent registration is not in itself a coherent statement of political purpose. It is, more than anything, a statement of rejection, a "No" in place of a "Yes." And while it's important to understand what we oppose before we can take positive action, it's also vital to understand what we should be working toward. In this respect, the growing Independent numbers give us little to go on: Independents have no ideology; no particular issue orientation. They are in no one's camp, as they have shown repeatedly over recent years.

Unlike committed Democratic or committed Republican voters, who have largely swung more left or more right over the last few years, Independent voters swing *between the parties*. In a nation in which just 11 percent of respondents, in a September 2011 Gallup poll, pronounced themselves "satisfied" with life in the United States,[3] Independent voters are like the tip of a spear. They are volatile and unpredictable—and, as recent elections have shown, they are also indispensable to either party's prospects of victory.

Just consider the last three election cycles. In 2006, Independents broke heavily toward the Democrats and against President George W. Bush and the Republicans. That year, the issue driving public discontent was the unrelenting bloodshed in Iraq and the sense that the president and his party simply had not provided the leadership the country needed. Nationally, Independents voted nearly six in ten for Democrats.[4] It was enough to end Republican control of the House of Representatives and the Senate, handing the GOP what President Bush accurately described as a "thumpin'." Two-thirds of Independent voters, according to the *New York Times*, "said they were dissatisfied or angry."

In 2008, Independents again broke for the Democrats. Thanks to the troop surge, Iraq had quieted down, but now the economy dominated all other issues, especially after the financial crisis hit that fall. With record numbers of housing foreclosures, rising unemployment, and concern about the stability of the global financial system, Independents gave Bush a kick on his way out the door, rejecting his designated successor, John McCain, in favor of Barack Obama. Obama won 52 percent of Independents, and Democrats nationally took the Independent vote, holding their majorities in both houses of Congress.

Two years later, however, the story was different. With the Great Recession showing no signs of ending and the enormously divisive passage of Obama's health-care reform package, Independents broke heavily for the GOP. Independents favored House Republicans over House Democrats, 55 percent to 40 percent. It was enough to retake control of the House for the Republicans, though Democrats held onto the Senate. But Obama would now face an emboldened conservative opposition.

What lesson can we draw from this seemingly schizophrenic voting behavior? A fairly simple one: Independents are intensely dissatisfied with the state of the country, with the economy, and with their own life prospects. There is no more vivid way of sending this message electorally than by continually throwing out incumbents. And while Democrats in 2006 and 2008, and Republicans in 2010, tried to attribute the friendly voting tide to their own party's ideas, the truth is otherwise: Independents were crucial to all three of those election results, and Independents were not lining up for either party. They were responding less to Democratic or Republican ideas than they were expressing their mounting discontent with the state of the country.

Specifically, a survey I conducted for the Independent Women's Forum last year demonstrated the depth of anger that Independents feel.

Only 7 percent of Independents surveyed said that they have confidence in the federal government. Clear majorities were strongly negative to both the Democratic and Republican parties. They had very low levels of confidence in American institutions, and they described themselves as being alienated and disconnected from the mainstream of political life.

Independents tend to want less government and less regulation, but it would be a mistake to describe them as closet conservatives. Independents have moved back and forth between the two parties and are enormously volatile—driven far more by anger than by interest, suspicion rather than support, for the established order and the two major parties.

President Obama himself is a perfect example of the way the Independent dynamic has worked. He harnessed them brilliantly in 2008, connecting with their discontent, inspiring their lingering idealism, and—most of important of all, for a bloc not always tuned in to politics—getting them out to the polls. But he has not been able to retain their support. While he entered office with a strong majority of Independent support, by 2011, he had lost them: in March, 40 percent of Independents still preferred that he be reelected versus 34 percent favoring a Republican. But by July, just 31 percent favored Obama, while 39 percent wanted to see a Republican elected.[5] An ominously low 34 percent of Independents now approve of Obama's handling of the economy.[6]

So while the two parties took the results of those elections—at least the ones in which they were successful—as endorsements from the American center, Independent voters meant no such thing. The truth is, they don't know what they believe: they've broken down, too, like the system itself. The common denominator in their recent voting behavior is rejectionism—a disavowal of both parties and a system from which they feel increasingly estranged and excluded.

Polling data makes clear how disgusted Independents are with Republicans and Democrats. In July 2011, 55 percent of Americans held an unfavorable view of the Republican Party, while 49 percent held an unfavorable view of Democrats. Both those figures match, or nearly match, record highs. "The combined unfavorable score for both parties—104 percent—is also a record," wrote Nate Silver, "and represents the first time that the figure has been above 100."[7] Meanwhile, 52 percent of Americans feel that a new, third major party is needed.

In my own polling of Independents, I've found this same rejection of the two-party system, but their dissatisfaction and anger doesn't end there. More broadly, Independents express disgust with the entire political system. Below are their responses to five key questions:

1. Do you feel that the wealthiest Americans have too much power and influence?

YES: 74%
NO: 26%

2. Both parties serve the political class and not ordinary people: Agree or Disagree?

AGREE: 81%
DISAGREE: 15%

3. Do special interests in Washington have too much power and influence on decisions that are made on Main Street, too little power and influence, or the right amount of power and influence?

TOO MUCH: 84%
TOO LITTLE: 4%
RIGHT AMOUNT: 5%

4. Is the economy headed in the

RIGHT DIRECTION: 24%
WRONG TRACK: 63%

5. Our democratic system has become a system driven by huge wealth, power, and special interests, and it is perpetuated by a revolving door between the private sector and Washington that links most of the same people to one another over time.

AGREE: 84%
DISAGREE: 10%

WHERE WILL THEY GO?

By now, it has become a common practice in American politics to try to handicap the Independent vote. It's an understandable impulse, more so now than ever, when the Independent line in voter-identification surveys is rising at the expense of both parties. But given the somewhat unique circumstances of our present moment, I don't think any crystal ball is possible regarding the future disposition and behavior of Independents. I'm skeptical for two key reasons. First, because they're so large, and getting larger, it's increasingly difficult to generalize about them. Second, they're angrier than the electorate as a whole, and whenever you're dealing with this level of anger, all bets are off.

As we've seen, the anger of committed Republicans and committed Democrats has led them to double down on their party loyalties and, to a considerable degree, on their ideological convictions. That's one kind of angry response. Another—the one often taken by Independents—is to say, in effect, "to hell with you."

To hell with you can mean, I'm voting against the incumbent party—as it did in 2006, 2008, and 2010. Or it can mean, I'm sitting this one out, I don't care anymore, I'm disconnected.

How Independents will respond in the years ahead is anyone's guess (though the signs don't look good for Democrats in 2012). Could Independents become involved and energized again? Certainly. We saw that scenario play out compellingly in 2008. But in 2009, we saw a different response: anger at the Obama health-care plan, as demonstrated memorably in the summer town hall meetings across the country. Within one year, a large swath of Independents went from involvement and commitment to anger. This is a volatile voting bloc united only by its abiding sense that the country is in bad shape.

In this conviction, Independents are an accurate reflection of America: they're economically stressed, they're middle class, they're worried about the future, and they're feeling the pinch in the present. They know what they're against: they're anti-Washington, anti-elite. They oppose high, redistributive taxation, but they also oppose tax cuts for the super-rich, and they generally want no part of extreme right-wing social agendas. As the 2010 Pew study put it:

> Owing to defections from the Republican Party, independents are more conservative on several key issues than in the past. While they like and approve of Barack Obama, as a group independents are more skittish than they were two years ago about expanding the social safety net and are reluctant backers of greater government involvement in the private sector. Yet at the same time, they continue to more closely parallel the views of Democrats rather than Republicans on the most divisive core beliefs on social values, religion and national security.[8]

So what are they for? That's been tough to pin down. Their anger doesn't translate into a fixed worldview. Some on the left claim that, due to their economic distress, Independents are a progressive bloc just waiting to be captured. I've seen little in my own or other polling indicating this is true. Others, like Matt Welch in his recent book, suggest that Independents are perhaps nascent Libertarians. Again, this seems a bit thin to me. Certainly Independents voice some Libertarian thoughts—and yes, they think they pay too much in taxes—but Independents are much more like pragmatic problem solvers than they are budding Libertarians. I think Independents probably do, on the whole, have more of a predilection toward the right, but it's not tied down to firm ideological commitments.

If Independents have demonstrated one bedrock principle over the last decade, it is that no incumbent is safe. The demonstrated willingness of Independents to switch between the two parties—radically, from one election cycle to another—is the fundamental statement of their dissatisfaction with our politics and the state of the country. It's not always clear or predictable what's going to trigger these shifts in allegiance or what's going to inspire their commitment or provoke their ire.

In the end, the very volatility of Independents is a statement in itself on the failures of the political class of both major parties. Put simply: the largest voting bloc in the country is angry, has no commitment to the Republicans or the Democrats, and is willing to change its vote on a moment's—or an election's—notice.

10

THE POWER OF MONEY

The fundamental problem . . . is that the lens through which Congress approaches issues is re-election. The lifeblood of their re-election campaigns is political contributions.

—Howard Schultz, Starbucks CEO[1]

In the case of the tax-exempt groups, citizens have absolutely no idea what's going on here. They have no way of knowing how groups are trying to influence their votes.

—Fred Wertheimer, Democracy 21 president and campaign-finance watchdog[2]

"This is an impressive crowd: the haves, and the have-mores," George W. Bush says to a fund-raising dinner, as shown in Michael Moore's *Fahrenheit 9/11*. "Some people call you the elite, I call you my base."

Bush's humor got an appreciative chuckle from the crowd, but he wasn't so much telling a joke as he was poking fun at reality. Because the truth is, the well-heeled attendees at fund-raising dinners are indeed a base of support—and not just for Republicans, but for Democrats, too. In the last six election cycles alone, the amount spent on the quest for the Oval Office has quadrupled.

One of this book's core arguments is that our two-party system has become so overrun with partisanship and ideological inflexibility that it no longer functions in ways that have anything to do with the needs of ordinary people. Multiple forces brought us to this point, as I've documented—historical, political, and economic. In this chapter, I want to look at one of the most important *structural* forces: the capture of both parties, and thus our democratic system, by political money. It's happened because narrow interest groups dominate the two parties. While these groups don't represent the broader electorate, they have increasingly vast financial resources with which they flood political action committees (PACs), state and national party committees, and individual candidates.

And because of the Supreme Court's 2010 *Citizens United* decision—which legalized unlimited independent expenditures to support or oppose federal candidates, effectively removing restrictions on political donations by corporations or unions—the power of political money is now greater than ever before. *Citizens United* is also directly responsible for the growing impact of independent expenditures by 501(c)(4) organizations.

The impact of the *Citizens United* ruling has been transformative in two key respects. First, it led directly to the creation of what are now called Super PACs, which allow independent groups to raise and spend political money essentially without contribution limits. Super PACs became possible when the Court ruled in *Citizens United* that limiting independent expenditures by corporations and unions on political campaigns violated their freedom of speech. The ruling opened up the floodgates to a new universe of campaign finance. In the 2010 elections, the first since the ruling, Super PACs spent $65.3 million—and that was with very little head start. They'll spend much, much substantially more in 2012.

Consider two leading examples of Super PACs: American Crossroads, which has ties to Bush strategist Karl Rove, and Make Us Great Again, the Super PAC devoted to electing Texas governor Rick Perry the next president of the United States. In the case of Crossroads (and its sister nonprofit, Crossroads GPS), the group hopes to raise and spend $240 million in 2012. Perry's Super PAC plans to spend $55 million just in the primary season.[3] These and many other Super PACs are part of what the Huffington Post's Paul Blumenthal calls a "shadow campaign apparatus" that operates with fewer restrictions than the parties or individual candidates.

Super PACs, however, are required to disclose the source of their contributions to the Federal Election Commission (FEC). Nonprofit groups, on the other hand—the 501(c)(4) groups—are not, though they do have to report to the IRS for tax purposes. These groups also reaped a windfall from *Citizens United.* Just months after that ruling, in *SpeechNow.org v. FEC,* a U.S. Appeals Court ruled that nonprofits, too, could accept unlimited contributions from corporations and unions—in addition to unlimited individual contributions. Nonprofit political groups were now in the driver's seat: already free of FEC disclosure requirements, they now had the right to accept unlimited contributions. The decision also allowed the nonprofits to spend money directly on ads supporting or opposing specific candidates. Undisclosed nonprofit spending, or what Blumenthal calls "dark money," exploded immediately after the ruling. Just 51 percent of nonparty outside spending was disclosed in 2010.[4]

And topping it all off, Super PACs can skirt the disclosure requirements themselves by accepting donations from these same nondisclosing nonprofits. They can say their money came from a 501(c)(4) group, which is true on its face—but where did the 501(c)(4) group's money come from? They're not obligated to tell.

It is these two spending traits—unlimited spending and secret spending—that now define the campaign-finance system in the United States. As the Center for Responsive Politics executive director Sheila Krumholz puts it: "The money has shifted to the fringes and it's become less and less transparent. It's shifting away from the parties, the candidates, the PACs, and shifting to these unregulated groups and becoming much more secret."[5]

"SUBSTITUTION OF THE RULE OF CASH FOR THE RULE OF LAW"

Citizens United is perhaps the culmination of developments that have been accelerating over the last decade and a half. Before then, in what now seems a bygone age, candidates for president and Congress relied on individual campaign donations. Since the late 1990s, a seismic shift has occurred, in which the candidates themselves are becoming irrelevant as political action committees, party committees, and independent expenditure committees have become more dominant, strengthening the power of the political class and the insider and DC elites who work on their own or in concert with party functionaries. Ultimately, this phenomenon has transformed a system with already questionable ethics to one even more distasteful and corrupt, granting the political elite and the wealthiest individuals unprecedented influence over election outcomes—and compromising the democratic process in ways not imagined even a generation ago.

To the political professionals who run elections, the special interests have come to have a predominant, and arguably determinative, influence on our elections.

This is a huge change, and it has only begun to be recognized by the media. Special-interest political money has distorted our democratic system by dominating political communications to the detriment of ordinary citizens, who cannot compete with their resources. Put another way, if a politician has to choose between speaking to a group of interest-group elites or ordinary voters—it's no contest.

The imbalance in the campaign-finance system has further isolated voters from politicians and contributed enormously to the deep disenchantment with Congress and Washington more generally. Distrust of our governing institutions has grown to heights never seen in the history of public polling. This distrust is rooted substantially in a conviction that the system has become a casino, not a true democracy. Special-interest money has also exacerbated polarization, not just between the two parties but also within the broader electorate. Because most of the money comes from groups with a strong ideological cast—whether labor unions on the left or the Club for Growth on the right—candidates are pulled away from the center and toward extreme positions.

Not too long ago, political campaigns raised funds through individual contributions. Those who could afford to give did; those who couldn't didn't. That still happens to a certain extent. But today, fund-raising—and thus, campaign spending—has become the nearly exclusive preserve of the elite few. To have any influence on the outcome of a race, you must be part of the "system"—a director of a party committee, the executive director of a special interest PAC or organization, or better yet, a multimillionaire or billionaire. The phrase *special interests* has long been a catchphrase of government critics, but it doesn't capture just how concentrated power has become in a few hands in just the last couple of years.

This is how Landon Rowland, a director and chairman emeritus of the Janus Capital Group, describes our current campaign-finance system: "Substitution of the rule of cash for the rule of law."[6]

This chapter is meant to be descriptive. It is meant to avoid casting judgment on the activities of any group based on its ideological orientation. Rather, its central theme is this: In politics today, ideological groups matter, party committees matter, and together they form a self-reinforcing, secret establishment that determines the outcome of elections and is far more important than what any individual candidate does on his or her own.

My intention here is to document the individuals and groups that make up this new universe of political money, to demonstrate the outsized influence they have attained over the political process, and to make clear why this system is so profoundly undemocratic and so necessary to change.

POLITICAL ACTION COMMITTEES

For sixty years, political action committees (PACs) have been the center of the fund-raising universe, generating untold millions for candidates. PACs are essentially slush funds for special-interest groups, from the conservative Club for Growth—which raises money for Republican candidates who pledge to support limited government and lower taxes—to the left-leaning feminist group Emily's List, which works to elect pro-choice Democratic women. PACs enforce orthodoxy in each party and exert enormous influence on the course of campaigns.

Under the Federal Election Campaign Act of 1971, organizations could become PACs after receiving contributions or making expenditures above $1,000 for the purpose of influencing a federal election. PACs enjoy higher donation limits than other campaign vehicles—individuals, unions, and corporations can donate a maximum of $5,000 per year to a PAC.[7] Today, some 4,600 PACs represent all kinds of trade groups, unions, businesses, and health organizations.

Candidates from both parties today cannot run for office without the tacit support—or at the very least approval—of Washington insiders in their respective party committee who have already determined which interest groups will directly or indirectly support their candidate. Hence, the idea of a Mr.-Smith-Goes-to-Washington-style campaign is, at the very least, highly improbable, if not completely extinct.

I say this not to cast aspersions on the current system but to describe the fundamental change that has occurred.

GOVERNORS' ASSOCIATIONS

Unlike political committees or candidates for federal office, neither the Democratic Governors Association (DGA)[8] nor the Republican Governors Association (RGA)[9] faces any limits on campaign donations. Both groups can receive unlimited amounts of money in their bids to support gubernatorial candidates across the nation, including money directly from corporate and union treasuries.

During the 2010 election cycle, the RGA raised a total of $117.1 million. Interest groups, corporations, and unions accounted for $73.1 million of these contributions. Of that sum, $60.3 million (82.5 percent) came from businesses, lawyers, and lobbyists. In all, eight people gave at least $500,000 to the RGA during the 2010 election cycle, including Perry Homes chief Bob Perry ($8 million), Elliott Management hedge fund honcho Paul Singer ($2.38 million), and Koch Industries co-owner David Koch ($1 million).[10] According to a Center for Responsive Politics analysis, of the top fifty donors to the RGA, thirty-nine are corporate entities, and together, they gave $19 million to support the organization.[11]

Topping the list of corporate contributors to the RGA is News America, at $1.25 million.[12] News America is a subsidiary of News Corporation, a company founded by media magnate Rupert Murdoch. News Corporation is the third-largest media conglomerate in the world, and it owns Fox News Channel, the *Wall Street Journal*, and the *New York Post*, among other conservative outlets.

Contran Corporation runs a close second, having made $1.125 million in contributions to the RGA during the 2010 election cycle.[13] Contran is a holding company that owns subsidiaries that specialize in chemical, metal, computer, and waste-management systems. In 2010 alone, the company also spent $340,000 to lobby the federal government.

The DGA, meanwhile, received $46.7 million of its overall $55.3 million in receipts during the 2010 election cycle from corporations, unions, or special-interest groups, and $32.7 million of that—about 70 percent—came from corporations, lobbyists, and lawyers. Of the DGA's top fifty donors, thirty-two are corporations from the health, energy, or telecommunications sectors—that is, industries that want special legislative dispensations and are willing to pay for them.

According to Opensecrets.com, a website that regularly tracks campaign donations, the largest portion of political donations comes from a widely defined financial sector that includes insurance, banking, investment, and real estate. These industries, which depend on long-term investment strategies, closely watch the winds of politics and carefully plan where to invest. Sometimes one party or the other will be the prime beneficiary, but large companies frequently back both parties, just to hedge their bets.

Generally speaking, Democrats get heavy support from unions (especially public-sector unions) and the tort bar—lawyers who make their living suing industry—while Republicans get theirs from the extractive industries and finance. As OpenSecrets summarized:

> Of the nine other business sectors, the only ones giving a majority of their dollars to Democrats have been Lawyers & Lobbyists (71 percent to Democrats) and Communications & Electronics (59 percent to Democrats). All the others give more to Republicans, but different patterns prevail in different industries. Some, like timber companies, mining firms and the oil & gas industry, have always been heavily Republican, no matter who's in power. Others shift their dollars with the prevailing winds in Washington, giving very generously to Republicans when they're in control of Congress and somewhat less generously to Democrats when they're in power.[14]

BUNDLERS

In the past few election cycles, national campaigns have tapped high-profile business leaders to become "bundlers"—point people who could dig deep into their Rolodexes and tap their contacts for contributions. These wealthy individuals pool contributions and funnel far more money into campaigns than they could give individually under campaign-finance laws. Bundlers who bring in large sums are rewarded with special access to the candidate, and in some cases, patronage jobs for friends and relatives. In turn, bundlers use their new political status to enhance their own business prospects.

Often, the most effective bundlers are industry lobbyists looking for access and special favors for businesses from lawmakers on key committees. Politico.com described how this process works in an article on the congressional deficit-reduction "super committee":

> Over the past year, more than two dozen of these "bundlers"—companies and lobbyists who cut big checks and pile up scores of smaller donations— have directed $1.6 million to several members of the supercommittee and

the House and Senate campaign arms, according to federal records. What makes these bundlers stand out above other lobbyists in Washington is the sheer size of their donations—bolstering their influence over the most critical issues before the supercommittee, including defense, health care and taxes.[15]

Both parties' front-runners rely on bundlers to assemble large packages of legal campaign cash. By the time of the Super Tuesday primaries in February 2008, more than 2,500 bundlers had raised almost $600 million for various presidential candidates.

Table 10.1.   Top Bundlers in 2010

Contributor	Total	Recipient
Club for Growth	$837,641	Pat Toomey (R-Pa.)
EMILY's List	$397,695	Martha Coakley (D-Mass.)
EMILY's List	$366,637	Barbara Boxer (D-Calif.)
Club for Growth	$356,862	Sharron Angle (R-Nev.)
Club for Growth	$353,891	Marco Rubio (R-Fla.)
EMILY's List	$343,053	Robin Carnahan (D-Mo.)
Boies, Schiller & Flexner	$204,364	Kirsten Gillibrand (D-N.Y.)
EMILY's List	$202,656	Patty Murray (D-Wash.)
Moveon.org	$179,156	Bill Halter (D-Ark.)
Microsoft Corp.	$176,775	Patty Murray (D-Wash.)
Simmons Cooper LLC	$155,950	Alexander Giannoulias (D-Ill.)
Davis, Polk & Wardwell	$152,750	Kirsten Gillibrand (D-N.Y.)
Club for Growth	$152,020	Joe Miller (R-Alaska)
Club for Growth	$151,553	Ken Buck (R-Colo.)
Senate Conservatives Fund	$150,346	Joe Miller (R-Alaska)
University of Wisconsin	$149,640	Russ Feingold (D-Wis.)
Senate Conservatives Fund	$147,377	Ken Buck (R-Colo.)
Paul, Weiss et al.	$145,550	Charles E. Schumer (D-N.Y.)
Paulson & Co.	$137,300	Charles E. Schumer (D-N.Y.)
Senate Conservatives Fund	$135,551	Sharron Angle (R-Nev.)
American Financial Group	$125,652	Rob Portman (R-Ohio)

527s

The so-called 527s—wholly unregulated, tax-exempt entities named for the section of the tax code that allows them to organize—have been a major force in campaign finance since the late 1990s. They're something of a precursor to today's Super PACS, and their influence remains great: 527s donated $415 million to campaigns on both sides of the aisle during the 2010 midterm elections. In the 2010 election cycle, 196 different 527s raised $251 million for Democrats and liberal politicians, while 165 Republican and conservative organizations picked up $231 million. (Midterm elections tend to bring out fewer dollars, however, than presidential contests.)

The organizers of 527s had a choice: they could register as PACs and give directly to candidates under FEC limits, or they could focus on hot-button issues like gun control, abortion, and taxes, allowing them to raise and spend unlimited amounts. The more issue-oriented 527s could not promote or attack candidates directly.

Essentially, however, the 527s exploited a loophole in the law. So long as the organization did not use such buzzwords as "vote *for* Candidate X" in its advocacy, it was protected by its 527 status, meaning that it was obliged neither to disclose its expenditures (to the FEC or IRS) nor to submit to caps on spending. Further, any expenditures the 527 made were not subject to taxation.

Legitimate issue advocacy might involve a commercial in which a prochoice group argues that abortions should be legal and safe. Even if the proabortion group argues not only that abortions should be legal and safe but also points out that Candidate X doesn't support them, it would still be protected by its 527 status so long as it doesn't encourage people to vote *against* Candidate X. This technique of using issue ads to implicitly (but not explicitly) attack candidates, which Loyola Law School professor Richard Hasen dubbed "sham issue advocacy," became widespread in the 1990s.[16]

527s, then, afford significant advantages to their organizers: they can influence elections almost as effectively as if they were directly advocating for their favored candidates, but they can dodge significant restrictions on their activities. According to David Storey of the *University of Indiana Law Review*, the initial laws governing 527s empowered organizers by protecting them from the usual accountability laws— allowing large donors to preserve their anonymity and avoid scrutiny:

A key method for PAC's to hide any questionable ties to a candidate and avoid the appearance of corruption is for the PAC to keep its contributors anonymous. Hence, if a PAC has a large paper products manufacturer as its major soft money contributor, and this information remains anonymous, then the PAC named Citizens against the Use of Plastics would appear completely legitimate. If it is disclosed, however, that the main contributor of a group advertising the benefits of paper bag use over plastic is a large paper products manufacturer, then the issue advertisement loses credibility and will not be as effective. Furthermore, disclosure of the fact that a large corporation paid for the advertisement may clue the public into a questionable connection between the candidate that the advertisement favors and the corporation funding the advertisement.[17]

Such anonymity enabled 527s to have an unprecedented, silent degree of influence. They grew quickly, as their advantages became clear to organizations and donors. They were branded "Stealth PACs" because, while they behaved like PACs in that they were formed to advance an issue or ideology, they were entirely unaccountable to the IRS—or, for that matter, to the American people. As Lauren Daniel notes, "Second only to state and national political party committees, 527s became the primary sponsors of political issue advertisements—many of which were undeniably linked to advocacy for a particular candidate."[18]

Then, thanks partly to three landmark federal court decisions in 2010 and 2011, the balance of political power and influence shifted even more dramatically toward 527s and their ilk—and helped create a new entity, the Super PACs.

Table 10.2. Top 527 Committees for 2012 Election (as of September 26, 2011)

Committee	Total Receipts	Total Expenditures
Citizens United	$3,928,367	$3,547,431
College Republican National Committee	$2,752,173	$2,290,560
EMILY's List	$1,760,646	$824,667
ActBlue	$1,559,482	$1,449,981
Gay & Lesbian Victory Fund	$1,534,776	$1,643,572
GOPAC	$1,008,032	$1,072,901
Progressive Change Campaign Committee	$966,280	$729,325
International Brotherhood of Electrical Workers	$957,623	$814,981
Plumbers/Pipefitters Union	$595,994	$333,373
National Education Association	$551,555	$59,408

A TURNING POINT: *CITIZENS UNITED*

In 2010, by a historic 5–4 vote in *Citizens United v. Federal Election Commission*, the Supreme Court ruled that the government cannot prevent corporations and unions from spending unlimited money to support or criticize specific candidates. The ruling dealt a major blow to the 2002 Bipartisan Campaign Reform Act, more commonly known as McCain-Feingold, which sought to limit certain aspects of campaign donations. The full ramifications of the decision will be debated for years, but few dispute that it will make money in politics more central than ever.

Citizens United, a conservative not-for-profit group, had sought to broadcast an unflattering documentary about Hillary Clinton, *Hillary: The Movie*, along with related ads on television during the 2008 Democratic primaries. The FEC prohibited the broadcasts on the grounds that the movie and ads constituted "electioneering communications" that were illegal under McCain-Feingold, which forbids such groups from even mentioning the name of an elected official in any communications within sixty days of an election.

Citizens United sued the FEC, arguing that such communications qualified as protected speech under the First Amendment. The Court agreed, and in doing so ruled that, under the First Amendment, corporate- or union-sponsored independent political expenditures—that is, spending not coordinated with or directed by a candidate's campaign—*cannot be limited*. A major portion of McCain-Feingold had been overturned.

Two months after the *Citizens United* decision, a federal appeals court ruled in *SpeechNow.org v. Federal Election Commission* that political committees making independent expenditures could accept donations unlimited in size. Finally came the May 2011 ruling by U.S. District Judge James Cacheris striking down the long-standing ban on direct corporate contributions to federal candidates—which *Citizens United* had actually left intact. *Citizens United* and its follow-on rulings have led to a free-for-all in campaign finance, opening the gates for the political elite to funnel even more money into politics with even less transparency than before.

Citizens United makes campaign-finance compliance even murkier and further limits public information about political money. It allows corporations, unions, and associations to report their donors to the FEC on a monthly or quarterly basis, meaning that they can make expenditures without immediate, full disclosure of the source of the funds. This all but guarantees that campaign-finance machinations won't be discovered until well after a victorious candidate has been sworn into office.

By allowing corporations and independent groups to raise unlimited amounts to promote candidates, *Citizen's United* has given birth to new kinds of PACs—Leadership PACs and Super PACs.

LEADERSHIP PACS AND SUPER PACS

A Leadership PAC, which can accept donations from individuals or other PACs, is a committee established by a member of Congress to support other candidates. Leadership PACs allow elected officials to set themselves up as kingpins, seeding the campaigns of others and thereby extending their influence and power. For example, House Majority Leader Eric Cantor's Every Republican Is Crucial PAC has so far taken in more than $1.4 million for the 2012 election cycle, disbursing $480,000 of that to other candidates in the first half of 2011.[19] While a Leadership PAC cannot spend funds to directly support the campaign of its sponsor (through mail or ads), it may fund travel, administrative expenses, consultants, polling, and other noncampaign expenses.

Super PACs, known formally as "independent expenditure-only committees," operate under few restraints, except that they must disclose their contributions and they cannot coordinate directly with candidates or political parties.

During the 2010 midterm elections, these independent groups functioned effectively as unregulated party committees—eighty-four Super PACs funneled billions of dollars into campaign advertisements, including $65,326,957 in reported expenditures to a wide range of candidates. As of August 2011, twenty-three groups organized as Super PACs have reported total expenditures of $1,715,235 for the 2012 cycle. To date, 135 Super PACs have filed with the FEC, and doubtless many more will have done so by the time this book is published.

Given the importance of Super PACS and the arcane rules governing them, it's no wonder that political satirist Stephen Colbert decided to spoof the system by starting his own Super PAC, giving it the Orwellian name "Making a Better Tomorrow, Tomorrow."

GOP presidential hopefuls Mitt Romney, Rick Perry, and Michele Bachmann were all backed by at least one Super PAC set up by their political allies with the explicit purpose of raising and spending millions of dollars in unrestricted campaign donations. Groups on the left and the right have taken advantage of the new rules.

According to research by the Center for Responsive Politics, all liberal Super PACs have raised a combined $7.61 million during the first half of 2011. More than 80 percent of their money came from just twenty-three donors—45 percent came from people in the entertainment industry, 26 percent came from chief executive officers, and 25 percent came from unions.

Meanwhile, conservative Super PACs have collected $17.61 million so far. More than 80 percent of their money came from just thirty-five donors—66 percent came from chief executive officers, 18 percent came from corporate treasuries, and 16 percent came from individuals employed by Bain Capital, the private-equity firm that Mitt Romney founded in the 1980s.

Table 10.3. Money Raised by Conservative and Liberal Super PACs as of September 2011

Top Conservative Super PACS

Organization	Total Raised	Independent Expenditures
Restore Our Future	$12,231,700	$0
American Crossroads	$6,643,257	$1,016,353
Club for Growth Action	$1,144,022	$114,642
Raising Red	$200,000	$2,125

Table 10.4. Top Liberal Super PACS

Organization	Total Raised	Independent Expenditures
Priorities USA Action	$3,161,535	$96,555
American Bridge 21st Century	$1,562,774	$0
Majority PAC	$1,082,407	$86,550
House Majority PAC	$985,000	$919,562

TOP GROUPS MAKING OUTSIDE EXPENDITURES
IN 2012 ELECTIONS

The political elite and corporations have developed many ways to game the election rules involving Super PACS.

Consider W Spann LLC, created strictly as a shell corporation with the purpose of funneling funds into Mitt Romney's campaign treasury. In 2011, it made a $1 million donation to a Super PAC known as Restore Our Future—and then, in July 2011, W Spann LLC was dissolved after only four months of incorporation. Why the sudden move to close down? Simple: wealthy contributors can set up a corporation, give millions to a Super PAC, and then dissolve it before they have to file annual reports to the FEC. As Paul Ryan, FEC program director and associate legal counsel at the Campaign Legal Center, puts it: "It takes nine months to create a human, decades for that human to be able to make judgments reaching the level of contributions to political causes, but only a matter of days to create a corporation."[20]

Large contributions to the 2012 race are just beginning to roll in. Ed Conard, a former top official at Bain Capital and a strong supporter of Romney's over the years, gave $1 million to Spann. John Paulson, the billionaire hedge-fund manager, also made a $1 million contribution to the Restore Our Future Super PAC.

OTHER INFLUENTIAL GROUPS

With the influence of regular Americans being buried by large donations from millionaires, large corporations, and interest groups, a number of PACs and other vehicles of both the left and right have arisen in response. They often cast themselves as anti-Washington and anti-business-as-usual, and they've originated some innovative techniques. But at core, they're principally dedicated to prevailing politically—like any other PAC or interest group.

ActBlue

ActBlue, "the online clearinghouse for Democratic action," allows individuals to channel the money of friends, family, and like-minded voters into a significant donation for their favorite candidates. The Web-based

Table 10.5. Top Groups Making Outside Expenditures in the 2012 Elections

Organization	Total	Independent Expenditures	Election Comm.	Comm. Costs	SSuper PAC	527s†	5501c
Democratic Congressional Campaign Cmte	$1,386,958	1,386,958	$0	$0			
National Republican Congressional Cmte	$1,277,342	$1,277,342	$0	$0			
American Crossroads	$1,016,353	$1,016,353	$0	$0	x		
House Majority PAC	$919,562	$919,562	$0	$0	x		
Republican Majority Campaign	$708,142	$708,142	$0	$0			
U.S. Chamber of Commerce	$200,000	$0	$200,000	$0			x
Service Employees International Union	$159,046	$150,054	$0	$8,992		x	
Campaign to Defeat Barack Obama	$132,913	$132,913	$0	$0		x	
Club for Growth	$114,642	$114,642	$0	$0	x	x	
Communications Workers of America	$107,000	$107,000	$0	$0	x	x	

PAC, which was established in 2004 by two young technology geeks who had met at an MIT summer program, has distributed nearly $200 million to Democratic candidates of all "ideological persuasions," ranging from Obama's presidential bid to small state and local races. Of this, only about $55 million has been reported, not because of any illegal contributions but "because much of that money comes in donations below the $200 threshold for itemized disclosure."[21]

Still, these figures may reflect a less democratic process than advertised. Given the open nature of the site, other Democratic PACs often use it as another platform to reach more donors and raise more funds for their existing causes.

The site lets individuals become fund-raisers for their favorite candidates or give to candidates at the suggestion of others. "The site . . . tells you what congressional and Senate Democratic candidates are in close races, and then lets you donate money to those candidates with a few clicks."[22] According to organizers Matt DeBergalis and Benjamin Rahn, it also allows users to create their own group of preferred candidates in an attempt to gain support from their friends, colleagues, and liked-minded others. For example, one page, titled "vegetarian candidates," would allow users to donate to their favorite "herbivorous Democrats."[23]

During President Bush's presidential campaign in 2000, professionals within Republican PACs developed the idea of combining many small donations into significant sums of cash . . . ActBlue takes a different tack, in that it allows "anybody with an Internet connection [to] become a bundler."[24] The site does take precautions to cap contributions at $2,000.[25]

As the site's donation page declares: "We think that American politics should reflect the patterns of American life, and that the American people shouldn't have to be politicos to be political. Washington D.C. speaks the language of money and influence. At ActBlue, we're working every day to help you be part of the conversation."[26] This is not all warm and fuzzy rhetoric: the user-created group with the top volume of contributions, "stop the Republican war on working families," has received $891,722 from 38,507 supporters—an average of just $23.16 per donation.

Such fund-raising power has attracted the "big dogs." Progressive Change Campaign Committee, a PAC that advocates electing progressive Democrats to Congress, created five of ActBlue's top ten fund-raising groups.[27] Another progressive advocacy PAC, MoveOn. org, is the creator of the second-largest group, which has raised just under a million dollars from 30,143 donations.[28] And the progressive blog Daily Kos created the top moneymaker: "Orange to Blue" raised $2,408,451.17 from 25,620 donors.[29] Even candidates have created groups advocating on their own behalf.

Club for Growth

Club for Growth, a not-for-profit organized in 1999 that advocates for conservative economic policies, offers a prime example of how money is legally and directly funneled to preferred candidates. The club raises money through its PAC and donates to candidates that adhere to its conservative views. It also solidifies its clout with independent expenditures via a separate 527 committee. The Club's PAC also acts as a conduit for federal candidates by accepting and transmitting earmarked contributions from the club's many members to federal candidates.

The Club also illustrates how special-interest money is driving politics to extremes. With its hard-right, laissez-faire economic philosophy, the Club has emerged as an irritant even in Republican politics by bankrolling right-wing primary challengers to centrist Republican officeholders or party-backed candidates. In the 2009 to 2010 election cycle, it gave more than $1.5 million to four Republican candidates: Pat Toomey (Pa.); Marco Rubio (Fla.); Joe Miller (Alaska); and Sharron Angle, who nearly unseated Senate Majority Leader Harry Reid in Nevada. The Club also donated to the campaign of Conservative Party nominee Doug Hoffman, who unsuccessfully sought a congressional seat in upstate New York.

Toomey, who headed the Club for some years, was a perennial challenger to longtime centrist GOP senator Arlen Specter, whom he ultimately drove out of the Republican Party (and out of his seat). Hoffman ran against establishment-backed liberal Republican Dede Scozzafava, splitting the GOP vote and so giving the seat to the Democrat—but illustrating the influence of the hard right.

The Club's PAC website notes, "At the beginning of the 20th century, federal taxes accounted for 3 percent of the nation's gross domestic product, and federal tax rules filled just a few hundred pages. Today, federal taxes account for more than 18 percent of GDP, and federal tax rules and regulations span over 60,000 pages."[30] The group champions a number of other conservative policies, including spending cuts, "federal death tax repeal," expanding trade freedoms, privatizing Social Security, reforming the medical malpractice and tort system, deregulation, and increased educational choices.[31]

In 2008, the group spent $3.4 million through its PAC on independent expenditures alone. It spent $2.5 million in 2010.[32] However, unlike sites like ActBlue, Club for Growth does not give contributors many options for where their money will go. Instead, it uses a "power-ranking" system, which allows members to vote for or against certain lawmakers. These rankings serve as a "real-time" confidence vote on conservative lawmakers. However, the PAC site does not make it clear to what extent, if any, these votes influence the Club's spending decisions.

American Crossroads

In 2010, in the wake of the *SpeechNow.org vs. FEC* and *Citizens United* decisions, independent Republican groups "battered" Democrats through "a wave of unlimited and, in part, undisclosed spending from the U.S. Chamber of Commerce and new outside groups led by American Crossroads."[33]

Crossroads is a Super PAC designed to give donors the ability to make a larger impact on politics by bundling their money. So far, anyway, most of the expenditures have been put toward rhetoric against Democrats. Of the $21.5 million spent on the 2010 election, $17 million was spent on anti-Democratic advertisements.[34] Crossroads' website mission statement includes a call for Americans to choose sides on the political battlefront: "We face a decision between two starkly different visions of America: one where the human creativity and initiative that are unleashed by liberty and free enterprise generate the economic growth this nation needs—and one where an increasingly powerful, all-controlling federal government decides how to allocate the economic spoils."[35]

American Crossroads' influential founders, huge financial backing, and goals for defeating Democrats through excessive spending embody the group's status as a Super PAC. Former chairman of the Republican National Committee Ed Gillespie and the former senior advisor to President George W. Bush, Karl Rove, were instrumental in its founding, though neither served officially on its board. In its first financial quarter, the group raised $4.2 million, and on a few occasions spent half a million dollars on independent expenditures in a single week. These actions had been illegal just months earlier.[36]

Furthermore, the group was not funded by bundling together small donations, as most other PACs had done. Instead, of the $4.2 million, 97 percent came from just *four* donors. Trevor Rees-Jones, president of Dallas-based Chief Oil and Gas, gave $1 million. Bradley Wayne Hughes, chairman of Public Storage, Inc., was American Crossroads' biggest donor at the time, contributing $1.55 million. A company called Southwest Louisiana Land LLC donated $1 million. And TRT Holdings, owned by Dallas's Robert Rowling, gave American Crossroads $1 million. (Three of these four donors are based in Texas.[37]) Though Crossroads claims that it is an "independent expenditure-only committee,"[38] in the 2010 election cycle, it donated $1.2 million to the Republican State Leadership Committee, which gives direct financial support to state and local Republican candidates.[39]

This year, Crossroads raised $2.7 million between July 1 and August 24, of which $2 million came from Texas homebuilder Bob Perry—the major funder of Swift Boat Veterans for Truth, the group that did so much to damage the presidential campaign of John Kerry in 2004. Perry has given $9.5 million since the group's founding. In fact, 98.6 percent of the group's total money raised in the 2010 election cycle came from donations of greater than $200 (an average donation of $32,648 from 814 individuals). American Crossroads also runs independent expenditures through its 501(c)(4), Crossroads GPS, which is *not required to disclose donor information.*

American Crossroads and Crossroads GPS hope to raise $240 million during the course of the 2012 election.[40]

THE MEGADONORS

For all of the power of Super PACs, the new world of campaign money is also being shaped by individuals—some of the wealthiest and most powerful people in the world. These "megadonors" have worked on their own or in concert with party committees or party luminaries to deploy huge sums of unregulated and frequently unreported money. The megadonor class includes hedge-fund billionaire John Paulson; Richard Mellon Scaife, a Pittsburgh newspaper magnate; George Soros, the Democratic financier and fund-raiser; Jeffrey Katzenberg, the

Hollywood producer; and most notably, the Koch brothers, wealthy industrialists who fund conservative organizations such as the Cato Institute and the Heritage Foundation—and most recently, Americans for Prosperity, the group that fuels the Tea Party.

The megadonors comprise a new "superclass" that has become disproportionately influential during political campaign season. They're part of a larger process that is fundamentally disenfranchising the American electorate. They and the systems and structures they support and manipulate have made American democracy unrepresentative and unresponsive to ordinary people. Individual voters, who have long pondered whether their vote really counts, have even less say than ever.

The Koch Brothers

Tied for eighteenth on *Forbes*'s world billionaires list,[41] Charles and David Koch are CEO and executive vice president of Koch Industries, the nation's second-largest private corporation. They inherited the company from their father and bought out their two brothers some time ago, but since then they have diversified and built the business. They operate oil refineries in Alaska, Texas, and Minnesota and control some four thousand miles of pipeline. They sell paper towels, toilet tissue, wall board and lumber, carpets, Lycra, and dozens of other products. Their presence is felt in virtually every community—indeed, almost every middle-class home—in America. And, along with Scaife, they've become among the biggest bugaboos of professional Democrats and left-wing populists.

The brothers' politics are simple: they are avowed Libertarians, against big government, and for lower taxes. They regularly rail against the policies of President Obama. They believe global climate change is a myth perpetuated by liberal science, and they oppose strict environmental laws, and, of course, the fines their companies have to pay for violating them. In past years, they've given more than $100 million to conservative causes and the politicians who support them.

According to the Center for Responsive Politics, the Koch brothers donated $11 million to mostly conservative candidates over the past two decades and have poured money into lobbying, academia, and think tanks since 1980.[42] In recent years, the Kochs have become much more active and visible in their efforts. Their direct campaign contributions have gone exclusively to Republican candidates, many of whom are Tea Partiers or Libertarians. As Charles Lewis, the founder of the Center for Public Integrity, told *The New Yorker*: "The Kochs are on a whole different level. There's no one else who has spent this much money. . . . They have a pattern of lawbreaking, political manipulation, and obfuscation. I've been in Washington since Watergate, and I've never seen anything like it."[43]

Along with their lobbying efforts, the Kochs' campaign contributions have escalated. In 2004, David Koch founded Americans for Prosperity, a group that quickly became a conservative powerhouse. It's estimated to have contributed $45 million during the 2010 midterm election cycle. Between 2007 and 2009, the Kochs donated $3.4 billion to the Americans for Prosperity Foundation, a nonprofit 501(c)(4) organization that supports the Tea Party, among other right-wing causes. They have also donated large sums to the infrastructural and intellectual foundations of the Republican Party, giving over a million to the Cato Institute, the Heritage Foundation, and a number of other conservative think tanks in the past five years.[44]

When Democrats gained control of the White House and Congress in 2008, Koch Industries and its subsidiaries suddenly quadrupled its spending on lobbying, from $5 million in 2007 to about $20 million in 2008. Of this, just under $18 million was appropriated to "oil and gas."[45]

In 2011, the Koch brothers involved themselves heavily in the controversial antiunion activities of Wisconsin governor Scott Walker. The Kochs were among the largest donors to Walker's campaign, and they stood by him as he took on the state's unions. Tim Philips, president of Americans for Prosperity, was dispatched to Wisconsin to organize counterprotests against the unions, fund Walker's efforts, and bring the message of fiscal responsibility to local and national media.[46]

As a tax-exempt 501(c)(4), Americans for Prosperity is legally forbidden from endorsing candidates. That hasn't stopped the brothers from donating $10,000 to Michele Bachmann, making her the only Republican candidate to receive Koch money at the time of this writing. (Texas governor Rick Perry has held private meetings with the Koch brothers, who have supported him in the past, but he has not yet received any funds.[47]) It's unclear so far, then, which Republican the Kochs will support for the GOP presidential nomination. Regardless of how the Republican primary turns out, however, it's clear that Koch money will play a larger role than ever in the advancement of the far-right agenda.

Unlike other Republican groups, who have focused on electability, the Kochs are unrelenting in their ideological pursuit of Libertarian goals: they use their money to support causes that square with their principles.[48]

George Soros

One of the world's richest men, George Soros, is also one of the most controversial.

A Hungarian-born child survivor of the Holocaust, he has made his billions as a financier, gaining nations' ire for shorting their currencies and other supposed market manipulations. At the same time, he has used his fortune to become a philanthropist with few rivals. His charitable organization, the Open Society Foundation, has channeled some $7 billion into a staggering array of causes—from supporting the Polish Solidarity Movement, to providing Russian universities with access to the Internet, assisting New York artistic and educational organizations, to supporting Pakistani flood victims.

Soros has been credited and condemned for his philanthropic activities, which, according to some of his critics, seek to unravel capitalism and democracy in favor of a one-world government. But it is his bankrolling of left-wing political organizations in America that has made Soros a lightning rod for populist agitation.

Soros's deep political involvements date to 2004, when he declared that he would devote himself to defeating George W. Bush's reelection attempt. He explained in an interview with the *New York Times*: "The government of the most powerful country on earth has fallen into the hands of extremists." He proceeded to give $15.8 million to anti-Bush groups and promised to give more if necessary. Most of this money was funneled into the 527 organizations Americans Coming Together and the MoveOn.org Voter Fund, since they were some of the only means through which such large quantities of money could legally be spent on the election.[49]

Soros therefore set in motion what would become an enormous wave of 527 contributions. His clout and fame paved the way for others to join him, demonstrating the potential for 527s to receive massive contributions from incredibly wealthy donors. Also in 2004, Soros gave significant funds to conservative-turned-liberal attack journalist David Brock to set up the website Media Matters for America. A provocative mudslinger, Brock describes the group's mission as an all-out campaign of "guerrilla warfare and sabotage" aimed at the Fox News Network, which Brock considers an arm of the GOP. Since its founding, the site has grown enormously.

By the end of the 2004 elections, Soros had spent $17 million. In 2005, he pulled back considerably, donating only half a million dollars. By 2006, however, he had ramped spending back up to $3.2 million. The 527 money went to a variety of causes, including founding the Secretary of State Project, which sought to elect Democratic secretaries of state in battleground states where John Kerry had lost by slim margins. The organization focused on that office because it presides over elections in each state, giving it significant influence over the outcome.[50] Soros also donated nearly a million dollars in hard-money contributions to federal candidates and PACs, along with undisclosed donations to organizations such as Catalyst LLC, a Democratic consulting agency, and the Democratic Alliance, an organization that shelled out millions to Democratic think tanks and media groups.[51] But most of his 527 money—nearly $3 million—went to America Votes, a progressive voter registration and mobilization group.[52]

Soros's *modus operandi* of funneling his money through a variety of 527s and PACs remained the same from year to year. In 2008, Soros ramped up his spending again to assist the Obama campaign, giving at least $5 million to 527s in 2008.[53]

Soros-funded groups produced a number of advertisements in favor of Obama and against McCain, including a controversial ad entitled "General Petraeus or General Betray Us?," which was eventually condemned by Congress.[54]

In 2010, Soros announced his official exit from partisan politics. In a brief interview, he explained to the *New York Times* that he was pulling out because, fittingly, he did not think that the odds were in his favor, no matter how much money he pumped into Democratic causes. Though Soros seems to be moving on to policy rather than electoral goals, his record of partisan contributions has set a precedent and established a network that will continue to influence elections for years to come.

CONCLUSION

The idea that we have a representative democracy, where candidates raise their own money based on levels of overall popular support, is simply gone.

Today, professional politicians have their eyes on a single issue, first and foremost: raising enough money to get reelected. This is especially true for House members. As soon as a freshman member of Congress is sworn in, he or she must immediately begin fund-raising for the next two-year term. With the growing importance of money and short election cycles, the time legislators actually spend making laws is shrinking. They must spend more time fund-raising. Getting reelected gives them seniority, and seniority leads to important committee assignments. It's a vicious cycle.

Given the current direction of campaign-finance law, it's likely that our political system will grow even more polarized. The two parties will be even less willing to put forth constructive solutions, and candidates will become deferential only to their most generous donors—who are, almost invariably, those with the most extreme ideological views, right wing or left wing. The ordinary voter, who lacks both ideological commitment and financial clout, is left standing on the sidelines.

I believe that the public's understanding of the political system—as an unequal, undemocratic system run by and for the powerful, elite few—is fundamentally correct. Everything I've documented in this chapter bears out this conclusion.

Unless there is a national movement to radically reform the role of money in politics, the system will likely continue to reward those wealthy individuals who commit large sums to "causes" and candidates equally committed to those causes. Even those in positions of power seem to recognize this. A group of about two hundred business executives have formed a bipartisan organization calling on companies to be more transparent in their political activity and have urged Congress to pass new disclosure laws.[55] Efforts like this are urgently needed; otherwise, in the words of Trevor Potter, the president and general counsel of the Campaign Legal Center and a former FEC chairman, "the whole country is going to see a situation where corporate interests are going to be electing members of Congress" to serve their interests.[56] Only wholesale, systemic change can address the stranglehold that megadonors, power brokers, and Super PACs now have on our political system.

11

THE K STREET EFFECT

How Lobbyists Have Saturated Public Policy

It's going to be pain versus pain for a lot of people. There's going to be a focus on the 12 [lawmakers] and a focus on the leadership and a focus on the administration. Decisions will get made by a smaller number of people than you learned about in high school.

—Veteran lobbyist Tony Podesta of the Podesta Group

Jack Abramoff and Elizabeth Warren would appear to have very little in common.

Abramoff is the quintessential American "super lobbyist" who went to jail for a myriad of crimes—most notably the collection of tens of millions extorted from Indian tribal gambling operations.

Elizabeth Warren is a Harvard Law School professor, and Democratic Party candidate in the 2012 United States Senate election in Massachusetts. She is a liberal populist who advocated for the creation of a new Consumer Financial Protection Bureau and who has said—with some justification—that she "created much of the intellectual foundation" for Occupy Wall Street.

The two individuals could not be more different in life experience and approach.

Yet, in interviews in the fall of 2011, and in his new book *Capitol Punishment: The Hard Truth About Washington Corruption From America's Most Notorious Lobbyist*, Jack Abramoff said that Washington is awash with lobbyists who corrupt every aspect of the political process.

Abramoff has been frank in repenting and trying to seek a new life, and in so doing has called for an absolute ban on anyone who has ever worked on Capitol Hill—be they congressmen or staffers—from ever working as a lobbyist. He has also urged banning political contributions from anyone doing business with the government and closing the revolving door between Congress and lobbying firms.

Warren has not gone as far as Abramoff, but has acknowledged that "there are now a zillion lobbyists for every single member of Congress."

In a November 2011 *New York Times Magazine* profile in all of her dealings with the Obama administration, she has been outnumbered by lobbyists, describing the "phalanxes" of lobbyists who forced her to move aside in congressional hallways; by how, after a meeting, she might head back to her office to look up figures while lobbyists would "get on cellphones to an army of well-trained lawyers preparing to do a customized memo."[1]

Put simply, Warren has routinely felt overwhelmed by a process that is simply out of control.

And this was no more evident than in the failure of the Super Committee to reach a deal to make a relatively moderate $1.2 trillion in cuts in the federal budget.

Welcome to Capitol Hill, late 2011. I'm sure you remember the basic concept of the Super Committee. It was formed with the best of intentions: an honest effort to temper extremist rhetoric, partisan bickering, and legislative extortion and get our government working again. A bipartisan panel, made up of six Republican and six Democratic lawmakers, was formed as part of a hasty August deal to raise the U.S. debt ceiling and avoid default. It meets for the first time as I'm writing this in September and must deliver a report to the public by Thanksgiving. If the Super Committee fails to reach an agreement on how we, as Americans, should manage our finances—if Congress does not endorse its plan—automatic budget cuts are triggered. It is both entitlements and defense equally—without regard to policy or logic.

There was some logic behind the formation of the Super Committee. A group, isolated from politics and from political pressures, making decisions based on what is right rather than on partisan and political considerations.

But in fact, just the opposite has proven to be the case.

Herein lies the problem: the influence peddlers. Nearly one hundred registered lobbyists who formerly worked for members of the Super

Committee are now representing defense companies, health-care conglomerates, Wall Street banks, and others with a vested interest in the outcome of the panel's work, according to a *Washington Post* analysis of disclosure data. Three Democrats and three Republicans on the panel also employ a bevy of former lobbyists on their staffs.

The presence of so many lobbyists did nothing for the credibility of the Super Committee. Even before its first formal meeting, the panel had already come under criticism from watchdog groups for planning its activities in secret and allowing members to continue fund-raising while they attempted to negotiate a budget deal.

"When the committee sits down to do its work, it's not like they're in an idealized, platonic debating committee," said Bill Allison, editorial director of the Sunlight Foundation, which is tracking ties between lobbyists and the panel. "They're going to have in mind the interests of those they are most familiar with, including their big donors and former advisers."

And indeed, at the time of this writing, the twelve members of the Super Committee had raised in excess of $41 million from the special interests—special interests who by their very nature demand and enjoy special access to the Committee members they support.

Despite the challenge of cutting $1.2 trillion from the deficit, the leaders of Congress and the twelve members of the Super Committee have yet to abandon long-standing cherished special interests that benefit their home state interests. John Kerry, a committee member, continues to back a special tax break for the beer industry because of a Massachusetts brewery. Mitch McConnell, the majority leader, continues to believe it is essential to offer incentives to the Kentucky thoroughbred racing industry. And President Obama, while lacking parochial concerns that face individual senators and members of Congress, attacks benefits for corporate interests that help him win favor from the populist left—specifically, the oil industry and corporate jet owners.

As George Mason professor Jason Fichtner told the *New York Times*, "These special interests are getting carve outs . . . from Congress and both sides—Democrats and Republicans . . . are guilty of picking their favorite interests to support."

There is nothing new about this, of course. Lobbying is about contacts and money and persuasion. It has been that way since shortly after the country was formed. But the nature of lobbying is changing, and with it, the way politics is conducted. Increasingly, ordinary voters are shut out of the democratic process. For those who believe that representative democracy hasn't been terribly representative of their interests, there is more bad news: it's even less so today than it was just a few years ago. Government is becoming more and more insular, but in ways that are so subtle that few people even notice it. A much smaller and select circle of elite policy makers is now making the major decisions in Washington that affect how we live. And it's not just the senators you see on the Sunday morning political talk shows. It's the senior staff aides that remain in the background, as well, rarely quoted in the local news media. It is the unprecedented ability of these policy makers and lobbyists to bypass the American people completely that sets the current system apart from anything that has come before. The average citizen's voice in public policy is diminishing more and more each day.

THINK NATIONALLY, LOBBY LOCALLY

It is clear that lobbyists have special influence, special access, and a greater ability to influence policy than ever before. It is because they contribute money, have frequently served on the staffs of the people they are trying to influence, and in a highly polarized environment, they are able to communicate directly with members who frequently don't have the time or, frankly, the inclination to pursue independent policy judgments.

Moreover, the lobbyists have figured out a way to influence public opinion through high-tech means that effectively take the public out of the process. Both sides do it; both sides deny its impact. But lobbying has gone from just an inside-the-Beltway business to a highly sophisticated public relations and communications vehicle that involves techniques and tools that most people do not understand yet have an enormous ability to mobilize millions of unsuspecting people on behalf of special interests.

Specifically, there has been a palpable shift in the geography of persuasion. It's now called grassroots and grass tops lobbying—a subject we will return to later in this chapter.

Power inside the Beltway is now often exercised from the outer regions of the nation, where legislators have district offices and local interests to protect. The federal budget debate has exposed how the system operates. Lobbyists and trade groups have turned to the companies in the hometowns and states of Super Committee members to put a local face on their causes, which includes protecting oil and gas incentives and corporate accounting rules.

What this means is that inside-the-Beltway firms will be hired to influence both political elites with a direct interest in a subject as well as ordinary citizens who can be persuaded that matters of life and death to them are being decided at that very moment in Washington.

Lobbyists frequently use manipulation, evasion, exaggeration, and just plain scare tactics to convince people that their most coveted benefits like Medicare and Social Security are at risk—and can be saved *only* if they take some particular action.

Needless to say, when millions of dollars are spent on this sophisticated form of mobilization—using electronic phone calls, the Internet, and phone banks, frequently located outside of the United States—the result can be jammed phone lines, not to mention extraordinary amounts of communication and confusion on Capitol Hill, exactly what the lobbyists want to create. This allows them greater opportunity to make a case to lawmakers who are frequently worried that their political positions will be jeopardized by unseen forces, and huge—seemingly spontaneous—outpourings of support for frequently arcane policy positions.

Thanks to a powerful public backlash—almost everyone is aware of special interests and their representatives—legislators have become somewhat gun shy. They want it to *look* as though they're limiting the influence of lobbyists. "This day and age, members of Congress don't want to listen to people in K Street as much as they want to listen to their own constituents who are engaged every day in trying to make it," said Judith Thorman of the International Franchise Association (IFA), trying to put a positive spin on her own lobbying efforts—which involve sophisticated mobilization of franchisees in individual districts in individual states. If it were only spontaneous, organic, and reflected grassroots concern, we would be a lot better off as a nation and have a much more responsive political system.

The IFA, along with groups like the American Petroleum Institute, are looking for their best state-based members—particularly large local employers—to make a personal case to the Super Committee. In September 2011, the IFA flew in local franchisees and franchisers such as Dunkin' Donuts, Baskin-Robbins, Handle with Care Packaging, and McDonald's as part of an annual event. The IFA made sure the locals met with Super Committee members, including Senators Patty Murray (D-Wash.), Pat Toomey (R-Pa.), John Kerry (D-Mass.), and Representative Fred Upton (R-Mich.).

"We're trying to search for folks looking for a different way to get access and get their message out to a member of Congress," Jeff Morris of K-Global, which counts AARP among its clients, told Politico.com. Morris sent an email blast that promoted his firm's ties with key Super Committee members, noting that the firm's Montana operatives had "personal relationships with the senator [Max Baucus, D-Mont.], his new wife and state director by spending annual weekend getaways with them on the Bighorn River and at local watering holes." He also wrote that K-Global's ties to Senator Kerry go back more than twenty-five years. "They remain close to his inner circle, participating in a steering committee for President Obama at a downtown Boston law firm with a slew of Kerry's longtime friends and advisers."

And the lobbyist groups like IFA recruited to help these efforts brag specifically about how they reach members of Congress and the special influence and access they enjoy.

GRASS ROOTS AND GRASS TOPS

The Super Committee's visibility in the national news for two months in the fall of 2011 caused lobbyists and their clients to quickly realize that a full frontal assault on Congress's budget crisis was not a particularly fruitful strategy. *The ultimate goal of lobbyists is to look like they're not lobbying, and the ultimate goal of their clients is to look like they're not sponsoring or facilitating techniques of persuasion.* Some committee members and senior congressional staffers were up front about the image of K Street shops and hinted that they weren't welcome at the negotiating table—at least, not when the TV cameras were rolling.

The best offense sometimes turns out to be the end run. Lobbyists were forced to use indirect techniques to get their clients' messages into the hearts and minds of the Super Committee members and their staff aides. "They're going to have a bit of a firewall—that's exactly what's going to happen," predicted Dave Wenhold of Miller/Wenhold Capitol Strategies, a former American League of Lobbyists president. Wenhold, whose clients include municipal governments, public colleges, and construction companies, said creativity from his colleagues was essential.

"Grass roots, grass top—don't just approach the D.C. office, go to the district offices, too. There will be a media aspect to it—you're going to see some interesting campaigns," he said. "The more facets of a diamond, the more opportunity for sparkle to get noticed."

Sponsored fund-raisers and aggressive check writing are the other options for special interests hoping to make an impression on the committee members. Paid media campaigns and outside-the-Beltway efforts also are a means for corporations and organizations hoping to convey messages to Super Committee members and their constituencies. The chosen twelve have already trumpeted their bipartisanship, independence, and the fact that they are not beholden to moneyed interests—all the while taking predictable political positions reflecting the basic outlooks of their parties and their chief supporters. And they have continued the fund-raising process without interruption.

As Holland & Knight partner Rich Gold put it: "There is no way to totally cut themselves off." After all, each member's reelection coffers must be replenished every two or six years—and that is the fundamental reality in Washington.

THE REVOLVING DOOR BETWEEN K STREET AND THE CAPITOL

It is more than just money and campaign contributions that connects K Street and the Capitol. It is a level of intimacy and connection that cannot be overstated.

The relationships are long lasting and deep, and it will be very difficult for the Super Committee to keep a hands-off posture. Among them, the twelve lawmakers have seven current staffers who formerly worked as lobbyists; ninety former staffers of the twelve now work as lobbyists in the following areas:

forty-three on health care
twenty-two on defense
forty on energy and transportation
thirty-seven on technology and medicine
twenty-nine on agriculture
twenty-seven on financial
fifty-eight on other sectors[2]

Overall, two-thirds of the lobbyists with committee ties are Democrats, including about two dozen former aides to Senator Max Baucus, the powerful chairman of the Senate Finance Committee. Baucus alumni include three former staff chiefs: David Castagnetti, who represents health insurers, oil producers, and other corporate clients; Jeff Forbes, who lobbies for medical-device makers and other health-care firms; and Peter Prowitt, who leads GE's Washington lobbying team. Senator Patty Murray, who serves as cochairman of the Super Committee, has employed more than a dozen currently registered lobbyists. Murray's counterpart, Representative Jeb Hensarling (R-Tex.), has a former lobbyist as a senior adviser, but only two of his former employees now work on K Street. Murray, a four-term senator, is widely known for her ardent defense of industries important to the Pacific Northwest, including computer software firms and defense contractors. At least two former Murray staffers represent Boeing, including former legislative affairs aide Shay Michael Hancock, who also represents GE and several other defense contractors.[3] Such close ties run along both ends of Pennsylvania Avenue.

BOTH SIDES HAVE BEEN COMPROMISED

The Super Committee is only the most visible example of how Washington works. A more highly explosive and potentially criminal scandal developed in September 2011. This potential scandal has landed squarely at the White House doorstep, and much of it involves lobbying and a possible quid pro quo stemming from campaign contributions. We might not have heard about it had the company—a solar-energy firm named Solyndra—not gone bankrupt and laid off 1,100 employees after receiving a $535 million loan guarantee from the federal government.

Solyndra made a huge lobbying effort in Washington, and President Obama visited its Fremont, California, headquarters to highlight it as a prime example of a renewable-energy company worthy of economic stimulus funding. In the first quarter of 2009, Solyndra paid McBee Strategic Consulting $20,000 to lobby on issues related to the Energy Department's loan-guarantee program, and it paid $30,000 in early 2008 to Dutko Worldwide to handle Solyndra's loan application. In all, the solar outfit spent nearly $2 million lobbying in a four-year period—just before White House officials urged that the loan be approved.

Arousing further suspicion was the fact that George Kaiser, one of the company's primary investors, donated $53,000 to Obama's 2008 campaign (while others connected to the company gave thousands, as well).

Republicans, of course, were livid, and attacked the administration for its seemingly unsavory behavior. Texas Republican representative Ted Poe, a member of the House Judiciary Committee, called it "old-fashioned Chicago cronyism." Even some Democrats were critical, as taxpayers were on the hook for the loan.

Old-fashioned or not, cronyism-via-lobbying runs rampant in the other party camp as well, especially as the 2012 campaign season began revving up. In the dogfight for the Republican nomination for president, Texas governor Rick Perry felt the heat for his lobbying ties.

Forty Perry aides have either left the governor's administration to become registered state lobbyists or gone from lobbying into Perry's inner circle. Some of them have made multiple trips through the revolving door, according to Huffington Post. At least five of Perry's closest campaign aides have been registered lobbyists, including his communications director, his spokesperson, and his political director.

These lobbyists have done good work for their clients, winning lucrative state contracts for everything from private toll roads to a nuclear waste dump to the now infamous HPV vaccine mandate. A review of financial disclosures filed with the Texas Ethics Commission revealed that during the past ten years, former Perry staffers have earned tens of millions of dollars in lobbying contracts. And indeed, Perry has received tens of millions of dollars in campaign contributions from them and their allies.

"The revolving door turns at torrential speeds in Texas," explained Andrew Wheat, research director for the nonpartisan watchdog group Texans for Public Justice. "It's like it's driven by a hurricane and Perry's office has been part and parcel of it." When it comes to lobbying, it is difficult to imagine a bigger juggernaut than Patton Boggs, which specializes in representing the nation's banks, real-estate interests, consumer-electronics companies (Sony, for instance), hospitals, pharmaceuticals, Indian tribes, unions, colleges (Baylor and Clemson, to name just two), and cities (several, from Denver to Baton Rouge). Patton Boggs is a law firm, but it is also in the business of influence peddling. These days, everyone needs or wants something from government—whether federal, state, or local—and Patton Boggs has the currency of the moment: people who know people in power. They stand and deliver. Or they merely pick up the phone. From 1998 through the first half of 2011, Patton Boggs was the clear leader in lobbying income—$411,287,000, according to the website Opensecrets.com, distancing itself from the number-two firm by more than $70 million.

Nearly 5,400 former congressional staffers have left Capitol Hill to become federal lobbyists in the past ten years, according to a new study that documents the extent of the revolving door between Congress and K Street.

The data published by the online disclosure site LegiStorm found close to four hundred former U.S. lawmakers also have made the leap to lobbying. The report, which tallies a greater number of workers moving between Congress and lobbying than found in previous studies, underscores the symbiotic relationship: Thousands of lobbyists are able to exploit experience and connections gleaned from working inside the legislative process, and lawmakers find in lobbyists a ready pool of experienced talent.

Of the 5,400 lobbyists with recent Hill experience, the study found that 2,900 were registered to lobby on behalf of clients this year. Twenty-five powerhouse firms and organizations each employ ten or more former Hill workers. The largest number is at the Podesta Group, followed by the U.S. Chamber of Commerce, which employs at least twenty-one. "For every person the American people have elected to sponsor legislation of public benefit, special interests have more than one former legislative advocate now working on the inside in Congress," reveals Jock Friedly, the founder of LegiStorm. "That represents a large network of people to influence decisions and to provide valuable intelligence." In the House, the study found at least eleven former lobbyists working on the Republican staff of both the Energy and Commerce and Ways and Means committees. Democratic members of those committees together employ five former lobbyists.[4]

CASE STUDY: HOW THE BIG OIL LOBBY WORKS

It is not just the Democrats who have been compromised. When the Republicans controlled the White House during the George W. Bush administration, big oil was able to have a disproportionate amount of influence to the point where lobbyists were apparently even writing legislation.

Let's look at the power of lobbying just within one industry. During his first month in office, President George W. Bush appointed Vice President Dick Cheney to head a task force charged with developing the country's energy policy. This group, which conducted its meetings in secret, relied on the recommendations of the industry's key players: namely, Exxon Mobil, Conoco, Shell Oil, BP America, and Chevron. It would be the first of many moves to come during the Bush administration that would position oil and gas companies well ahead of other energy interests, with billions of dollars in subsidies and tax cuts—quid pro quo for an industry with strong ties to the administration and plenty of money to contribute to congressional and presidential campaigns. While Bush and Cheney, both former oil executives, were in the White House, the oil and gas industry spent $393.2 million on lobbying the federal government. This put the industry among the top nine in lobbying expenditures. The industry has also contributed a substantial $82.1 million to federal candidates, parties, and political action committees, according to the Center for Responsive Politics.

Eighty percent of the industry's contributions have gone to Republicans. This support has not gone unrewarded. In 2005, Bush, who received more from the oil and gas industry than any other politician, signed an energy bill designed by the Republican-controlled Congress that gave $14.5 billion in tax breaks for oil, gas, nuclear power, and coal companies. The Energy Policy Act of 2005, which was based on recommendations by Cheney's energy task force, also rolled back regulations the oil industry considered burdensome, including exemptions from some clean-water laws. All of this transpired only one year after Congress passed a bill that included a tax cut for domestic manufacturing expected to save energy companies at least $3.6 billion over a decade.

None of this should surprise us. "Political action committees, lobbyists and executives do not give money to politicians or parties out of an altruistic support of the principles of democracy," says Tyson Slocum, director of Public Citizen's Energy Program. "They are savvy investors expecting a return on their investments. Politicians routinely deliver on campaign contributions that are provided to them . . . [by] giving goodies to the industry." And the size of those contributions matters.

To be sure, the slew of organizations that oppose the rampant corporate power wielded in the government also have lobbyists, and they give money to their causes, as well. It's just a lot less. In comparison, environmental groups and alternative-energy production and supply companies, which didn't see similar benefits come out of the Republican Congress's legislation, have made paltry contributions. The Sierra Club, League of Conservation Voters, and the Nature Conservancy, which often push for policies counter to those favoring big oil, have given nearly eleven times less than the oil industry since 2001. The disparity is simply a financial reality for these smaller competing interests. Exxon Mobil, for example, reported the largest annual profit on record for a U.S. corporation in 2006, bringing in $39.5 billion. By contrast, the nonprofit Sierra Club Foundation—which funds organizations in addition to the Sierra Club—reported income in 2006 of just $29 million.

By paying so much special attention to big oil, our elected representatives produce policies that don't reflect the interest of the public, which wants affordable, reliable, clean sources of energy. A 2006 survey by the Pew Research Center found a majority of Americans across the political spectrum want an energy policy that emphasizes renewable and alternative sources of energy. "Energy companies have a right to have a say in energy policy. Do they have a right to dictate energy policy, to be the only people at the table? Absolutely not. That was the main problem with the Cheney task force—[the industry] was the only one at the table," says Public Citizen's Tyson Slocum.[5]

THE FLIP SIDE OF THE COIN: BIG LABOR

But it's not just the Republicans who are beholden to a major industry like big oil. The Democrats are similarly beholden to big labor. Labor provides a disproportionate amount of political contributions to the Democratic Party, and has recently set up organizations to allow them to influence not only their own members but also the broader electorate. Their levels of independent expenditures rival those of conservative groups.

Under President Obama, the National Labor Relations Board has very publicly worked to block Boeing from setting up a plant in South Carolina—a nonunion state—by instead encouraging them to operate in unionized Washington.

The Obama administration has worked to make union organizing easier to accomplish. In the health-care reform bill, they worked to exempt high-dollar union plans from any limitations. Though for labor, these concessions were not enough.

The head of the AFL-CIO Richard Trumka has made it very clear that labor is prepared to go its own way in the 2012 election. President Obama responded shortly thereafter that he is both solicitous of labor, supportive of collective bargaining for public employees, and prepared to maintain the close ties between the movement and the Democratic Party that have traditionally existed.

One thing is for sure: between now and election day 2012, it is unlikely that there will be much daylight between a labor movement that, although losing members daily, remains able to raise large sums of money and a president and Democratic Party that desperately need their support to remain competitive in the 2012 election.

LOBBYISTS: THE WAY IT USED TO BE AND THE WAY IT IS NOW

Not long ago, Americans had a much different image of lobbyists. Call it a necessary uneasiness. Compared with today, lobbyists were less powerful, less nefarious, less corrupt, and most importantly, less visible. They were more like bothersome gnats that politicians with a modicum of integrity could just swat away from their outer offices or relegate to talking to staff aides, who were perhaps rewarded with a dinner in a pricey Georgetown bistro. They didn't yet wield the clout to instantly stall a bill in committee that threatened their client's bottom line. They were more like gentle persuaders, not yet fixated in voters' minds as part of "what's wrong with government" or a major cause of gridlock on Capitol Hill.

That was a kinder, gentler era, when politics was about civil discourse and disagreement, and not the blood sport it is today. Now a lobbyist can significantly influence the passing of a piece of legislation (or the derailing of it) as he rakes in millions of public dollars for a client. It's not just about the rights of gun owners and senior citizens (think the NRA and AARP). Now, every trade association, every public-interest group, every group of any kind—foreign and domestic—representing any cause you can think of has a lobby. When last counted in 2008, there were more than 7,600 trade associations in the United States, and around 2,000 were headquartered in Washington. That's a lot of special interests.

If the press is the Fourth Estate, then lobbying has become what we might think of as the Fifth Estate. And this Estate—encompassing the most important industries and corporate entities—is located on K Street, a canyon of nondescript office buildings just a few blocks north of the White House. In Washington, insiders speak of K Street as the epicenter of lobbying the way the financial industry talks about Wall Street as the primary theater of finance.

In 2010, the amount spent on lobbying efforts in the United States totaled about $3.5 billion, two and a half times more than the $1.44 billion just ten years earlier. What explains such massive growth? "Congressional staffs are extremely busy, and often there aren't enough staffers to do everything," says a lobbyist who specializes in representing cities. "Our job is to facilitate communication, package priorities, and make sure that requests for funding meet deadlines and get included in legislation." Others who defend their profession point out that the junkets taken by our public servants actually save the taxpayers money. They claim that privately funded travel, both overseas and domestic, enables members of Congress and senior staff members to gain knowledge and experience without spending taxpayers' money. When candidates running for public office burnish their foreign policy credentials with a speech beginning, "I've been to Iraq and Afghanistan. . . .," you can be sure that they didn't pay their own way. Some company or trade group rolled out the Gulfstream VI.

Whatever the explanation for the influx of money from outside interest groups, the amount spent on lobbying has steadily increased for more than a decade and shows few signs of slowing. "The federal government is handing out billions of dollars by the day," says former Center for Responsive Politics executive director Sheila Krumholz, "and that translates into job security for lobbyists who can help companies and industries get a piece of the payout." Perhaps the ultimate justification for lobbying comes from those who are masters of engineering pork-barrel legislation. If they are really good at what they do, they ensure that the congress member or senator whose industries are benefiting can keep a straight face and rail against earmarks on C-SPAN while ensuring that their district gets its fair share.

Lobbyists will continue to claim that contributions do not buy votes, but few will dispute the notion that money does indeed provide "access." Today's lobbyists are far from the turn-of-the-century caricatures of shady characters who stuffed hundred-dollar bills into the pockets of lawmakers. Today, the best lobbyists are the ones who understand the subtleties of persuasion. That art is one that lobbyists have perfected especially over the last generation, a period in which the American people were slowly awakened to the power lobbyists had begun to wield in Washington.

MILESTONES OF THE MODERN LOBBYING ERA

In 1978, undercover FBI agents along with convicted swindler Melvin Weinberg began posing as American representatives of wealthy Arab businessmen eager to make sizable investments in the United States. Under the auspices of a company called "Abdul Enterprises Limited" (from which the name ABSCAM derived), they let it be known to public officials that their clients were willing to pay heavily for influence and favors, especially visas from the Immigration and Naturalization Service (INS). The first politician snared in the sting was U.S. congressman Michael J. Myers, who was videotaped accepting a $50,000 bribe.

As ABSCAM spread its tentacles and word of easy money circulated, more politicians fell prey, including U.S. Senator Harrison A. Williams Jr. and five other congressmen. Geographical considerations and the sheer number of defendants necessitated several trials. The first began in Brooklyn, New York, on August 11, 1980, before Judge George C. Pratt.

In opening his case, Thomas P. Puccio, who would handle most of the ABSCAM prosecutions, brought to the stand Anthony Amoroso, a federal undercover agent. Amoroso and Weinberg had run the sting in a New York hotel room. The videotaped transaction was played to the packed, hushed courtroom. Amoroso handed Myers an envelope containing $50,000, saying, "Spend it well." Myers, who sat next to fellow defendant Mayor Angelo J. Errichetti of Camden, New Jersey, boasted of the influence he wielded in Congress. "As leader of the Philadelphia delegation, I control four and then six when we go into state matters . . . I'm going to tell you something real simple and short—money talks in this business . . . and it works the same way down in Washington."[6]

One of the most startling examples of lobbyist influence is the story of the "Keating Five." In 1983, Charles Keating, a financier and real-estate developer, bought Lincoln Savings and Loan Bank, a conservatively run, California-based bank. At the time it was purchased,

Lincoln was experiencing what could at best be called moderate growth and had no more than $1.1 billion in assets. By 1989, under Keating's management, profits began to increase and the bank's assets were valued at over $5.5 billion.

Keating was able to so dramatically improve Lincoln's fortunes in so short a time by encouraging risky, aggressive investment strategies and amassing large amounts of debt. In 1987, the Federal Home Loan Bank in San Francisco—responsible for regulating, among other things, savings and loan banks like Lincoln—recommended that the federal government take over Lincoln and curb its hazardous practices. Keating deferred.

Later that year, Edwin J. Gray, then head of the Federal Home Loan Bank Board, was summoned to a meeting, arranged by Senator Donald Riegle Jr. (D-Mich.), in the offices of Senator Dennis DeConcini (D-Ariz.). At that meeting, Gray testified that he was asked, "on behalf of their friend and contributor" at Lincoln, to rescind regulations on one of Lincoln's risky practices, direct investment.[7] A week later, at a meeting arranged by Mr. Gray, five senators found themselves sitting across from San Francisco Federal Home Loan Bank officials who wanted to shut Lincoln down. The senators succeeded in keeping Lincoln open temporarily; two years later, Lincoln went bankrupt, and along with it American Continental Corporation, its parent company.

Aside from Senators DeConcini and Riegle, three other senators were present at either one or both of the meetings: Senator Alan Cranston (D-Calif.), Senator John McCain (R-Ariz.), and Senator John Glenn (D-Ohio).

Senator DeConcini and Senator Riegle received $48,100 and $76,100, respectively, from Keating for their 1988 reelection campaigns. After the scandal broke, however, they both pledged to return the money. Arizona's other senator, John McCain, had, over the years, received $112,000 from Keating for various campaigns. McCain also, on occasion, flew on Keating's private jet to Keating's private spa in the Bahamas. Senator Cranston received $39,000 from Keating for his 1986 reelection campaign. In 1984 Senator Glenn tried to capture his party's presidential nomination, and Keating donated $34,000 to his ill-fated White House run.[8]

In the end, thousands of investors lost their savings, the American taxpayer had to foot a $3 billion bailout, and Keating was convicted on seventy-three counts of fraud and served four years in prison.[9] Only

Senator Cranston was officially reprimanded by an ethics commission for acting improperly. Senators Reigle and DeConcini were criticized for acting improperly, and Senators Glenn and McCain were cleared of any wrongdoing but criticized for poor judgment.[10]

In the mid-1990s, Tom DeLay and his colleagues in the Republican leadership, notably Senators Rick Santorum and Grover Norquist— a lobbyist who founded Americans for Tax Reform at the behest of President Reagan—struck a bargain with Washington's lobbyists that was both brazen and remarkably creative: if the lobbyists would help raise hundreds of millions of dollars to support Republicans and help preserve their majority in Congress, DeLay would invite them into the legislative process and allow them to propose entire bills and suggest changes to legislation proposed by others. The partnership helped the Republicans increase contributions received from $358 million to $782 million between the election years of 1994 and 2004.

DeLay's involvement with the lobbying industry included a pointed effort on the part of the Republican Party to parlay the congressional majority into dominance; they dubbed this the K Street Project. The K Street operatives were less than subtle. They pored over lists of corporations that made substantial political contributions. Firms that had Democrats in positions of authority, DeLay suggested, would not be granted access to majority party members. "K Street used to be a barrier to sweeping change in Washington," wrote Nicholas Confessore in *Washington Monthly*. "The GOP has turned it into a weapon."

POINT OF NO RETURN: THE ABRAMOFF SCANDAL

When did the American public *really* sour on lobbyists? It's hard to pinpoint a specific time, but the Jack Abramoff scandal was likely the nadir. Gallup conducts an annual poll on the publically perceived honesty and ethical standards of people in various professions. In 2007 the firm found a new entry at the bottom of the list. For the first time, Gallup asked the public to rank the moral standards of lobbyists, and only 5 percent of respondents described their ethics as "very high" or "high." Lobbyists, car salesmen, and advertising practitioners were the lowest-rated professions. (Ratings of congress members were the worst Gallup has ever recorded, and I'm certain lobbyists haven't helped their cause.) A more recent Gallup poll revealed that when it comes to groups and institutions that the public thinks has *too much power*, lobbyists top the list—ahead of major corporations, banks, the federal government, and labor unions.

These surveys showed how far the image of lobbyists had fallen among ordinary Americans, and it's no coincidence that they were conducted in the aftermath of the Abramoff scandals.

Washington "super lobbyist" Jack Abramoff engaged in a number of schemes to extract money from clients, sometimes working directly against their interests so that they felt the need to pay huge retainers for dramatic change. In 2002, then Texas attorney general John Cornyn was convinced that Speaking Rock Casino, owned by the Tigua tribe, was in violation of a federal statue and tried to have it shut down. Abramoff, who already represented a myriad of several other Indian tribes, decided that instead of trying to represent the Tigua and to try to get the statute amended by Congress before the casino was closed, it would be more profitable to first have the casino shut down.

Abramoff, along with one of his top aides, Michael Scanlon, paid conservative activist and gambling foe Ralph Reed to drum up public support for closing the casino, which it was eventually closed in February of 2002. Ten days later, Abramoff emailed a Tigua representative and told him that a "gross indignity" was "perpetuated by the Texas state authorities" and that he wished to help the Tigua rectify it. Abramoff then boasted that he had "a couple of senators willing to ram this through." The Tigua ended up paying $4.2 million to Abramoff to lobby for the changes, which never ended up making it into the legislation.[11]

Abramoff enjoyed a close relationship with House Majority Whip Tom DeLay (R-Tex.). In 2000, DeLay flew with his wife, two aides, and two lobbyists to the United Kingdom to meet with conservative lawmakers and play golf at St. Andrews. Although the trip was officially planned and paid for by the National Center for Public Policy Research, Abramoff provided the real financing. Abramoff suggested the trip and arranged for it to be partially paid for; the day DeLay left for the UK, two $25,000 checks arrived at the National Center. One was from the Mississippi band of the Choctaw, the other from eLottery—both Abaramoff's clients. Later that year, DeLay helped kill the Internet Gambling Prohibition Act, opposed by both the Choctaw and eLottery.

That same year a DeLay aide named Tony Rudy, who went with DeLay on the UK trip, left the Whip's office to work for Abramoff. At least one other DeLay aide was taken, via private jet, to the 2001 Super Bowl in Tampa by Abramoff. The aide was then taken to one of Abramoff's casino boats anchored off Tampa. The trip was never disclosed. When news of this broke, DeLay spokesperson Dan Allen explained, "The staffer went down to participate in a National Republican Congressional Committee party, so it was considered political travel," which does not have to be disclosed.[12]

U.S. Family Network was a public advocacy group in the mid-1990s with close ties to DeLay. In 2005, long after the group became defunct, it was revealed that the group received almost all of its founding from Abramoff clients.

Two associates of Edwin A. Buckham, founder of U.S. Family Network and previous DeLay chief of staff, claim that Buckham told them that Russian oil and gas executives gave the group $1 million in 2000 to sway DeLay's vote on legislation concerning an IMF bailout for Russia. In fact, Abramoff represented two Russian oil and gas companies at that time.

Similarly, textile companies from the Mariana Islands donated $500,000 to the Network. Those very same companies also hired Abramoff to lobby DeLay so that he would publicly oppose legislation that would have increased labor costs. DeLay came out against the legislation. Lastly, it has come out that DeLay's wife Christie was hired by U.S. Family Network to supply them with the list of lawmakers' favorite charities. For three years, she was paid $3,200 a month for this.[13]

The abuse of power in the Abramoff affair was a shock to even the most cynical observers of the quid pro quo relationship between business and government. Abramoff induced four Indian tribes flush with gambling profits into paying his firm huge fees to protect their interests—which Abramoff pledged to do by exploiting his connections with the White House and conservative Republicans in Congress. He did practically nothing and pocketed an estimated $85 million. In one case, he and his partners secretly orchestrated lobbying against their own clients in order to force them to pay for lobbying services.

EFFORTS AT REFORM—AND THEIR LIMITATIONS

"Congress has always had, and always will have, lobbyists and lobbying," said Robert Byrd, the Democratic senator from West Virginia in a speech in 1987. "We could not adequately consider our workload without them . . . At the same time, the history of the institution demonstrates the need for eternal vigilance to ensure that lobbyists do not abuse their role."

While recent reforms and regulations have stalled the growth of the *number* of lobbyists on Capital Hill, the *amount* spent on lobbying efforts continues to increase. This phenomenon has left some claiming that many are using loopholes to avoid declaring themselves as lobbyists and becoming subject to regulations. To cut back on this type of behavior, Congress has enacted a series of reforms, including the Lobbying Disclosure Act of 1995, the Legislative Transparency and Accountability Act of 2006, and the Honest Leadership and Open Government Act of 2007.

The last of these acts was the strictest and is what governs Washington lobbyists today. The bill, among other sanctions, requires lawmakers to disclose any earmarks before introducing them into legislation. In addition, they identify any lobbyist who raises over $15,000 in a six-month period by bundling campaign donations from a group of people. Members can only accept funds that are designated for "official duties" and "not create the appearance that they are using their public office for private gain."

Another stipulation that received widespread attention is that "former Senators and high-ranking executive branch officials will have to wait two years before lobbying Congress; ex-House members will have to wait one year." This measure is meant to minimize the practice of revolving door lobbying, which uses the connections individuals have in order to gain leverage for their efforts. While still an Illinois senator, Barack Obama called the legislation "the most sweeping ethics reform since Watergate."

Will staving off free agency for a short period of time make a difference? Perhaps. The immediate effect was positive. While the total number of lobbyists rose significantly between 1998 and 2007 (from 10,405 to 14,874), it seems likely that the law Obama was referring to led to a significant drop—around 28 percent—in registered lobbyists (in 2011 there were 10,812).

Private groups spent $6.5 million on travel for the 111th Congress during 2009 and 2010, less than half the $15 million spent in 2005 to 2006. The increased disclosure efforts make lobbyists more accountable for their actions. They cannot (directly, anyway) line the pockets of legislators—and therefore it requires more money per lobbyist to influence legislation.

Our political representatives are finding it more uncomfortable than ever to accept any benefit that ultimately could be questionable, if not directly unethical. Their staffs think twice before accepting a junket that could end up costing them votes in an upcoming reelection campaign. In some cases, it's easier just to say no than worry about the video of a stroll on the beach in a foreign resort popping up on YouTube in a matter of hours.

But for all of that, the total amount of money spent has increased dramatically. One explanation for this is that the rules apply only to those who spend at least 20 percent of their time lobbying. This loophole exempts a vast army of public relations, grassroots, and strategic consultants who have redefined the industry. There is even "grass tops" lobbying that provides communications from prominent individuals, community leaders, and key decision makers. (The emphasis of grassroots lobbying tends to be of quantity; grass tops, of quality.) Grassroots and grass tops lobbying have also been called "stealth lobbying."

A lobbyist can navigate the corridors of Washington power wearing two or three different hats. Here's a telling example of how this works. Rick Berman is one of the more visible influence peddlers, mainly for the food industry, and he has a number of well-heeled corporate clients. In his day job, he's a principal in Berman and Company, a public relations company that does the work of promoting new products launched in supermarkets and groceries. He also heads a nonprofit group called the Center for Consumer Freedom. According to the organization's website, it was founded to defend "the right of adults and parents to choose . . . what they eat and drink, . . . and how they enjoy themselves." (The group was founded mainly as an antidote to the increasingly vocal nutrition outfit, the Center for Science in the Public Interest.)

Financial support for the Center for Consumer Freedom comes from companies like Philip Morris, Cargill Processed Meat Products, Anheuser-Busch, Coca-Cola, Tyson Foods, Perdue Farms, Outback Steakhouse, Wendy's, and White Castle—and this is far from a complete list. Because Berman draws a nominal salary from this "foundation," he's able to set up what is nothing less than a lobbying arm for the food industry. So now, when you see an ad that basically argues that junk food isn't that bad for you or that calorie counts on restaurant menus are unnecessary, you know who's probably paying for it.

We have to remind ourselves that lobbying interests are represented on both sides of the aisle, and on both sides of an issue. But lobbying is primarily about money and the party in power. True grass roots and nonprofits—public interest groups that do not receive large inflows of money—must rely primarily on public relations and press visibility.

While legal loopholes allow well-funded corporate lobbyists to side-step regulations, Center for Responsive Politics president Larry Ottinger worries that that if all lobbyists were required to register, it would have "a devastating impact" on nonprofit and public-interest lobbyists, who have been the "collateral damage" of new executive-branch restrictions.

It is a difficult issue to resolve. Clearly, in the interests of fairness, more specific definitions of lobbying should be created to ensure that those groups working on behalf of the public interest without funding still have a voice in the national discourse. And we need to tighten the rules so that the activities of the Rick Bermans of the world do not spiral out of control; failing that, they could at least become more transparent.

THERE'S MORE THAN ONE WAY TO LOBBY

The public blowback caused by lobbyists peddling special interests over the past few years has inspired more stealth attempts in an effort to cover the tracks laid down by big money as well as those organizations without deep pockets. Phony movements often pop up days before a critical vote on a major bill. "Astroturf lobbying," so named because of its artificial nature, has been a tool for some time. Usually it means that a campaign is brewing on the web or via direct mail and that there's a call to get people to write their congress members because "we've had enough" of one thing or another. Thousands of identical postcards go through the Capitol Hill mailroom or hundreds of calls will flood the phone lines on the same day.

Many of today's efforts come from long-running grassroots movements that create longer-lasting pressure on legislators from their constituents. Is this a form of "lobbying"? Of course. But no regulations hinder this scattershot approach, and it may help to account for the discrepancy between rising spending and the shrinking number of lobbyists.

In addition to grassroots activities, those who are defined as lobbyists in the more traditional sense have also changed course to accommodate public sentiment. Grass tops lobbying is the practice of tapping local civic, business, and labor leaders to push lawmakers to support or oppose federal legislation—shutting out ordinary constituents from the process. Here is a perfect example. Richard Pinsky was a former campaign operative for Pat Robertson and Bob Dole. While Pinsky's past government contacts do not grant him direct access—especially with today's major players—he has found a clever way around this obstacle. He uses secondary connections to reach decision makers almost subconsciously. For example, the Dewey Square Group, a public relations and political consulting firm, hired Pinsky to gather support for fast-track legislation. He called an old ally, former Republican governor Bob Martinez. Martinez, in turn, discussed the issue with fellow Tampa resident and Democratic congressman Jim Davis. Davis, an impressionable freshman, is now a firm "yes" on the free-trade measure. Although Davis's spokesman insists the Martinez talk didn't affect the congressman's vote, the little chat certainly didn't hurt.

Then there are what I call the "trench lobbyists"—those foot soldiers without name recognition—that can also have a significant impact on legislation. These are people, often high-level congressional aides, who do not appear in the press very often. More importantly, they understand the back channels of Washington and how they interconnect. Again, they're not subject to the revolving-door restrictions.

For instance, a senior Republican senate aide recently joined a prominent GOP-leaning lobbying firm. BGR Government Affairs hired Erskine Wells, the former deputy chief of staff to Senator Roger Wicker (a Mississippi Republican). Wells is now a vice president at the firm, owned by BGR Group and formerly known as Barbour Griffith & Rogers. (While working in the Senate, Wells had a top-secret security clearance and dealt with the Defense Department, the State Department, and intelligence and homeland security issues. "It continues to give me the opportunity to work on a wide range of issues, like I did on Capitol Hill," Wells said of his new job. "I will be on the other side of the table, but I think I have some knowledge and experience that I can share with the firm's clients." That's certainly true.)

BEHIND-THE-SCENES PLAYERS

Examples abound about how behind-the-scenes players are able to influence the legislative process.

To take one example, the story of a Canadian pipeline project provides a primer on how this works. There is a plan to build a $7 billion extension that will complete a long route from the Alberta oil fields to the Gulf of Mexico. The project, known as the Keystone XL pipeline, has not been without controversy; environmental groups, eager to scuttle it, have held protests with guest celebrities outside the White House. The company that will build it, TransCanada, already has spent close to $2 million on lobbying since 2009. Paul Elliott, the principal lobbyist for TransCanada, was national deputy director of Hillary Clinton's campaign when she ran for president in 2008.

According to OpenSecrets.org, TransCanada has engaged substantial political firepower. It also has paid outside firms Bryan Cave LLP, McKenna Long & Aldridge, and Van Ness Feldman to lobby on its behalf. These firms have well-connected personnel. Jeff Berman of Bryan Cave was the national delegate director for Obama's 2008 presidential campaign. Berman's colleague, Brandon Pollak, worked as deputy regional political director on John Kerry's unsuccessful 2004 presidential run. Another colleague, David Russell, was chief of staff to the late Ted Stevens, a long-serving and influential Republican senator. Bandele McQueen at McKenna was chief of staff to the late Democratic congresswoman Juanita Millender-McDonald. McQueen also put in a stint at the Chicago mayor's office, the original hub for many of Obama's top aides, including former senior adviser David Axelrod.

CONCLUSION

The bottom line is this: without radical change, we will see more abuses, more shocking scandals, and more calls for ethics reforms in the future. Perhaps some reforms will be enacted and even do some good on the margins. But the one constant will be that average citizens will continue to have less and less impact on the way their lawmakers conduct public policy. Of this I am certain.

12

REDISTRICTING, RACE, AND THE POLITICAL CLASS

Twenty thousand is nothing to keep your seat. I spend $2 million (campaigning) every year. If my colleagues are smart, they'll pay their $20,000, and [our consultant] will draw the district they can win in. Those who have refused to pay? God help them.

—Congresswoman Loretta Sanchez (D-Calif.)[1]

Redistricting potentially pits brother against brother and sister versus sister. It's the ultimate political cage match and makes you run against an adversary who you've worked with for years. It's three-dimensional chess.

—GOP fund-raiser and former congressman Bill Paxon[2]

In May 2003, Federal Aviation Administration (FAA) employees fielded a call from a senior aide to House Majority Whip Tom DeLay of Texas, asking the agency to track the location of a private aircraft with tail number N711RD. It belonged to Texas House Speaker Pete Laney, a Democrat, who was using the plane to join other Democrats across the state border in Ardmore, Oklahoma. The group of Democrats, dubbed the Killer D's in the media, had fled the state to avoid voting on a new redistricting plan being pushed by DeLay and his Republican allies—a plan that would radically alter voting districts to Republican advantage and effectively end Democratic dominance in Texas.[3]

DeLay wasn't called "The Hammer" for nothing. States are permitted to redraw their congressional districts every ten years in line with the census, but here was DeLay trying to revamp a state map that had been approved by a federal court just two years earlier. His new map targeted several incumbent Democrats, forcing them to compete in newly minted Republican districts, which would surely cost them their seats. Determined to find Laney, DeLay had no hesitation in using a federal agency to track his adversary down. Eventually thirteen FAA employees in three state offices—Washington, Texas, and Oklahoma—were drawn into the search. Several said later that they assumed there was a safety issue with the plane; others conceded that they were aware of the political dispute in Texas. Not stopping there, DeLay also directed his staffers to enlist the support of both the Department of Homeland Security and the Justice Department, though neither acted on his request.[4]

For all of that, a reporter from the *Dallas Morning News* first spotted Laney. Eventually he and the Killer D's had to face reality and return to Texas, where votes in both the state House and Senate ratified the DeLay-sponsored redistricting plan. The following year, in the 2004 elections, the Texas delegation in the U.S. House of Representatives went from seventeen to fifteen Democrat to twenty-one to eleven Republican. Tom DeLay had won a smashing victory in one of the most audacious—and notorious—redistricting battles in recent history. (A Supreme Court decision would eventually uphold it, while also affirming states' rights to gerrymander more frequently.)

DeLay took it to an extreme, but the fact is, politicians will do most anything to prevail in redistricting battles. Partisan tensions, already at a boiling point in Washington, can explode when the maps come out. But the corrosive effect of redistricting also creates intense battles *within* the parties, since newly drawn district lines often force longtime incumbents out of comfortable seats and into struggles for survival against their colleagues. In the wake of the 2010 census, it's happening again.

"F___ you. Thanks for your help." That's what Missouri congressman Russ Carnahan reportedly told his fellow House Democrat, Lacy Clay, on the House floor in September 2011. Carnahan was infuriated by the refusal of Clay and Emanuel Cleaver (chairman of the Congressional

Black Caucus) to join him in opposition to a GOP redistricting plan for their state. The new plan would force Carnahan either to run a primary race against Clay, a black Democrat, in a heavily black district or to take on a Republican in a GOP-leaning district.[5]

Why does redistricting arouse such passions? Because next to money, it's perhaps the most essential tool of the political class, ensuring their hold on power—just so long as they can control the process. For the last generation or so, the political class of both parties has mastered the art of redistricting—or gerrymandering, in the less flattering term—and they have used it to expand and consolidate power. Along the way, they have further corrupted our political system and made a mockery of representative government.

The Constitution mandates that district lines in each state be redrawn every ten years to account for population shifts. It didn't take long for abuses to show up: the term *gerrymander* dates back to the nation's early days. It refers to Massachusetts governor Elbridge Gerry, a signer of the Declaration of the Independence, who became adept at drawing new districts to his party's advantage. Redistricting today goes far beyond what Gerry and others could contrive. Recreating congressional districts based not on geography but on race or demography, both parties have manufactured homogeneous districts where most voters are either registered Democrats or registered Republicans. In the process, the parties have created scores of "safe" seats and reduced competitive races for the House of Representatives to an ever-dwindling number. Between 2000 and 2008, the number of "close-call" elections—those determined by a 51–49 percent margin or narrower—declined by 37 percent compared with the period between 1990 and 1998.[6]

Envisioned by the Founding Fathers as the most democratic organ of government, the House of Representatives has instead become a bastion of entrenched privilege. Only a relative handful of the 435 House seats— perhaps as few as 45, according to the Cook Political Report—are true toss-ups. The rest are highly predictable contests, thanks to districts in which either Democrats or Republicans have been handed a significant advantage by their states' legislatures. Even in 2006, when Democrats took back the House and the Senate, only fifty-eight House races were decided by a margin of ten percentage points or less. In 2008, the year when change swept through the nation, only sixty-six House and eight Senate races were truly competitive. The data clearly show that most congressional races are blowouts. In House races, incumbents won 95 percent of the elections, and in openly contested House seats, the candidate that raised the most money won 84 percent of the time.

As I've written elsewhere, redistricting has reversed the core process at the heart of democracy: that is, instead of voters picking their candidates and representatives, the political parties pick their own voters. They successfully render the general election a fait accompli, with the only real voter input coming in low-turnout party primaries (in 2010, primary voter turnout was under 20 percent as a percentage of the voting-age population).[7] And primaries are often restricted to registered party members, thus excluding Independents and moderates.

All of this would be bad enough, but redistricting has also increased polarization, both in Washington and among mainstream Americans. By remaking districts so that they are uniformly aligned with a political persuasion—or uniformly composed of a specific racial group—redistricting has all but eliminated the need, at least on the congressional level, to build broader coalitions. Putting whites with whites, blacks with blacks, and segmenting an electorate by regional, neighborhood, and cultural characteristics has driven Americans—the most diverse electorate in the history of the world—increasingly into self-contained voting blocs. This segmenting only furthers the sense of division among disparate groups in our country, and it encourages politicians to "play to the base" at the expense of the center.

Look no further than today's House GOP caucus, in which 234 of 240 members have signed the Taxpayer Protection Pledge from Americans for Tax Reform, committing them to oppose all tax increases, no matter what.[8] All eight Republican presidential candidates at the Fox News Iowa debate in September 2011 said that they would refuse to sign a bill that cut *ten* dollars in spending for each *one* dollar raised in taxes.

Redistricting has become an essential tool of the political class: it protects politicians' fiefdoms, it blunts the power of voters, and it sows the partisan divisions that keep the electorate polarized—and politicians in their jobs.

THE TOOLS OF THE TRADE

The redistricting revolution wouldn't have been possible without remarkable improvements in computer technology. Consultants, working with state lawmakers, have used sophisticated tools to identify the preferences of voters into ever-smaller and more precise segments. District drawing has become such an art that legislators are essentially able to select the voters they wish to represent. Some districts have become so homogeneous that even the pretense of competition is gone: in 2004 alone, there were thirty-four uncontested House elections.[9]

With so many districts essentially rigged, it's much tougher for voters to hold their representatives accountable. In California, for example, *not one* of the 153 seats in the state legislature changed hands in 2004. (The same is true of California's representatives in the U.S. House that year.) No House incumbent in Tennessee lost reelection between 1980 and 2004.[10] Few Americans are aware of just how sophisticated this technology has become or how adept both parties have become at deploying it.

I speak from close experience here, because, together with my former partner Mark Penn, I developed the practice of "microtargeting" voters by their demographics and "psychographics." By identifying a person's economic, cultural, and social status, often summarized by their ZIP code, we developed techniques to target voters in a way never before possible. Where people send their children to school, where they shop and what they buy, and any number of additional datasets offer insight into how people in certain areas vote—and why. Using that information enables a politician to send a particular message to particular voters. Our pioneering use of microtargeting revolutionized modern campaigning. By now, political consultants can identify the political preferences of voters on a *block-by-block* basis.

It should be noted, with a modicum of optimism, that redistricting is strictly a phenomenon affecting the House, not the Senate. Because senators compete for votes statewide, there are no districts to gerrymander, which means their races are impervious to the partisan manipulations that have plagued House contests. In 2000, only 10 percent of House races were decided by ten points or less, while 29 percent of Senate races were decided by the same margin. In 2008, one-quarter of House candidates faced no opposition *at all*. Because of gerrymandering, it doesn't matter how unpopular Congress might become. The system is rigged to reelect incumbents to the House and maintain one-party control in most congressional districts.

HOW REDISTRICTING THWARTS DEMOCRACY

Most Americans would agree that our political system wasn't set up with the goal of protecting incumbents from democratic challenge—let alone accountability. But redistricting places both of those goods in jeopardy. At this point, many incumbents hire their own consultants to help them draw district lines that will guarantee their political futures. As a study from the Brennan Center for Justice documented:

> Many incumbents each paid a consultant at least $20,000 to have their districts custom-designed, with enough friendly voters to make it extremely likely that they would win the election. As one member of Congress [Democrat Loretta Sanchez of California] explained: "Twenty thousand is nothing to keep your seat. I spend $2 million (campaigning) every year. If my colleagues are smart, they'll pay their $20,000, and [our consultant] will draw the district they can win in. Those who have refused to pay? God help them."[11]

Whatever party holds the cards of power will usually try to isolate members of the opposition party in bizarrely shaped districts that essentially disenfranchise opposition voters and blunt their impact on the party in power. They'll often try to concentrate opposition-party voters into just a few districts. Those districts will vote overwhelmingly for their party, but they'll have little impact on state houses or the state's congressional coalition because they count for only a few representatives.

That's been the case in Texas for some time, and it didn't start with Tom DeLay or the Republicans. For both DeLay and the Texas GOP, the 2003 redistricting triumph must have been sweet payback. In the 1990s, Democrats redistricted the state so that *Republicans* were tightly concentrated into a few districts. Republicans and Democrats essentially split the vote, but Democrats held 70 percent of the seats in the state legislature because of their districting advantage. DeLay would eventually turn the tables.

Therein lies another cost of redistricting. It becomes a toxic battleground between the two parties, perpetuating political feuds while doing little good for constituents.

The two parties have shown, again and again, that they will use redistricting expansively and ruthlessly—even to the extent of intentionally endangering popular public servants. Both parties have proven adept at "poaching" opposition incumbents by redrawing the map to place them in less friendly districts—or, as in the case of Russ Carnahan of Missouri, by placing them in districts where they would have to go head-to-head against another popular party member, thereby ensuring that one is eliminated in the primary. The Brennan Center's redistricting study offers an example:

> After the 2000 elections in Virginia, the Republicans who controlled the redistricting process targeted Richard Cranwell, the leader of the Democrats in the state house, who had represented his constituents for 29 years. They surgically carved his house out of the district he had represented, and drew it into the district of his 22-year colleague, Democrat Chip Woodrum. Woodrum's district looked like it had a tiny grasping hand reaching out to grab Cranwell's home. Rather than run against the hometown favorite in an unfamiliar district, Cranwell decided not to run for reelection.[12]

Even primary challenges can be guarded against, so long as your party's running the redistricting show. The parties have found ways to remove challengers from incumbents' districts, especially if those challengers seem like they could be trouble. That's how Barack Obama was removed from his district in 2000 after losing a primary election for Congress against Democratic incumbent Bobby Rush. Obama only won 30 percent of the vote, but he had thrown his campaign together hastily, and under the circumstances, winning nearly a third of the vote against a powerhouse like Rush was rather impressive. Might he do better next time? Never mind: "When Illinois redrew its districts . . . the block around Obama's house was carved out of the district."[13] The Democrats made sure that Rush was protected.

While not explicitly related to redistricting, the primary process itself often serves to limit voter choice. Increasingly, more states have adopted a closed-primary system, which limits voter participation to registered Republicans or Democrats only, excluding Independents. As Mark Siegel has written: "By excluding independent voters, who generally are ideological moderates, the restrictions narrowed the internal debate within both parties and accelerated the radicalization of American politics."[14] A good example of this is the fate of Utah GOP senator Bob Bennett, who, over eighteen years in the Senate, earned lifetime ratings of 84, 100, 88, and 100, respectively, from the American Conservative Union, Right to Life, Family Research Council, and the U.S.

Chamber of Commerce. But just a few deviations from conservative orthodoxy, like voting for TARP and pursuing a bipartisan health-care solution, was enough to sink him in the 2010 state primary, where hard-core conservative voters ended his Senate career.[15]

According to Siegel, about 70 percent of Democratic primaries, and twenty-five of forty-two Republican primaries, will be closed for next year's presidential election. The closed-primary system helps create what he calls "a Congress of ideologues representing a country of pragmatists who increasingly feel alienated by partisan rancor."[16]

I should note, surprising as it might seem, that redistricting has its defenders—and not just in Washington. Some, like Jamelle Bouie[17] of *The American Prospect*, have argued that redistricting improves the quality of legislative representation because it ensures that voters, now grouped into homogenous districts, get what they want from their representatives. Republicans or Democrats who represent politically diverse districts are bound to disappoint some, or all, of their constituents, whereas a Republican from a uniform Republican district, or a Democrat from a uniform Democratic district, is much more likely to satisfy voter demands. Bouie also argues that more partisan districts generate more creative policy solutions—as opposed to a mad rush to the center, in which everyone ends up sounding like one another.

I'm not persuaded by these arguments, though they're certainly creative defenses of gerrymandering. Bouie and other redistricting defenders seem to assume that everyone is a hard-core liberal or conservative; where are the districts for centrists and Independents? And no mention is made of the toxic effect of a system that encourages the election of rigid ideologues, left and right, who have little interest in solving problems in a bipartisan fashion.

One thing defenders and critics *do* agree on, however: redistricting undoubtedly contributes to ideological polarization, whether one sees that as a good thing or not.

There is one other important constituency that defends redistricting. In fact, it is the most powerful and influential constituency of all: those who argue that racially homogenous districts are necessary as a matter of racial justice and political equality. Their efforts go back to the civil rights movement and the reforms that almost all Americans embrace. Yet these same reforms have also produced some major unintended consequences that continue to shape our politics today.

RACE, REDISTRICTING, AND THE VOTING RIGHTS ACT

The Voting Rights Act, passed in 1965 at the height of the civil rights movement, has undoubtedly created unparalleled opportunities for minority representation in Congress. Unfortunately, in its nearly fifty-year history it has also devolved into yet another political tool for lawmakers to use for their own partisan advantage. Increasingly, the VRA's main function seems to be to increase polarization along ideological and racial lines—and not only between the two parties in Washington, but also between members of the electorate, whites and blacks, tensions among whom the law's original passage was intended to lessen.

I should make myself clear up front: the Voting Rights Act, as originally written, passed, and applied, was a triumph of American democracy and a desperately needed reform. It put an end to a century's worth of post–Civil War legal and electoral chicanery and intimidation in the South. Blacks were denied their voting rights through a host of measures ranging from poll taxes to "good character" requirements for voting. The VRA banned any such obstacle that made voting difficult or impossible for Americans, black or white.

The results speak for themselves: in 1964, five blacks held seats in Congress, none from the South. Today, forty-two blacks hold seats in Congress, including seventeen from the South. In just a few years, black voter registration increased in Mississippi from 6.7 percent before the Act was passed to an astonishing 59.8 percent in 1967.[18] In overcoming century-old barriers to black electoral participation, the Voting Rights Act could hardly have been more successful.

Two key sections of the Act did the work. Section 2 banned states from enacting or enforcing laws that barred Americans from voting on the basis of their race. Section 5 required that states or districts with a history of discrimination "pre-clear" changes to their voting laws with the Department of Justice. Whereas section 2 eradicated the laws that kept minorities from the polls, section 5 was designed to prevent such laws from being rewritten in another form.[19]

So far, so good, but the VRA's terms were such that it soon became susceptible to the same motives that are at work across our entire political spectrum: the desire to maximize and concentrate political power at the expense of democratic principles.

The VRA has a long history of court decisions, which have continued to the present day. That history is available elsewhere, but I'll note two key rulings: first, the 1982 Supreme Court decision in *Thornburg v. Gingles*. In that case, the court set out three criteria for minority-voter representation and equal access to polls, which became known as the "*Gingles* prongs." If the prongs were not met, then, under the terms of the VRA, the minority group in question would justifiably be grouped into a district of its own, in which it would likely elect one of its own ethnic members to Congress. The three prongs were as follows:

> [f]irst, the minority group [is] able to demonstrate that it is sufficiently large and geographically compact to constitute a majority in a single-member district . . . Second, the minority groups [is] able to show that it is politically cohesive. . . . Third, the white majority votes sufficiently as a bloc to enable it . . . usually to defeat the minority's preferred candidate.[20]

The *Gingles* decision accelerated the motive and rationale to create what came to be known as "majority-minority" districts, under the often-questionable reasoning that these voters were otherwise not being adequately represented. Many Democrats, especially black Democrats, instinctively supported the expansion of the VRA's mandate, believing that anything that increased black representation in Congress—as indeed, it has increased since 1982—would be by definition a good thing.

What they overlooked, among other things, was that this same goal served *Republican* interests: by packing blacks into all-black or mostly black districts, the Republicans heightened their chances of winning most of the other districts, now devoid, or mostly devoid, of minority voters more inclined to vote for Democrats.

Within a decade after *Gingles*, the pace of minority redistricting rapidly accelerated. Between 1990 and 1993, the number of majority-minority districts doubled. During that period, black representation in Congress increased by 50 percent, Hispanic representation increased by 38 percent, and minority representation in state legislatures increased by approximately one-fifth. These gains were most pronounced in Southern states, particularly Mississippi and Louisiana, where black representation increased by 100 percent and 60 percent, respectively. These gains represented a combination of both the original workings of the VRA and the heightened partisan maneuverings of both parties as they began redrawing districts along racial lines.[21]

The second crucial case is the Supreme Court's ruling in *Shaw v. Reno*, in 1993, because it demonstrated the growing awareness of the abuses of the VRA as a political tool. The case concerned the drawing of a 160-mile-wide district in North Carolina after the 1990 census. Democrats initially planned to draw a black congressional district in the southeastern part of the state, but they realized this would threaten one of their incumbents. So, in the now-familiar pattern, they fashioned a bizarre patch of the state—dubbed as the "snake district" by some, and "political pornography" by the *Wall Street Journal*—as a majority-minority district. But the Court struck the district down, arguing that it violated the rights of *white* voters. As Sandra Day O'Connor wrote for the majority, the district bore

> an uncomfortable resemblance to political apartheid. It reinforces the perception that members of the same racial group—regardless of their age, education, economic status, or the community in which they live—think alike, share the same political interests, and will prefer the same candidates at the polls. We have rejected such perceptions elsewhere as impermissible racial stereotypes.[22]

The Court ruled that racial-redistricting decisions had to be subjected to "strict scrutiny" to confirm that a "compelling state interest" is at stake. Few would argue with that language on its face, but by the time of *Shaw*, the racial-redistricting game had become well advanced, and little between then and now has changed. For one thing, these decisions are only made every ten years, with the Census (unless you're Tom DeLay). For another, the polarization of our politics has increased exponentially since the *Shaw* decision; both Democrats and Republicans are as motivated as ever to gerrymander in any way possible to enhance their advantages—and that motivation very much includes racial gerrymandering.

The parties have continued to draw majority-minority districts, furthering the marginalization and polarization of black voters. They did it in the last election cycle: in the historically black Mississippi Delta, the 2010 census packed more blacks into majority-black districts, decreasing the efficiency of the Democratic vote and driving black legislators away from the political center, as well as from their colleagues. As the local *Enterprise-Journal* put it astutely:

> The last time the Legislature drew new lines, Republicans and blacks struck an unspoken bargain: each would pick up seats as a result of

packing districts with one race or the other. That appears to be the direction the process is going again. That may be terrific for these two interest groups, but not so great for everyone else, as it tends to produce legislators with less of a reason to move the state forward through consensus and compromise.[23]

Racial gerrymandering has many things wrong with it in principle, but looking merely at its results, there are at least three to be concerned about: first, it's highly questionable whether majority-minority districts really end up doing blacks that much good by "increasing their representation"—they might gain a black representative, yes, but whether that adds up to a greater voice in our politics is another thing entirely. Second, and related to the first, racial gerrymandering frequently leads to greater marginalization of blacks, not enhanced political power. And third, and most ominously for our politics, racial gerrymandering has fostered polarization between whites and blacks, Republicans and Democrats, and played a leading role in the hyperpartisanship of the last two decades.

As University of South Carolina professor David Lublin has chronicled, while blacks were more represented in Congress in the 1992 and 1994 elections, their *interests* were not, because the Democratic Party ended up losing seats as a result of the redistricting mandated under *Gingles*. Packed into majority-minority districts, blacks were not available to provide crucial votes to white Democrats running in closer races in other districts. Lublin estimates that the Democrats lost nine seats in 1992 and twelve in 1994 as a result of redistricting. Those are substantial numbers of seats, and holding them in Democratic hands would have given the party a much stronger chance of achieving the policies favored by large majorities of blacks.

"There is a trade-off," as Lublin puts it, "between the symbolic and the substantive representation of black interests."[24] That's a sobering way to put it: it's almost as if, the more Democrats achieve their post-VRA goal of increasing the number of black-held seats in Congress, the fewer seats the party itself actually holds. (And what of those minority groups that don't gain seats from the Voting Rights Act? Smaller minority communities become pawns in the hands of redistricting politicians, split up at a whim, their votes diluted because they're politically expendable. A good example is in Los Angeles, where Koreatown, barely over one square mile in area, is divided into *four* city council districts and *five* state assembly districts. Koreans' needs are poorly addressed in the legislature because no politicians are substantively accountable to the Korean population.[25])

Residing increasingly in majority-minority districts, black voters become marginalized politically. While their single legislator might advocate for their interests, white members from neighboring districts have little political incentive to advance those goals, and white voters in these districts have no electoral incentive to take them on, either. Before the explosion of racial redistricting, minority voters may not have been able to point to as many black legislators, but they represented an important part of many Democrats' electoral constituencies—thus exerting influence on what representatives did in office.

So the most empirically obvious result of racial redistricting—more black seats—actually works a perverse result, weakening the political power of any "black agenda." As black Democrats increasingly become the representatives of black populations, their ability to strike deals with their counterparts decreases, as the factions simply don't have enough in common to work together.

Many legislators from majority-minority areas are also seen as legislators with racially driven agendas—even when the legislator himself is not from the racial group in question. Consider Steve Cohen, Tennessee's first Jewish congressman, who represents a district that's 60 percent black. Cohen is one of the House's most liberal members: he's a member of the Progressive Caucus, he introduced a resolution apologizing for slavery and Jim Crow, and he compared Republican criticism of President Obama's health-care law to the "Big Lie" employed by Nazi propagandist Joseph Goebbels.[26] In 2010, Cohen faced a primary challenge from former Memphis mayor Willie Herenton, the first black mayor of Memphis. Cohen won handily.

Legislators like Cohen might excel at partisan warfare, giving bracing and controversial speeches, but they're usually not so effective at crafting major resolutions or helping bring it to a vote. They rarely receive important legislative appointments,[27] and though many are long-serving, they're never considered serious contenders for higher office—usually not the Senate, certainly not the presidency either.

Finally, racial redistricting has increased, rather than lessened, racial polarization among the electorate. Today, as has been the case for two generations, blacks tend to be Democrats—and thus, a "safe" black district is a safe Democratic district. Whites, the majority to begin with and now often clustered into districts nearly "bleached" of blacks, find it easier to empower Republicans. Blacks become less important to the electoral prospects of whites; whites become almost irrelevant to the electoral prospects of blacks. The chance—let alone the need—for cooperation between the two groups' legislative representatives is greatly lessened, while the two voting populations can only view one another with increased suspicion.

The redistricting process has institutionalized this dynamic. In the Southern states particularly, VRA-driven redistricting has encouraged the two parties to heighten racial and ideological divisions in the electorate.[28] It shouldn't require a political science degree to understand that this is a woeful development, and not just for our national harmony, but also for our democracy.

Partisan redistricting is antidemocratic, self-interested, and quite simply, corrupt. When conducted specifically on the racial level, it is all of those things, and worse.

CONCLUSION

Redistricting might be *the* emblematic practice defining our governing elite. It perfectly sums up the self-interested, antidemocratic ethos at the heart of the Washington political class. Explicitly and aggressively redrawing political maps so that they serve the career interests of professional politicians—and to hell with the needs of the people—pretty well captures what so many Americans detest in our political system.

Ultimately, the abuse of redistricting represents nothing less than the *disenfranchisement of the American voter*—black voters, white voters, everyone. Through the denial of meaningful choice in elections, the redistricting revolution has thwarted democracy and accountability. Like so many other traits of the political class, redistricting has its own internal logic that only bolsters its negative effects: politicians winning elections in gerrymandered districts arrive in Washington to hear immediately the demands of political groups with narrow ideological and policy agendas. The politician, eager to keep his seat, toes their line. Thoughts of compromise are few and far between and are in a real sense beside the point.

In my concluding chapter, I'll offer solutions that might break the stranglehold of the political class in Washington. When it comes to redistricting, the fundamental solution is fairly simple: the power to redraw districts must be taken away from legislators. Nothing short of that can possibly begin to reverse the violence that Democrats and Republicans have worked on the American political map.

CONCLUSION

Reform or Fail

Finally our political system has become paralyzed by partisanship to a degree that has many citizens, and investors, depressed and wondering whether we are capable anymore of collective action.

—Thomas Friedman, *New York Times,*
September 10, 2011[1]

I've been inundated with messages from people I've never met. They are all sharing their stories that have one common theme: "We don't feel represented, and we don't recognize the country."

—Howard Schultz, CEO, Starbucks[2]

Since I began writing this book, the main argument that I wished to make has only become more compelling. When I began, I thought that it had become fairly clear, over the last several years, that the political class has been systematically dividing America—isolating ordinary people from decision making and heightening public anger and distrust of government. I saw this principally as a political crisis, albeit a serious, emerging one. I didn't anticipate that by the summer of 2011, what I had seen as an important argument would become a compelling—indeed, *the* compelling—national issue.

The divide between the political class and mainstream Americans, which Standard & Poor's aptly described in its announcement of its downgrading of the United States' credit rating; the anger that the debt-ceiling negotiations produced; and the concomitant financial crisis that was created both on Wall Street and on Main Street: all would become a central topic of conversation from the boardrooms of high finance to the bedrooms of middle America. Undergirding them all was a common theme. Put directly: the American people now understand far better than their leaders do that the U.S. political system has lost so much public confidence as to be unsustainable in its present form.

To be sure, elites in Washington and in the media almost certainly will regard this argument as overblown and exaggerated. It has always been the case in times of crisis, whether in the United States or around the world, that those with vested interests in the system are most reluctant to recognize the unraveling of the system. But that being said, now not only S&P but also Wall Street senior executives, and leading politicians on both sides of the aisle, but, most of all, ordinary Americans recognize that our democratic system is no longer working. Polarization and partisan division are keeping America from maintaining its competitive position in the world. Our global stature and our democracy are at risk.

In an interconnected world, what America does has implications, both for our financial situation and for our reputation. When people from around the world focused on our debt-ceiling debacle in summer 2011, they saw it as more than just a political logjam; they also recognized that there was a mounting crisis both in the United States and around the world. Of course, the events of summer 2011 were not entirely manufactured here at home. A significant international component was also at work, involving European sovereign debt, the stability of the banking system, and the ability of the European Union to find the funds to bail out Greece and stabilize the rest of the continent. But America—still the central focus for most financial and political elites around the world—became a laughingstock. Listening to the views of friends and colleagues around the world, I saw clearly that President Obama, who had inspired such hope and confidence on assuming the presidency in 2009, had come to be viewed as another representative of a failing American political system.

Blame for this systemic failure surely can be equally accorded to both major political parties. What, then, is to be done? I'm among those who believe that we need systematic, fundamental change. But I'm not a legislator, so allow me to sketch broadly here some things we need to address as soon as possible. The specifics—assuming they could ever be agreed upon—will be for others to formulate and implement.

If this book shows anything, it's that we need campaign-finance reform. I say this not because the Supreme Court's 2010 *Citizens United* decision was necessarily wrongly decided on legal merits, although certainly over the last few years that decision has been the main exhibit in campaign-finance reformers' arguments. For me, however, the real problem (which predates that ruling) is that our political system has effectively become a casino dominated by huge financial interests—in fact, much more of a casino than a democracy that's responsive to the voices of ordinary people. Liberal and conservative special-interest groups, most notably labor on the left and business on the right, continue to wage a titanic struggle for control of the Congress and the White House. Even just since 2008, the problems have grown worse. Lobbyists have become embedded in politics to an unprecedented degree, writing legislation and, indeed, coming to dominate lawmaking by both parties. The system has become insulated (and alienated) from public opinion.

To address the increasingly outsized influence of lobbyists, we certainly need lobbying reform, with broader disclosure. We also need campaign-finance reform that effectively takes the lobbyists out of the game. At the very least, we must preclude lobbyists from making financial contributions during legislative sessions. Stricter limits on PAC contributions and independent expenditures should also be imposed. I recognize that these steps may involve legislation—or even constitutional change—that neither party might want to support. So be it. My purpose is not to wring my hands and say how terrible everything is but to make a more fundamental point: the system is not working, and it does not achieve its purposes.

Would anyone not working as a congressional staffer or for the administration seriously challenge that assertion?

We also need, as I indicated in chapter 12, redistricting reform. Yes, the Constitution mandates that congressional districts be redrawn every decade in line with the Census, but I think it's pretty safe to say that the Framers did not envision what a racket redistricting would become. I'll say it again: the power to redraw districts must be taken away from legislators. Period.

We need open primaries, too, as I've discussed. We must explore whatever might break the hold of partisanship on the democratic process. Most ordinary citizens—again, in contrast to the two major parties—would wholeheartedly support the expansion of ballot access. We should broadly open ballot access for state, local, and national offices as part of an overall political reform, making it much easier for Independent candidates to get on the ballot and reducing petition and filing requirements. Locally, we should promote more nonpartisan elections—as New York mayor Michael Bloomberg tried to do in 2003, without success.

Of course, at a higher level, we need alternatives to the two major parties. It is simply self-deluding to believe that the two-party system as presently constituted can in any way represent ordinary people. The Democratic Party is dominated by left-wing special-interest groups—environmentalists, unions, and ideological pressure groups, frequently funded by the ultrarich. Republicans are beholden either to large corporate interests, conservative special interests and pressure groups, or economic or cultural conservatives such as the Club for Growth and the Religious Right. I'm not interested in singling out one group or another, one party or another. They all plainly have their faults. The point is that the system itself is in crisis.

The American people broadly understand this. In early August 2011, when it appeared that America might go into default rather than raise its debt ceiling, Starbucks CEO Howard Schultz took out a full-page ad in the *New York Times* in the form of an open letter to his fellow citizens. He implored them to withhold political donations until lawmakers agreed upon a comprehensive debt-and-deficit package and a plan for addressing the nation's unemployment crisis. The reaction he received from people around the country was overwhelmingly supportive:

> I've been inundated with messages from people I've never met. They are all sharing their stories that have one common theme: "We don't feel represented, and we don't recognize the country." The extremes on both sides have completely overwhelmed the silent majority of the country. I am not afraid to say to both extremes: the ideology that you represent is

not the country. A person at Starbucks sent me an e-mail the other day with the Pledge of Allegiance and underlined was one word: "indivisible." The people in Washington should reread the Pledge of Allegiance and look up "indivisible."[3]

Not long after Schultz published his open letter, I conducted a poll for *Newsweek*. While some of my findings were familiar—76 percent thought the country was on the wrong track, while 70 percent felt we were better at solving problems twenty-five years ago—I wanted to learn more about what Americans thought should or could be done. I found that, for all of our problems and worries about national decline, the American spirit of self-help and independence remains very much alive. When I asked which people or institutions were most likely to solve our problems, the top choice (75 percent) was "involved citizens." In other words, people said that if the problems were to be fixed, we'd have to do it ourselves.[4]

Why shouldn't they believe that? Not only is such a spirit part of our national heritage but also Americans can see that those supposedly responsible for our national well-being aren't getting the job done. An astonishing 91 percent said that we have failed to address the nation's problems; and 78 percent said the reason why we haven't is lack of political will on the part of our elected politicians from both parties.

Fortunately, a number of movements have sprung up in recent years that seek to encourage bipartisan cooperation and/or develop political alternatives to the two major parties. No Labels is one: a group founded by a Democratic fund-raiser, Nancy Jacobson, but whose founding members include such conservative luminaries as David Frum and Mark McKinnon. The group articulates a statement of five core principles that it feels will unite America's "vital center," and from my own polling, I think it's on solid ground in making that claim:

- Americans are entitled to a government and a political system that works—driven by shared purpose and common sense.
- Americans deserve a government that makes the necessary choices to rein in runaway deficits, secure Social Security and Medicare, and put our country on a viable, sound path going forward. Americans support a government that works to spur employment and economic opportunity by encouraging free and open markets, tempered by sensible regulation.

- Americans want a government that empowers people with the tools for success—from a world-class education to affordable health care—provided that it does so in a fiscally prudent way.
- America should be free from discrimination and should embrace the principle of equal opportunity.
- America must be strong and safe, ready and able to protect itself in a world of multiple dangers and uncertainties.

Americans Elect is another promising independent group working to provide alternatives to the American voter, although in a different way. It has constituted itself as a separate political party and focused its efforts on offering voters an online presidential nominating convention in 2012, a process that would include participation in platform development. So far, Americans Elect has gained ballot status in four states—Arizona, Kansas, Nevada, and Alaska—and it's working to achieve accreditation in every state in order to get its presidential candidate on the ballot nationwide. (Nearly a third of my *Newsweek* respondents told me they would prefer a candidate not affiliated with either party.)

My point is not that any one of these emerging organizations is a panacea, although I've done polling work for Americans Elect and am personally committed to its goals and values. Rather, I'm seeking to stress the notion that our system broadly and fundamentally needs change of the type I'm describing.

Some, like those in the Tea Party, argue that the fundamental change is relatively simple: We need to return to core constitutional principles. As I've indicated earlier, I'm sympathetic to the Tea Party's frustration with Washington and the desire for a smaller, more accountable government. But the problem with advocating a return to "constitutionalism" is that it's very hard to do in a world dominated by Super PACs, super lobbyists, and the super-rich. We have a dysfunctional political system; trying to return to the understanding of a document written more than two hundred years ago, before the kind of technological changes that have altered our society and our politics, is bound to be futile.

I bow to none in my profound respect for our nation's Founders. They remain our first and greatest stroke of fortune as a nation. But consider what George Washington warned about in his Farewell Address:

Let me . . . warn you in the most solemn manner against the baneful effects of the spirit of party . . . in [governments] of the popular form, it is seen in its greatest rankness, and is truly their worst enemy. . . .

The alternate domination of one faction over another, sharpened by the spirit of revenge natural to party dissension . . . is itself a frightful despotism . . . the common and continual mischiefs of the spirit of party are sufficient to make it the interest and duty of a wise people to discourage and restrain it. It serves always to distract the public councils and enfeeble the public administration. It agitates the community with ill-founded jealousies and false alarms, kindles the animosity of one part against another.[5]

That spirit of faction—today's rampant partisanship—has overcome our political system in ways Washington and his contemporaries would not have recognized.

Reading this, you might think I'm a disillusioned member of the political class or a longtime participant in the system who has become radicalized and found religion in middle age. Not so: I still participate, work for political and business interests, offer commentary on television, and publish op-eds and articles. I do all of that, and I do it proudly. But my experience, and it's a diverse one over forty years, has convinced me that unless we fix our system, we face a bleaker, more troubled future. The dark possibilities that my friend and colleague Scott Rasmussen has written about—in one of his polls, 51 percent of Americans suggested that there could be some kind of social instability in America in the next few years—could come to reality.

It might seem that I'm focused too closely on process-related issues. But processes have real-world consequences. We have an economic crisis in this country. Combined, the unemployed, underemployed, and discouraged workers in the United States now comprise between 16 to 18 percent of the population. Another portion, perhaps between 10 to 15 percent, holds down jobs but finds it nearly impossible to pay its bills. Forty percent of home mortgages are underwater; unemployment among young people, especially among minority youth, is cresting to dangerous levels. Underpinning it all is the breakdown of governance and leadership. As Tom Friedman puts it: "We underestimate how much the toxic political rancor casts a pall over the whole economy and makes everyone hold fast to what they have."[6]

Is the American Dream dead? Millions believe so, as I've chronicled in this book. If you don't buy that premise, we might all agree, at a minimum, that the possibility for success and advancement in America is more limited than it has been than at any time since the Great Depression. For many, hope is gone, and opportunity minimal. For others, merely paying their bills is a great accomplishment. Beyond bread-and-butter economics lies the pervasive sense of worry, uncertainty, and despair that our economic difficulties inflict. A June poll I conducted for *Newsweek* found that one in three respondents felt uneasy about getting married, starting a family, or being able to buy a home. Most said that their relationships had been damaged by economic woes and/ or the stress that accompanies them.

None of this is an exaggeration; I wish it were. Read the economic data; browse a few polls on how the middle class is feeling; talk to your neighbors. The picture that emerges, while complex, is not ambiguous.

My interest is less in arguing that we must adopt Policy A or Policy B, or that we must cut taxes by a given percentage, or that we must limit this or that regulation. I want to conclude by suggesting that, unless we have a broad-based commitment to change and to a national dialogue about our systemic problems, we are going to fail.

People like me who promote centrist, bipartisan cooperation are often denigrated as being unable or unwilling to make political choices. That's wrong. Centrists have views and take positions, but our broader goal is to promote cooperation based on shared values to achieve results that can benefit the greatest number of people. At the end of the day, we *know* what will work; we know the kinds of policies, broadly speaking, that will promote the change we need in America.

If we don't recognize the threat we face from the corruption of our system, and work to change that system, we *will* fail—all of us. That much is certain.

NOTES

CHAPTER 1

1. Richard Clark, "Has the Great American Apocalypse Begun?," OpEdNews. com, April 30, 2011. Accessed October 22, 2011, at http://www.opednews.com/ articles/Has-the-Great-American-Apo-by-Richard-Clark-110430-275.html.

2. Employment Situation Summary, United States Department of Labor Bureau of Labor Statistics, October 7, 2011. Accessed October 22, 2011, at http:// www.bls.gov/news.release/empsit.nr0.htm.

3. Elizabeth Kneebone and Emily Garr, "Income and Poverty," Brookings.edu. Accessed October 22, 2011, at http://www.brookings.edu/metro/ MetroAmericaChapters/poverty_income.aspx.

4. Gordon H. Wadsworth, "Sky Rocketing College Costs," InflationData.com, October 19, 2001. Accessed October 22, 2011, at http://www.inflationdata .com/inflation/inflation_articles/Education_Inflation.asp.

5. Mortimer B. Zuckerman, "America's Fading Exceptionalism," U.S.News.com, June 10, 2011. Accessed October 22, 2011, at http://www .usnews.com/opinion/mzuckerman/articles/2011/06/10/americas-fading -exceptionalism?PageNr=3.

CHAPTER 2

1. Jon Prior, "Foreclosures in 2011 to Break Last Year's Record: RealtyTrac." Accessed October 22, 2011, at http://www.housingwire.com/2011/01/12/ foreclosures-reach-record-high-in-2010-realtytrac.

2. Daniel Golden, "Countrywide's Many 'Friends,'" Portfolio.com, June 12, 2008. Accessed October 22, 2011, at http://www.portfolio.com/news-markets/top-5/2008/06/12/Countrywide-Loan-Scandal.

3. Angelo M. Codevilla, "America's Ruling Class—And the Perils of Revolution," Spectator.org, July–August 2010. Accessed October 22, 2011, at http://spectator.org/archives/2010/07/16/americas-ruling-class-and-the/print.

4. Chrystia Freeland, "The Rise of the New Global Elite," Atlantic.com, January/February 2011. Accessed June 2011, at http://www.theatlantic.com/magazine/archive/2011/01/the-rise-of-the-new-global-elite/8343/.

5. Joseph Soares, *The Power of Privilege: Yale and America's Elite Colleges.* Stanford, CA: Stanford University Press, 2007.

6. G. William Domhoff, *Who Rules America?* New York: McGraw-Hill, 2010.

7. Matt Taibbi, "Wall Street's Big Win," Rolling Stone.com, August 6, 2010. Accessed October 22, 2011, at http://www.rollingstone.com/politics/news/wall-streets-big-win-20100804?print=true.

8. "David Brooks on Fannie Mae," *New York Times*, June 17.

9. Samuel Huntington, "Dead Souls: The Denationalization of the American Elite," National Interest, Spring 2004.

10. Chrystia Freeland, "Getting By without the Middle Class," NYTimes.com, June 9, 2011. Accessed October 22, 2011, at http://www.nytimes.com/2011/06/10/us/10iht-letter10.html?_r=1.

11. Edward N. Wolff, "Recent Trends in Household Wealth in the United States: Rising Debt and the Middle-Class Squeeze—an Update to 2007," Levy Economics Institute Working Papers Series No. 159.

12. Freeland, "Getting By without the Middle Class."

13. Nathan Vardi, "The Top 5 Cities with Rising Home Prices," MSN.com. Accessed October 22, 2011, at http://realestate.msn.com/article.aspx?cp-docu mentid=26389371.

14. Arthur C. Brooks, "Happy Now?" National Review Online, June 2, 2010. Accessed at American Enterprise Institute for Public Policy Research, June 16, 2001, at http://www.aei.org/article/102127.

15. "Pay Disparity Ratio," AFL-CIO.org. Accessed October 22, 2011, at http://www.aflcio.org/corporatewatch/paywatch/paydisparityratio.cfm#_ftn1.

16. "Study: Gap Growing between Rich and Poor," MSNBC.MSN.com, October 21, 2008. Accessed October 22, 2011, at http://www.msnbc.msn.com/id/27295405/ns/business-world_business/t/study-gap-growing-between-rich-poor/.

17. "Pessimism about National Economy Rises, Personal Financial Views Hold Steady," Pew Research Center, Peoplepress.org, June 23, 2011. Accessed October 22, 2011, at http://people-press.org/2011/06/23/section-2-views-of-personal-finances/.

18. Bob Willis and Alex Tanzi, "Consumer Confidence Out of Sync with U.S. Stock Gains since '09," Bloomberg.com, June 16, 2011. Accessed October 22, 2011, at http://www.bloomberg.com/news/2011-06-17/wall-street-divergence -from-main-street-widening-with-jobless-exceeding-9-.html.

19. Chrystia Freeland, "The Rise of the New Global Elite," TheAtlantic.com, January–February 2011. Accessed October 22, 2011, at http://www.theatlantic .com/magazine/print/2011/01/the-rise-of-the-new-global-elite/8343/.

20. Andrew Ross Sorkin, Diana B. Henriques, Edmund L. Andrews, and Joe Nocera, "As Credit Crisis Spiraled, Alarm Led to Action," NYTimes .com, October 1, 2008. Accessed October 22, 2011, at http://www.nytimes .com/2008/10/02/business/02crisis.html?pagewanted=print.

21. Jacob S. Hacker and Paul Pierson, *Winner-Take-All-Politics: How Washington Made the Rich Richer—and Turned Its Back on the Middle Class*. New York: Simon and Schuster, 2010.

22. Hacker and Pierson, *Winner-Take-All Politics*.

23. Michael Beckel, "More Political Action Committees to get 'Super' Powers?," Opensecrets Blog, June 15, 2011. Accessed June 2011, at http://www .opensecrets.org/news/2011/06/more-political-action-committees-to.html.

CHAPTER 3

1. The ultrarich, in my formulation, are NOT the super class; rather, they are a rung below, very successful and often influential individuals but not people who have direct access to power or whose wealth can be used as a political tool in the manner of a George Soros or David Koch.

2. History of the Dow Jones Industrial Average, MDLeasing.com. Accessed October 22, 2011, at http://www.mdleasing.com/djia.htm.

3. Marcus Walker, Damian Paletta, and Brian Blackstone, "Global Crisis of Confidence," WSJ.com, August 13, 2011. Accessed October 22, 2011, at http:// online.wsj.com/article/SB10001424053111903918104576504493072650756 .html.

4. For the survey, I identified political class members using the Rasmussen Political Class Index described in chapter 2.

5. "Most Voters Are Unhappy with Both Sides in the Debt Ceiling Debate," RasmussenReports.com, July 22, 2011. Accessed October 22, 2011, at http://www. rasmussenreports.com/public_content/politics/general_politics/july_2011/ most_voters_are_unhappy_with_both_sides_in_the_debt_ceiling_debate.

6. Lydia Saad, "Americans Decry Power of Lobbyists, Corporations, Banks, Feds," Gallup.com, April 11, 2011. Accessed October 22, 2011, at http://www .gallup.com/poll/147026/americans-decry-power-lobbyists-corporations -banks-feds.aspx.

7. Jeffrey Jones, "Americans Most Confident in Military, Least in Congress," Gallup.com, June 23, 2011. Accessed October 22, 2011, at http://www.gallup.com/poll/148163/americans-confident-military-least-congress.aspx.

8. NIMA, "Rasmussen: 75% Say Free Markets Better Than Government Management of Economy, Political Class (*Shockingly*) Disagrees," EconomicsJunkie.com, August 4, 2010. Accessed October 22, 2011, at http://www.economicsjunkie.com/rassmussen-75-say-free-markets-better-than-government-management-of-economy-political-class-shockingly-disagrees/.

9. "Only 14% Prefer Government-Regulated Economy over Free Market," RasmussenReports.com, October 26, 2010. Accessed October 22, 2011, at http://www.rasmussenreports.com/public_content/business/general_business/october_2010/only_14_prefer_government_regulated_economy_over_free_market.

10. "Are You Overtaxed? 64% of Americans Say Yes, Political Class Says No," IHateTheMedia.com, April 11, 2011. Accessed October 22, 2011, at http://www.ihatethemedia.com/are-you-overtaxed-64-of-americans-say-yes-political-class-says-no.

11. Midas Mulligan, "Rasmussen: 68% Prefer a Government with Fewer Services, Lower Taxes," AtlasShrugsinBrooklyn.wordpress.com, January 23, 2011. Accessed October 22, 2011, at http://atlasshrugsinbrooklyn.wordpress.com/2011/01/23/rasmussen-68-prefer-a-government-with-fewer-services-lower-taxes/.

12. "Voters Put Spending Cuts ahead of Deficit Reduction," Rasmussen Reports.com, December 10, 2010. Accessed October 22, 2011, at http://www.rasmussenreports.com/public_content/business/federal_budget/december_2010/voters_put_spending_cuts_ahead_of_deficit_reduction.

13. "Health Care Law: 58% Think Repeal of Health Care Law Likely," RasmussenReports.com, October 17, 2011. Accessed October 22, 2011, at http://www.rasmussenreports.com/public_content/politics/current_events/healthcare/health_care_law.

14. "68% Say Bailout Money Is Going to Those Who Caused the Economic Crisis," RasmussenReports.com, March 19, 2009. Accessed October 22, 2011, at http://www.rasmussenreports.com/public_content/business/federal_bailout/march_2009/68_say_bailout_money_is_going_to_those_who_caused_the_economic_crisis.

15. "80% Say Wall Street, Not Taxpayers, Benefited More From Bailout—As Goldman Sachs Announces Record Profit," RasmussenReports.com, July 17, 2009. Accessed October 22, 2011, at http://www.rasmussenreports.com/public_content/business/federal_bailout/july_2009/80_say_wall_street_not_taxpayers_benefited_more_from_bailout_as_goldman_sachs_announces_record_profit.

16. "53% Say Bailouts Have Been Bad for the Country," RasmussenReports .com, January 19, 2011. Accessed October 22, 2011, at http://www.rasmussen reports.com/public_content/business/federal_bailout/january_2011/53_say_ bailouts_have_been_bad_for_the_country.

CHAPTER 4

1. "Text of S&P Downgrade of U.S. Rating," Marketwatch.com, August 5, 2011. Accessed October 24, 2011, at http://www.marketwatch.com/story/text -of-sp-downgrade-of-us-rating-2011-08-05.
2. "New Low: 17% Say U.S. Government Has Consent of the Governed," Ras- mussenReports.com, August 7, 2011. Accessed October 24, 2011, at http://www .rasmussenreports.com/public_content/politics/general_politics/august_2011/ new_low_17_say_u_s_government_has_consent_of_the_governed.
3. Washington Post poll, August 9, 2011. Accessed October 24, 2011, at http://www.washingtonpost.com/wp-srv/politics/polls/postpoll_080911.html.
4. "Will There Be Blood? The Revival of American Populism Is Partly Syn- thetic, but Mostly Real," Economist.com, March 26, 2009. Accessed June 2011, at http://www.economist.com/node/13375986?story_id=13375986&source=hp textfeature.
5. Nate Silver, "Why the Republicans Resist Compromise," NYTimes.com, July 7, 2011. Accessed October 24, 2011, at http://fivethirtyeight.blogs.nytimes .com/2011/07/07/why-the-g-o-p-cannot-compromise/#more-12913.

CHAPTER 5

1. See www.americanthinker.com/2011/11/why_occupy_wall_street_is_ no_tea_party_html#ixzz1ex3x2LCp
2. "Reich: Washington Needs Bold Solution for Middle-Class," Marketplace. PublicRadio.org, December 15, 2010. Accessed October 24, 2011, at http:// marketplace.publicradio.org/display/web/2010/12/15/pm-reich-washington -needs-a-bold-solution-for-middleclass/.
3. Paul Krugman, "No, We Can't? or Won't?," NYTimes.com, July 10, 2011. Accessed October 24, 2011, at http://www.nytimes.com/2011/07/11/ opinion/11krugman.html?ref=opinion.
4. "In Bad Economy, Countries Contemplate Protectionist Measures," PBS .org/newshour, February 19, 2009. Accessed October 24, 2011, at http://www .pbs.org/newshour/bb/business/jan-june09/trade_02-19.html.

5. Alan Hassenfeld, "The New Populism," NYTimes.com, May 14, 2009. Accessed October 24, 2011, at http://www.nytimes.com/2009/05/15/opinion/15iht-edlet.html.

6. Tula Connell, "Buy American Opponents: Un-American," AFL-CIO .org, February 6, 2009. Accessed October 24, 2011, at http://blog.aflcio .org/2009/02/06/buy-american-opponents-un-american/#more-10080.

7. "In Bad Economy, Countries Contemplate Protectionist Measures."

8. President Lyndon B. Johnson's Remarks at the University of Michigan, May 22, 1964, Lyndon Baines Johnson Library and Museum.edu. Accessed October 24, 2011, at http://www.lbjlib.utexas.edu/johnson/archives.hom/speeches.hom/640522.asp.

9. Jerome Armstrong and Markos Moulitssas, *Crashing the Gate: Netroots, Grassroots, and the Rise of People-Powered Politics*. White River Junction, VT: Chelsea Green, 2006.

10. Brian Knowlton, "91% Support President, Poll on Speech Shows: Americans Back Bush's Ultimatum to Taleban," NYTimes.com, September 22, 2001. Accessed October 24, 2011, at http://www.nytimes.com/2001/09/22/news/22iht-terr_ed3__7.html?scp=10&sq=From+this+day+forward%2C+any+nation+that+continues+to+harbor+or+support+terrorism+will+be+regarded+by+the+United+States+as+a+hostile+regime&st=cse&pagewanted=print.

11. Johnathan Chait, "The Left's New Machine," NewRepublic.com, May 7, 2007. Accessed October 24, 2011, at http://www.tnr.com/print/article/the-lefts-new-machine-how-the-netroots-became-the-most-importantmass-movement-us-politics.

12. DailyKos.com. Accessed October 24, 2011, at http://www.dailykos.com/comments/2004/4/1/144156/3224/16#c16.

13. Chait, "The Left's New Machine."

14. Kelly Wallace, "$1.35 Trillion Tax Cut becomes Law." CNN.com, June 7, 2001. Accessed June 13, 2011, at http://edition.cnn.com/2001/ALLPOLITICS/06/07/bush.taxes/.

15. Joseph E. Stiglitz, "The Economic Consequences of Mr. Bush," Vanity Fair.com, December 2007. Accessed October 24, 2011, at http://www.vanityfair.com/politics/features/2007/12/bush200712?printable=true.

16. Zach Carter, "Small Business Owners Demand Repeal of Bush Tax Cuts for the Rich," HuffingtonPost.com, May 4, 2011. Accessed October 24, 2011, at http://www.huffingtonpost.com/2011/05/04/small-business-owners-bush-tax-cuts-rich-repeal_n_857204.html.

17. Ari Berman, "Obama Caves on Tax Cuts, Endorses 'Bush-McCain' Philosophy," TheNation.com, December 6, 2010. Accessed October 24, 2011, at http://www.thenation.com/blog/156852/obama-caves-tax-cuts-endorses-bush-mccain-philosophy.

CHAPTER 6

1. www.washingtonpost.com/business/economy/occupy-wall-street-protest ers-confront-obama-in-nh-descend-on-dc/2011/11/22/gIQA1ZyulN_story.html

2. Paul Krugman, "Reform or Bust," NYTimes.com, September 20, 2009. Accessed October 24, 2011, at http://www.nytimes.com/2009/09/21/ opinion/21krugman.html.

3. William Kristol, "Pelosi's Reactionary Liberalism," WeeklyStandard.com, July 28, 2011. Accessed October 24, 2011, at http://www.weeklystandard.com/ blogs/pelosis-reactionary-liberalism_577709.html.

4. Ron Fournier, "Obama: It's Kids versus Corporate Jets on Debt-Ceiling Talks," NationalJournal.com, June 30, 2011. Accessed October 24, 2011, at http://www.nationaljournal.com/whitehouse/obama-it-s-kids-versus-corpo rate-jets-on-debt-ceiling-talks-20110629.

5. Stephanie Condon, "Obama: Time to 'Eat Our Peas' and Pass Debt Deal," CBSNews.com, July 11, 2011. Accessed October 24, 2011, at http://www.cbs news.com/8301-503544_162-20078418-503544.html.

6. Jackie Calmes, "Rightward Tilt Leaves Obama with Party Rift," NYTimes.com, July 30, 2011. Accessed October 24, 2011, at http://www.nytimes .com/2011/07/31/us/politics/31dems.html?ref=todayspaper.

7. Robert Reich, "Anyone Who Thinks the Debt Deal Is a Victory for America Understands neither Economics nor Politics," InvestmentWatchblog.com, August 1, 2011. Accessed October 24, 2011, at http://investmentwatchblog .com/robert-reich-anyone-who-thinks-the-debt-deal-is-a-victory-for-america -understands-neither-economics-nor-politics/.

8. Frank Rich, "Obama's Original Sin," NYmag.com, July 3, 2011. Accessed October 24, 2011, at http://nymag.com/print/?/news/frank-rich/obama-econ omy/presidents-failure/.

9. Jim Hightower, "Populism Is Not a Style," Huffington Post.com, May 14, 2009. Accessed October 24, 2011, at http://www.huffingtonpost.com/jim -hightower/populism-is-not-a-style_b_203658.html.

10. Sheryl Gay Stolberg and Stephen Labaton, "Obama Calls Wall Street Bonuses 'Shameful,'" NYTimes.com, January 29, 2009. Accessed October 24, 2011, at http://www.nytimes.com/2009/01/30/business/30obama.html.

11. Macon Phillips, "The White House Blog: New Rules," Whitehouse.gov, February 4, 2009. Accessed October 24, 2011, at http://www.whitehouse.gov/ blog_post/new_rules/.

12. Paul Krugman, "Reform or Bust," NYTimes.com, September 20, 2009. Accessed October 24, 2011, at http://www.nytimes.com/2009/09/21/ opinion/21krugman.html.

13. Michael Hirsh, "The Wisdom of Crowds," DailyBeast.com, January 28, 2010. Accessed October 24, 2011, at http://www.thedailybeast.com/news week/2010/01/28/the-wisdom-of-crowds.html.

14. Route66, "More Questions on Iowa AG Tom Miller Campaign Contributions from Banks," DailyKos.com, May 6, 2011. Accessed October 24, 2011, at http://www.dailykos.com/story/2011/05/06/973605/-More-questions-on-Iowa -AG-Tom-Miller-campaign-contributions-from-banks.

15. "Brief Summary of the Dodd-Frank Wall Street Reform and Consumer Protection Act," United States Senate Committee on Banking, Housing & Urban Affairs. Accessed June 22, 2011, at http://banking.senate.gov/public/ _files/070110_Dodd_Frank_Wall_Street_Reform_comprehensive_summary_ Final.pdf.

16. Rich, "Obama's Original Sin."

17. Robert Creamer, "Growing Income Inequality the Root Cause of Economic Stagnation," HuffingtonPost.com, July 11, 20011. Accessed October 24, 2011, at http://www.huffingtonpost.com/robert-creamer/growing-economic -inequali_b_894311.html?ref=email_share.

18. Kate Thomas, "President Obama: 'I Am a Pro-Union Guy,'" Service Employees International Union. Accessed July 1, 2011, at http://www.seiu .org/2010/04/president-obama-i-am-a-pro-union-guy.php.

19. Steven Greenhouse, "Organized Labor Hopes Attacks by Some States Help Nurture Comeback," New York Times, March 5, 2011, Section A, p. 18.

20. Nate Silver, "The Effects of Union Membership on Democratic Voting," NYTimes.com, February 26, 2011. Accessed October 24, 2011, at http:// fivethirtyeight.blogs.nytimes.com/2011/02/26/the-effects-of-union-member ship-on-democratic-voting/.

21. James Parks, "McCain Stiffs U.S. Workers, Helps Europeans Win Air Tanker Deal," blog.aflcio.org, March 12, 2008. Accessed October 24, 2011, at http://blog.aflcio.org/2008/03/12/mccain-stiffs-us-workers-helps-europeans -win-air-tanker-deal/.

22. Steven Greenhouse, "Boeing Labor Dispute Is Making New Factory a Political Football." New York Times, June 30, 2011, p. 1.

23. Greenhouse, "Boeing Labor Dispute Is Making New Factory a Political Football."

24. U.S Department of Energy, "Buy American Provision," American Recovery and Reinvestment Act. Accessed July 4, 2011, at http://www1.eere.energy .gov/recovery/buy_american_provision.html.

25. Jason Riley, "The Election Choice: Unions," WSJ.com, October 27, 2008. Accessed July 1, 2011, http://online.wsj.com/article/SB122506674992670591 .html.

26. Peter Wallsten, "Obama and Unions: Many in Labor Movement Frustrated with President." WashingtonPost.com, February 19, 2011. Ac-

cessed July 2, 2011, at http://www.washingtonpost.com/wp-dyn/content/article/2011/02/18/AR2011021807507.html.

27. Paul Harris, "Barrack Obama Attacked by Democratic Rebel over US Healthcare Reform," Guardian.co.uk, January 10, 2010. Accessed June 14, 2011, at http://www.guardian.co.uk/world/2010/jan/10/obama-attack-democrats.

28. "Howard Dean Criticizes Health Reform Bill," gohealthinsurance.com, December 16, 2009. Accessed October 24, 2011, at http://www.gohealthinsurance.com/blog/coverage/entry/20091216.

29. Peggy Noonan, "The GOP Wins by Bruising," WSJ.com, October 22, 2011. Accessed October 24, 2011, at http://online.wsj.com/article/declarations.html.

30. Ina Jaffe, "Liberal Bloggers: Obama 'Not Our Boyfriend Anymore,'" NPR.org, June 17, 2011. Accessed October 24, 2011, at http://www.npr.org/2011/06/17/137238072/liberal-bloggers-obama-not-our-boyfriend-anymore.

31. Jaffe, "Liberal Bloggers: Obama 'Not Our Boyfriend Anymore.'"

32. "Progressive Change Campaign Committee Threatens to Pull Obama Support Ahead of 2012," HuffingtonPost.com. Accessed October 24, 2011, at http://www.huffingtonpost.com/2011/07/15/progressive-change-campaign-committee-obama_n_900155.html?ref=email_share.

33. Matt Negrin, "Is Obama Losing Rich Liberals?," Politico.com, July 14, 2011. Accessed October 24, 2011, at http://dyn.politico.com/printstory.cfm?uuid=CB7B89B3-0FA3-437F-A4AA-5429B6CE439E.

34. Calmes, "Rightward Tilt Leaves Obama with Party Rift."

CHAPTER 7

1. Jonathan Allen and John Bresnahan, "Sources: Joe Biden Likened Tea Partiers to Terrorists," Politico.com, August 11, 2011. Accessed October 24, 2011, at http://www.politico.com/news/stories/0811/60421.html.

2. Bernard Goldberg, "Tea Party 'Terrorists' and the Mainstream Media," FoxNews.com, August 3, 2011. Accessed October 24, 2011, at http://www.foxnews.com/opinion/2011/08/03/tea-party-terrorists-and-mainstream-media/.

3. Thomas L. Friedman, "Can't We Do This Right?," NYTimes.com, July 26, 2011. Accessed October 24, 2011, at http://www.nytimes.com/2011/07/27/opinion/27friedman.html?_r=2&partner=rssnyt&emc=rss.

4. Peter S. Goodman, "Republican Debt Ceiling Tactics Hold National Interest Hostage," HuffingtonPost.com, July 25, 2011. Accessed October 25, 2011, at http://www.huffingtonpost.com/peter-s-goodman/republican-terrorism-debt_b_908839.html.

5. Joe Nocera, "The Tea Party's War on America," NYTimes.com, August 1, 2011. Accessed October 25, 2011, at http://www.nytimes.com/2011/08/02/opinion/the-tea-partys-war-on-america.html?ref=economy.

6. Libertarian Party 2010 Platform, LP.org, May 2010. Accessed October 25, 2011, at http://www.lp.org/platform.

7. Marc Lacey, "Tea Party Group Issues Warning to the G.O.P.," NYTimes.com, February 26, 2011. Accessed October 25, 2011, at http://www.nytimes.com/2011/02/27/us/politics/27teaparty.html?pagewanted=print.

8. Lacey, "Tea Party Group Issues Warning to the G.O.P."

9. Matt Cover, "When Asked Where the Constitution Authorizes Congress to Order Americans to Buy Health Insurance, Pelosi Says: 'Are You Serious?,'" CBSNews.com, October 22, 2009. Accessed October 25, 2011, at http://www.cnsnews.com/node/55971.

10. Charles Krauthammer, "Constitutionalism," WashingtonPost.com, January 7, 2011. Accessed October 25, 2011, at http://www.washingtonpost.com/wp-dyn/content/article/2011/01/06/AR2011010604379.html.

11. Ronald Reagan, "A Time for Choosing," UTexas.edu, October 27, 1964. Accessed October 25, 2011, at http://www.reagan.utexas.edu/archives/reference/timechoosing.html.

12. "Calbuzz Dustbin: When Jarvis Stormed the Capitol," Calbuzz.com, May 24, 2009. Accessed October 25, 2011, at http://www.calbuzz.com/2009/05/calbuzz-dustbin-of-history-when-howard-jarvis-stormed-the-capitol/.

CHAPTER 8

1. Lynn Hulsey, "Tea Party Pushing Republican Politicians to the Right," DaytonDailyNews.com, April 25, 2010. Accessed October 24, 2011, at http://www.daytondailynews.com/news/election/tea-party-pushing-republican-politicians-to-the-right-670761.html.

2. Robert Pear, "G.O.P. Freshmen Say Debt Concerns Them More Than Re-election," NYTimes.com, July 16, 2011. Accessed October 25, 2011, at http://www.nytimes.com/2011/07/17/us/politics/17debt.html?ref=todayspaper.

3. Dana Milbank, "Conservatives Criticize Bush on Spending; Medicare Bill Angers Some Allies," Washington Post, December 6, 2003.

4. Jeff Zeleny, "The Other Texas Republican on Book Tour," New York Times, November 8, 2010. Accessed June 21, 2011, at http://thecaucus.blogs.nytimes.com/2010/11/08/ the-other-texas-republican-on-book-tour/.

5. Veronique D. Rugy, "Spending under President George W. Bush," Mercatus.org, March 2009. Accessed October 25, 2011, at http://mercatus.org/publication/spending-under-president-george-w-bush.

6. Rugy, "Spending under President George W. Bush."

7. Carl Hulse, "Conservatives Viewed Bailout Plan as Last Straw," New York Times, September 27, 2008.

8. Ryan Lizza, "New Hampshire Debate: The Ghost of George W. Bush," NewYorker.com, June 14, 2011. Accessed October 25, 2011, at http://www.newyorker.com/online/blogs/newsdesk/2011/06/new-hampshire-debate-the-ghost-of-george-w-bush.html.

9. Nicole Gelinas, "TARP's Shadow," City-Journal.com, July 15, 2011. Accessed October 25, 2011, at http://city-journal.com/2011/eon0715ng.html.

10. James F. Smith, "Ron Paul's Tea Party for Dollars," December 16, 2007. Accessed October 25, 2011, at http://www.boston.com/news/politics/political intelligence/2007/12/ron_pauls_tea_p.html.

11. "Ron Paul: 'We Will Default because the Debt Is Unsustainable,'" Real ClearPolitics.com, July 19, 2011. Accessed October 25, 2011, at http://www.realclearpolitics.com/video/2011/07/19/ron_paul_we_will_default_because_the_debt_is_unsustainable.html.

12. Accessed October 25, 2011, at http://www.amconmag.com/pdfissue.html?Id=AmConservative-2011aug01&page=12.

13. Gerald Seib, "Populist Vein Resurfaces in Protests," WSJ.com, September 15, 2009. Accessed October 25, 2011, at http://online.wsj.com/article/SB125295374286409541.html.

14. Jennifer Steinhauer, "Debt Bill Is Signed, Ending a Fractious Battle," NYTimes.com, August 2, 2011. Accessed October 25, 2011, at http://www.nytimes.com/2011/08/03/us/politics/03fiscal.html?ref=todayspaper.

15. Nate Silver, "Why the Republicans Resist Compromise," NYTimes.com, July 7, 2011. Accessed October 25, 2011, at http://fivethirtyeight.blogs.nytimes.com/2011/07/07/why-the-g-o-p-cannot-compromise/#more-12913.

16. Robert Draper, "How Kevin McCarthy Wrangles the Tea Party in Washington," July 13, 2011. Accessed October 25, 2011, at http://www.nytimes.com/2011/07/17/magazine/how-kevin-mccarthy-wrangles-the-tea-party.html?pagewanted=print.

17. Clark S. Judge, "The Debt Battle Is Good for the GOP," WSJ.com, July 18, 2011. Accessed October 25, 2011, at http://online.wsj.com/article/SB1000142405270230452130457644783266317361 2.html?mod=djemEditorialPage_h.

18. Declaration of Tea Party Independence, SaveOurMovement.com. Accessed October 25, 2011, at http://www.saveourmovement.com/.

19. Lynn Hulsey, "Tea Party Pushing Republican Politicians to the Right."

20. Lynn Hulsey, "Tea Party Pushing Republican Politicians to the Right."

21. Ezra Klein, "The Tea Party and the Debt Ceiling," WashingtonPost.com, July 14, 2011. Accessed October 26, 2011, at http://www.washingtonpost.com/blogs/ezra-klein/post/the-tea-party-and-the-debt-ceiling/2011/07/11/gIQA HaldEI_blog.html.

22. About, CorydonTeaParty.org. Accessed October 26, 2011, at http://www.corydonteaparty.org/index.php?option=com_content&view=article&id=113&Itemid=108.

23. Peter J. Boyer, "House Rule," NewYorker.com, December 13, 2010. Accessed October 26, 2011, at http://www.newyorker.com/reporting/2010/12/13/101213fa_fact_boyer.

24. Peter J. Boyer, "House Rule."

25. Olympia Meola, "Va. Tea Party Activists Frustrated with Cantor," Times-Dispatch.com, October 26, 2011. Accessed October 26, 2011, at http://www2.timesdispatch.com/news/virginia-politics/2011/mar/13/tdmet01-va-tea-party-activists-frustrated-with-can-ar-902140/.

26. "Allen West Blasts Tea Party 'Schizophrenia' over Debt Ceiling," Huffing tonPost.com, July 29, 2011. Accessed October 26, 2011, at http://www.huffing tonpost.com/2011/07/29/allen-west-tea-party-schizophrenia-debt_n_913283 .html.

27. Jeffrey H. Anderson, "Paul Ryan Tops the 2012 Tea Party Presidential Poll," PJMedia.com, March 11, 2011. Accessed October 26, 2011, at http://pjmedia.com/blog/paul-ryan-tops-the-2012-tea-party-presidential-poll/.

28. Ezra Klein and Dylan Matthews, "Everything You Need to Know about the Debt Ceiling in One Post," WashingtonPost.com, July 22, 2011. Accessed October 26, 2011, at http://www.washingtonpost.com/blogs/ezra-klein/post/everything-you-need-to-know-about-the-debt-ceiling/2011/07/11/gIQA 3mPTTI_blog.html.

29. Michael D. Shear, "Obama: Republican Leaders Must Bend on Taxes," NYTimes.com, June 29, 2011. Accessed October 26, 2011, at http://thecau cus.blogs.nytimes.com/2011/06/29/obama-republican-leaders-must-bend-on -taxes/?hp.

30. Chris Moody, "Poll: Majority of Republicans and Tea Partiers Not Worried about Debt Ceiling Deadline," July 19, 2011. Accessed October 26, 2011, at http://news.yahoo.com/blogs/ticket/poll-majority-republicans-tea-partiers -not-worried-debt-153417525.html.

31. Robert Pear, "G.O.P. Freshman Say Debt Concerns Them More Than Re-election," NYTimes.com, July 16, 2011. Accessed October 26, 2011, at http://www .nytimes.com/2011/07/17/us/politics/17debt.html?ref=todayspaper&page wanted=print.

32. Adele Stan, "In Bid for Control of GOP, Tea Party Brings U.S. to Brink of Economic Calamity," AlterNet.org, July 23, 2011. Accessed August 3, 2011, at http://www.alternet.org/teaparty/151750/in_bid_for_control_of_gop,_tea_ party_brings_u.s._to_brink_of_economic_calamity/?page=entire.

33. Binyamin Appelbaum, "After Aiding Republicans, Business Groups Press Them on Debt Ceiling," July 26, 2011. Accessed October 26, 2011,

at http://www.nytimes.com/2011/07/27/us/politics/27chamber.html?scp=3 &sq=chamber%20of%20commerce&st=cse.

34. Appelbaum, "After Aiding Republicans, Business Groups Press Them on Debt Ceiling."

35. Patricia Murphy, "Tea Party Takes on Boehner," TheDailyBeast.com, July 27, 2011. Accessed October 26, 2011, at http://www.thedailybeast.com/ articles/2011/07/27/debt-ceiling-tea-party-leader-calls-boehner-plan-an-em barrassment.html?om_rid=CTiDLi&om_mid=_BOMAhOB8chCPVg.

36. Michael D. Shear, "Can the Debt Ceiling Genie be Put Back in the Bottle?," NYTimes,com, August 3, 2011. Accessed October 26, 2011, at http:// thecaucus.blogs.nytimes.com/2011/08/03/can-the-debt-ceiling-genie-be-put -back-in-the-bottle/.

37. Henry Blodget, "Sarah Palin Eggs on Tea Partiers—Threatens to Get Them Fired if They Vote to Raise Debt Ceiling," BusinessInsider.com, July 28, 2011. Accessed October 26, 2011, at http://www.businessinsider.com/sarah -palin-eggs-on-tea-partiers-2011-7.

38. Robert Draper, "How Kevin McCarthy Wrangles the Tea Party in Washington," NYTimes.com, July 13, 2011. Accessed October 26, 2011, at http:// www.nytimes.com/2011/07/17/magazine/how-kevin-mccarthy-wrangles-the -tea-party.html?pagewanted=print.

39. Michael Shear, "Republicans Seeking Election Remain Unsure about Embracing Tea Party," NYTimes.com, August 2, 2011. Accessed October 26, 2011, at http://www.nytimes.com/2011/08/03/us/politics/03repubs.html.

CHAPTER 9

1. "GOP Makes Big Gains among White Voters," People-press.org, July 22, 2011. Accessed October 26, 2011, at http://people-press.org/2011/07/22/gop -makes-big-gains-among-white-voters/.

2. John Avlon, "In 2011, It's Truly Independents Day," CNN.com, July 4, 2011. Accessed October 26, 2011, at http://articles.cnn.com/2011-07-04/opin ion/avlon.independents.day_1_independent-voters-party-political-debates?_ s=PM:OPINION.

3. Satisfaction with the United States, Gallup.com. Accessed October 26, 2011, at http://www.gallup.com/poll/1669/General-Mood-Country.aspx.

4. Jeff Zeleny and Megan Thee, "Exit Polls Show Independents, Citing War, Favored Democrats," NYTimes.com, November 8, 2006. Accessed October 26, 2011, at http://www.nytimes.com/2006/11/08/us/politics/08exit .html?pagewanted=print.

5. Obama Loses Ground in 2012 Reelection Bid, People-press.org, July 28, 2011. Accessed October 26, 2011, at http://people-press.org/2011/07/28/obama-loses-ground-in-2012-reelection-bid/.

6. Karl Rove, "The Rise of Democratic Discontent," WSJ.com, September 14, 2011. Accessed October 26, 2011, at http://online.wsj.com/article/SB10001424053111903927204576570330619243552.html.

7. Nate Silver, "Unfavorable Ratings for Both Major Parties Near Record Highs," NYTimes.com, July 23, 2011. Accessed October 26, 2011, at http://fivethirtyeight.blogs.nytimes.com/2011/07/23/unfavorable-ratings-for-both-major-parties-near-record-highs/.

8. Independents Take Center Stage in Obama Era, People-press.org, May 21, 2009. Accessed October 26, 2011, at http://people-press.org/2009/05/21/independents-take-center-stage-in-obama-era/.

CHAPTER 10

1. Joe Nocera, "Boycott Campaign Donations!" NYTimes.com, August 12, 2011. Accessed October 27, 2011, at http://www.nytimes.com/2011/08/13/opinion/nocera-boycott-campaign-donations.html.

2. Paul Blumenthal, "Super PACs and Secret Money: The Unregulated Shadow Campaign," HuffingtonPost.com, September 27, 2011. Accessed October 27, 2011, at http://www.huffingtonpost.com/2011/09/26/super-pacs-secret-money-campaign-finance_n_977699.html?view=print&comm_ref=false.

3. Blumenthal, "Super PACs and Secret Money: The Unregulated Shadow Campaign."

4. Blumenthal, "Super PACs and Secret Money: The Unregulated Shadow Campaign."

5. Blumenthal, "Super PACs and Secret Money: The Unregulated Shadow Campaign."

6. Dave Leventhal, "Business Executives Call for End to Anonymous Cash," Politco.com, September 26, 2011. Accessed October 27, 2011, at http://www.politico.com/news/stories/0911/64448.html.

7. Contribution Limits 2011–12, FEC.gov. Accessed October 27, 2011, at http://www.fec.gov/pages/brochures/contriblimits.shtml#fn1.

8. Democratic Governors Assn: Top Contributors, 2012 Cycle, OpenSecrets.org. Accessed October 27, 2011, at http://www.opensecrets.org/527s/527cmtedetail_contribs.php?ein=521304889.

9. Republican Governors Assn: Overview, OpenSecrets.org. Accessed October 27, 2011, at http://www.opensecrets.org/527s/527cmtedetail.php?ein=113655877.

10. Koch Industries, OpenSecrets.org. Accessed October 27, 2011, at http://www.opensecrets.org/orgs/summary.php?id=D000000186.

11. "Lobbying Plus Public Relations, Super PAC Hopes to See Green and More in Capital Eye Opener: Oct. 27," OpenSecrets.org. Accessed October 27, 2011, at http://www.opensecrets.org/.

12. News Corp, OpenSecrets.org. Accessed October 27, 2011, at http://www.opensecrets.org/orgs/summary.php?id=D000000227&cycle=2010.

13. Contran Corp, OpenSecrets.org. Accessed October 27, 2011, at http://www.opensecrets.org/lobby/clientsum.php?id=D000000337&year=2010.

14. Interests behind the Money Are Predictable, OpenSecrets.org. Accessed October 27, 2011, at https://www.opensecrets.org/resources/dollarocracy/05.php.

15. Anna Palmer and Manu Raju, "Bundlers Poised for Power over Super-committee," Politico.com, September 18, 2011. Accessed October 27, 2011, at http://www.politico.com/news/stories/0911/63802.html.

16. Richard Hasen, "The Surprisingly Complex Case for Disclosure of Contributions and Donations Funding Sham Issue Advocacy," University of California, Los Angeles Law Review 48 (2000–2001).

17. David Storey, "The Amendment of Section 527: Eliminating Stealth PACs and Providing a Model for Future Campaign Finance Reform," University of Indiana Law Review 77 (Winter 2002).

18. Lauren Daniel, "527s in a Post–Swift Boat Era: The Current and Future Role of Issue Advocacy Groups in Presidential Elections," Northwest University School of Law, Northwestern Journal of Law and Social Policy Volume 5 (Spring 2010). Accessed October 27, 2011, at http://www.law.northwestern.edu/journals/njlsp/v5/n1/6/6Daniel.pdf.

19. Every Republican Is Crucial Act, OpenSecrets.org. Accessed October 27, 2011, at http://www.opensecrets.org/pacs/lookup2.php?strID=C00384701.

20. Paul Blumenthal, "Secret Corporate Money Powers Pro-Romney Super PAC," HuffingtonPost.com, August 4, 2011. Accessed October 27, 2011, at http://www.huffingtonpost.com/2011/08/04/w-spann-llc-restore-our-future_n_918051.html.

21. Heavy Hitters: Act Blue, OpenSecrets.org. Accessed September 2, 2011, at http://www.opensecrets.org/orgs/summary.php?id=D000021806.

22. David Bernstein, "Two Shmoes: How to Pump Young Democrats' Energy and Money into the Political Process," BostonPhoenix.com, September 24–30, 2004. Accessed October 27, 2011, at http://www.bostonphoenix.com/boston/news_features/other_stories/multipage/documents/04146120.asp.

23. Bernstein, "Two Shmoes: How to Pump Young Democrats' Energy and Money into the Political Process."

24. Bernstein, "Two Shmoes: How to Pump Young Democrats' Energy and Money into the Political Process."

25. Bernstein, "Two Shmoes: How to Pump Young Democrats' Energy and Money into the Political Process."

26. ActBlue—The Online Clearinghouse for Democratic Action. Accessed October 27, 2011, at https://secure.actblue.com/.

27. ActBlue, https://secure.actblue.com/.

28. ActBlue, https://secure.actblue.com/.

29. ActBlue, https://secure.actblue.com/.

30. "Economic Philosophies," Club for Growth Philosophy, ClubforGrowth. org. Accessed September 4, 2011, at http://www.clubforgrowth.org/philosophy/.

31. "Pro-Growth Tax Policy," Club for Growth Philosophy, ClubforGrowth. org. Accessed September 4, 2011, at http://www.clubforgrowth.org/philosophy/.

32. Club for Growth, "Money in Politics—See Who's Giving and Who's Getting," OpenSecrets.org. Accessed September 4, 2011, at http://www.open secrets.org/pacs/lookup2.php?strID=C00432260.

33. Ben Smith, "Liberal Group Uses Outside Money to Match GOP," Politico .com, November 24, 2010. Accessed September 5, 2011, at http://www.politico .com/news/stories/1110/45542.html.

34. Outside Spending, American Crossroads, OpenSecrets.org. Accessed September 5, 2011, at http://www.opensecrets.org/outsidespending/detail .php?cycle=2010.

35. Mission, AmericanCrossroads.org. Accessed September 5, 2011, at http://americancrossroads.org/mission.

36. Michael Beckel, "Karl Rove-Linked Conservative Group, American Crossroads, Adapts to New Campaign Finance Landscape," OpenSecrets.org, August 19, 2010. Accessed September 5, 2011, at http://www.opensecrets.org/ news/2010/08/karl-rove-linked-conservative-group.html.

37. Justin Elliott, "'Grassroots' Rove-linked Group Funded Almost Entirely by Billionaires," Salon.com, July 23, 2010. Accessed September 5, 2011, at http://www.salon.com/news/politics/war_room/2010/07/23/rove_group_ billionaire_donors.

38. Beckel, "Karl Rove-Linked Conservative Group, American Crossroads."

39. Outside Spending, American Crossroads.

40. Paul Blumenthal, "Karl Rove–Linked Super PAC American Crossroads Reports July and August Donations," HuffingtonPost.com, September 2, 2011. Accessed September 5, 2011, at http://www.huffingtonpost.com/2011/09/02/ karl-rove-kenneth-griffin-super-pac_n_946108.html?ref=mostpopular.

41. "The World's Billionaires," Forbes.com, March 9, 2011. Accessed August 30, 2011, at http://www.forbes.com/wealth/billionaires.

42. "The World's Billionaires," Forbes.com.

43. Jane Mayer, "Covert Operations," NewYorker.com, August 30, 2010. Accessed October 27, 2011, at http://www.newyorker.com/ reporting/2010/08/30/100830fa_fact_mayer.

44. John Aloysius Farrell, "Koch's Web of Influence," IWatchNews .org, April 6, 2011. Accessed August 27, 2011, at http://www.iwatchnews .org/2011/04/06/3936/kochs-web-influence.

45. Lobbying Spending Database–Koch Industries, 2011, OpenSecrets.org. Accessed August 31, 2011, at http://www.opensecrets.org/lobby/clientsum .php?id=D000000186.

46. Eric Lipton, "Billionaire Brothers' Money Plays Role in Wisconsin Dispute," NYTimes.com, February 21, 2011. Accessed August 27, 2011, at http:// www.nytimes.com/2011/02/22/us/22koch.html?pagewanted=all.

47. "Rick Perry Meets with Koch Brothers," Daily Kos, June 28, 2011. Accessed August 27, 2011, at http://www.dailykos.com/story/2011/06/28/989152/-Rick -Perry-Meets-With-Koch-Brothers.

48. Ben Smith and Kenneth Vogel, "Kochs' Plan for 2012: Raise $88 M," Politico.com, February 11, 2011. Accessed August 27, 2011, at http://dyn.polit ico.com/printstory.cfm?uuid=CB5926D0-C9D5-4AB0-A06D-DA2CEB824DF0.

49. Leslie Wayne, "And for His Next Feat, a Billionaire Sets Sights on Bush," NYTimes.com, May 31, 2004, Accessed August 25, 2011, at http://www.ny times.com/2004/05/31/politics/campaign/31soros.html?pagewanted=all.

50. "Secretary of State Project," DiscovertheNetworks.org. Accessed August 26, 2011, at http://www.discoverthenetworks.org/printgroupProfile.asp ?grpid=7487.

51. Kara Ryan and Stephen Weissman, "Soft Money in the 2006 Election and the Outlook for 2008," Campaign Finance Institute, cfinst.org, April 10, 2007. Accessed October 27, 2011, at http://www.cfinst.org/press/PReleases/07-04-10/ Soft_Money_in_the_2006_Election_and_the_Outlook_for_2008_The_Chang ing_Nonprofits_Landscape.aspx.

52. George Soros Contributions to 527 Organizations, 2006 Election Cycle, OpenSecrets.org. Accessed August 26, 2011, at http://www.opensecrets .org/527s/527indivsdetail.php?id=U0000000364&cycle=2006.

53. George Soros Contributions to 527 Organizations, 2008 Election Cycle, OpenSecrets.org. Accessed August 26, 2011, at http://209.190.229.99/527s/527 indivsdetail.php?id=U0000000364&cycle=2008.

54. Perry Bacon Jr., "MoveOn Unmoved by Furor over Ad Targeting Petraeus," Washington Post.com, September 21, 2007. Accessed August 26, 2011, at http://www.washingtonpost.com/wp-dyn/content/article/2007/09/20/ AR2007092001005.html?nav=hcmodule.

55. Dave Levinthal, "Business Executives Call for End to Anonymous Cash," Politico.com, September 26, 2001. Accessed October 27, 2011, at http://www .politico.com/news/stories/0911/64448.html.

56. Paul Blumenthal, "Super PACs and Secret Money: The Unregulated Shadow Campaign," HuffingtonPost.com, September 26, 2011. Accessed

October 27, 2011, at http://www.huffingtonpost.com/2011/09/26/super-pacs -secret-money-campaign-finance_n_977699.html?view=print&comm_ref=false.

CHAPTER 11

1. www.nytimes.com/2011/11/20/magazine/heaven-is-a-place-called-eliza beth-warren.html?pagewanted=4&ref=politics.
2. *Washington Post* analysis of data from the Center for Responsive Politics, the Sunlight Foundation, and congressional lobbying records. Published September 2, 2011.
3. Dan Eggen, "Members of Debt Panel Have Ties to Lobbyists," Washing tonPost.com, September 5, 2011. Accessed October 28, 2011, at http://www .washingtonpost.com/politics/many-members-of-debt-Super Committee-have -ties-to-lobbyists/2011/08/23/gIQANiLr4J_story.html.
4. T. W. Farnam, "Revolving Door of Employment between Congress, Lobbying Firms, Study Shows," WashingtonPost.com, September 12, 2011. Accessed October 27, 2011, at http://www.washingtonpost.com/study-shows -revolving-door-of-employment-between-congress-lobbying-firms/2011/09/12/ gIQAxPYROK_story.html.
5. Lindsay Renick Mayer, "Big Oil, Big Influence," PBS.org, August 1, 2008. Accessed October 28, 2011, at http://www.pbs.org/now/shows/347/oil-politics .html.
6. ABSCAM Trials: 1980 & 1981—Four-way Conspiracy, Untrustworthy Witness, Influential Senator Charged, Warning from Bench, No Acquittals, JRank.org. Accessed October 28, 2011, at http://law.jrank.org/pages/3323/ ABSCAM-Trials-1980-1981.html#ixzz1YVVIKBErPerhaps.
7. "The Lincoln Savings and Loan Investigation: Who Is Involved?," NYTimes.com, November 22, 1989. Accessed October 29, 2011, at http://www .nytimes.com/1989/11/22/business/the-lincoln-savings-and-loan-investigation -who-is-involved.html?src=pm.
8. Tom Fitzpatrick, "McCain: The Most Reprehensible of the Keating Five," PhoenixNewsTimes.com, November 29, 1989. Accessed October 28, 2011, at http://www.phoenixnewtimes.com/1989-11-29/news/mccain-the-most-repre hensible-of-the-keating-five/.
9. Alyssa Fetini, "A Brief History of the Keating Five," Time.com, October 8, 2008. Accessed October 28, 2011, at http://www.time.com/time/business/ article/0,8599,1848150,00.html.
10. Washington Corruption Probe, PBS.org, February 23, 2006. Accessed October 28, 2011, at http://www.pbs.org/newshour/indepth_coverage/law/ corruption/history.html.

11. http://www.washingtonpost.com/wpdyn/content/article/2004/09/26/AR2005040313244.html.

12. Susan Schmidt, "Papers Show Tribe Paid to Sway Bill," WashingtonPost.com, November 18, 2004. Accessed October 28, 2011, at http://www.washingtonpost.com/wp-dyn/content/article/2004/11/18/AR2005040313905.html.

13. R. Jeffrey Smith, "The DeLay-Abramoff Money Trail," WashingtonPost.com, December 31, 2005. Accessed October 28, 2011, at http://www.washingtonpost.com/wp-dyn/content/article/2005/12/30/AR2005123001480_2.html.

CHAPTER 12

1. John Avlon, "The Rigged Game of Redistricting," CNN.com, May 13, 2011. Accessed August 5, 2011, at http://articles.cnn.com/2011-05-13/opinion/avlon.redistricting_1_political-district-lines-partisan-primaries-florida-voters?_s=PM:OPINION.

2. Alex Isenstadt, "Redistricting Sparks Big-Time Feuds," Politico.com, September 11, 2011. Accessed October 28, 2011, at http://www.politico.com/news/stories/0911/63211.html.

3. Jeffrey Toobin, "Drawing the Line: Will Tom DeLay's Redistricting in Texas Cost Him His Seat?," NewYorker.com, March 6, 2006. Accessed October 28, 2011, at http://www.newyorker.com/archive/2006/03/06/060306fa_fact?currentPage=all.

4. Toobin, "Drawing the Line: Will Tom DeLay's Redistricting in Texas Cost Him His Seat?"

5. Jonathan Allen and John Bresnahan, "Russ Carnahan Confronts Emanuel Cleaver in House," May 4, 2011. Accessed October 28, 2011, at http://www.politico.com/news/stories/0511/54335.html.

6. One-party Domination, RangeVoting.org. Accessed October 31, 2011, at http://rangevoting.org/OneParty.html.

7. Brian J. McCabe, "Primary Voter Turnout Stays Low, but More So for Democrats," NYTimes.org, September 14, 2010. Accessed October 31, 2011, at http://fivethirtyeight.blogs.nytimes.com/2010/09/14/primary-voter-turnout-stays-low-but-more-so-for-democrats/.

8. The Taxpayer Protection Pledge Signers, 112th Congressional List, Americans for Tax Reform. Accessed October 31, 2011, at http://s3.amazonaws.com/atrfiles/files/files/Federal%20Pledge%20Signers%20112th%20Congress.pdf.

9. RT, "House Candidates Running Unopposed: Vote Totals," MyDD.com, November 22, 2006. Accessed October 31, 2011, at http://mydd.com/users/rt/posts/house-candidates-running-unopposed-vote-totals.

10. Examples of Our Unbiased District-Drawing Algorithm in Action/ Comparisons of Gerrymandered Districts Drawn by Politicians, MyDD.com. Accessed October 31, 2011, at http://rangevoting.org/GerryExamples.html.

11. "Why Redistricting Matters," The Brennan Center for Justice. Accessed August 11, 2011, at http://www.brennancenter.org/content/pages/why_redis tricting_matters1.

12. "Why Redistricting Matters," The Brennan Center for Justice.

13. "Why Redistricting Matters," The Brennan Center for Justice.

14. Mark A. Siegel, "How Closed Primaries Further Polarize Our Politics," WashingtonPost.com, September 4, 2011. Accessed October 31, 2011, at http:// www.washingtonpost.com/opinions/how-closed-primaries-further-polarize -our-politics/2011/09/02/gIQARBPb2J_print.html.

15. Andrew Romano, "Bennett Lost in Utah. Should Other Conservatives Be Scared?," DailyBeast.com, May 9, 2010. Accessed October 31, 2011, at http:// www.thedailybeast.com/newsweek/blogs/the-gaggle/2010/05/09/bennett-lost -in-utah-should-other-conservatives-be-scared.html.

16. Siegel, "How Closed Primaries Further Polarize Our Politics."

17. Jamelle Bouie, "In Defense of Partisan Gerrymandering," Prospect.org, January 27, 2011. Accessed October 31, 2011, at http://prospect.org/csnc/ blogs/tapped_archive?month=01&year=2011&base_name=the_case_for_par tisan_gerryman.

18. David T. Canon, *Race, Redistricting, and Representation* (Chicago: University of Chicago Press, 1999), 61.

19. Canon, *Race, Redistricting, and Representation*, 64.

20. *Thornburg v. Gingles* (1986).

21. Frank Parker, "Shaw v. Reno: A Constitutional Setback for Minority Representation," *PS: Political Science and Politics* 28 (March 1995), pp. 57–70.

22. *Shaw v. Reno* (1993).

23. Editorial: Redistricting Polarization, EnterpriseJournal.com, February 21, 2011. Accessed October 31, 2011, at http://www.enterprise-journal.com/ opinion/article_245361fe-3df4-11e0-ba6b-001cc4c002e0.html.

24. David Lublin, "Racial Redistricting Gives Minorities a Voice; Cost of Gerrymandering," *New York Times* (December 13, 1994).

25. "Why Redistricting Matters," The Brennan Center for Justice.

26. Jonathan Karl, "Say What? Democrat Compares Republicans to Nazis," ABCNews.go.com, January 19, 2011. Accessed October 31, 2011, at http://abc news.go.com/blogs/politics/2011/01/abc-news-jonathan-karl-reports-the-new found-civility-didnt-last-long-political-rhetoric-in-congress-doesnt-get-much/.

27. Lublin, "Racial Redistricting."

28. Abigail Thernstrom, "Redistricting, Race, and the Voting Rights Act," NationalAffairs.com, Spring 2010. Accessed October 31, 2011, at http://www

.nationalaffairs.com/publications/detail/redistricting-race-and-the-voting
-rights-act.

CONCLUSION

1. Thomas Friedman, "Getting Back to a Grand Bargain," NYTimes.com, September 10, 2011. Accessed October 31, 2011, at http://www.nytimes .com/2011/09/11/opinion/sunday/friedman-getting-back-to-a-grand-bargain .html.

2. Friedman, "Getting Back to a Grand Bargain."

3. Friedman, "Getting Back to a Grand Bargain."

4. "What Americans Find Important: A Newsweek Poll," DailyBeast.com. Accessed October 31, 2011, at http://www.thedailybeast.com/content/news week/2011/09/11/what-americans-find-important-a-newsweek-poll.html.

5. Washington's Farewell Address, 1796, The Avalon Project, Yale Law School. Accessed October 31, 2011, at http://avalon.law.yale.edu/18th_cen tury/washing.asp.

6. Friedman, "Getting Back to a Grand Bargain."

INDEX

134; politician influence from
big, 71; representative, collapse
of, 68; right-wing populism
antigovernment approach, 73;
smaller, 130–34, 152; spending,
17, 58, 72, 74, 132, 136, 146
Grand Bargain, 164–65
The Granny Peace Brigade, 85
grass roots and grass tops lobbying,
208–9, 223
Great Depression, 10, 12, 38, 88,
96–97, 110, 114
Great Divide, 22
Great Recession, 10, 11, 22, 37–38,
47, 118, 148, 173
Great Society, of LBJ, 98, 99, 140

Harris poll on big company influence
on politicians, 71
Hatch, Orrin, 168–69
Hayward, Tony, 34–35
Healthcare-NOW!, 87, 111
health-care reform, 20, 36, 86, 88;
constitutionalism and, 137–38;
data on, 58; Obama and, 17,
89, 110, 121–23, 149, 173;
socialization of, 84; Tea Party on,
133
health-care system failure, 9
Heritage Foundation, 198, 199
Hillary: The Movie, 190
Honest Leadership and Open
Government Act (2007), 222
housing. See mortgage crisis
Hurricane Katrina, 146

IFA. See International Franchise
Association
Immigration and Naturalization
Service (INS), 217
immigration legislation, 94

impeachment of Clinton, 100–101
income: median household decline in,
10; middle-class stagnation of, 6
income inequality, 27, 92, 110, 135;
Creamer on, 118; mainstream/
political class divide and, 38–39;
Occupy Wall Street on, 77;
Pew poll on, 39; technological
revolution and, 39
Independents, 1, 23, 66; anger of,
172–73; against Bush, 172; future
of, 175–77; growing numbers
of, 171–72; Libertarians and,
176; political system disgust by,
174–75
Independent Women's Forum, 173
individual contributions, 182
INS. See Immigration and
Naturalization Service
Inside Job, 80–81, 114
interest rates, the Fed lowering of, 40
International Franchise Association
(IFA), 207–8
Internet Gambling Prohibition Act,
220
Iraq war, 85, 102, 105, 139, 172;
antimilitarism and, 95; Bush and,
16–17; Obama and, 110, 123–24
isolationism, 20, 138, 146

James Capital Group, 182
job creation and protection: free
market, 94; globalization, 39, 95;
immigration legislation, 94; labor
unions, 94–95; left-wing populism
on, 93–95; protective tariffs, 94;
public sector, 86; public works
program for, 93
Johnson, Lyndon Baines (LBJ): Great
Society, 98, 99, 140; progressive
legislation, 98

ABOUT THE AUTHOR

Douglas E. Schoen is one of the premier political strategists in America today. For over thirty years, he has been involved in political campaigns and social initiatives around the world. He served as chief advisor to President Bill Clinton for six years between 1994 and 2000, and was named Pollster of the Year in 1996 by the American Association of Political Consultants for his contributions to the President Bill Clinton reelection campaign.

Schoen is a regular contributor to the *Wall Street Journal*, the *Washington Post*, and *Newsweek/Daily Beast*. He is also a Fox News contributor—making appearances on various news programs several times a week.

Schoen graduated magna cum laude from Harvard, and holds a degree from Harvard Law School as well as a doctorate in philosophy from Oxford University. He has lectured at the Institute of Politics at Harvard University John F. Kennedy School of Government, the Annenberg School for Communication at the University of Pennsylvania, and the School of International and Public Affairs at Columbia University.

He lives in New York City.